**Books are to be returned on or before
the last date below.**

Bᴏ

the las

1 6

2

Low-E Glazing Design Guide

Timothy E. Johnson

Department of Architecture
Massachusetts Institute of Technology

Butterworth Architecture

Boston   London   Oxford   Singapore   Sydney   Toronto   Wellington

Butterworth Architecture is an imprint of Butterworth-Heinemann.

Copyright © 1991 by Butterworth-Heinemann, a division of Reed Publishing (USA) Inc. All rights reserved.

Recognizing the importance of preserving what has been written, it is the policy of Butterworth-Heinemann to have the books it publishes printed on acid-free paper, and we exert our best efforts to that end.

Library of Congress Cataloging-in-Publication Data

Johnson, Timothy Edward, 1939-
    Low-e glazing design guide / Timothy E. Johnson
        p.   cm.
    Includes bibliographical references (p. 193) and index.
    ISBN 0-7506-9147-6 (acid-free paper)
    1. Glazing.   I. Title
TH8251.J64 1991
698' .5—dc20   90-26126
                                        CIP

British Library Cataloguing in Publication Data
Johnson, Timothy E. (Timothy Edward) 1939-
   Low-e glazing design guide
   1. Buildings. Glazing. Design
   I. Title
   721.823

   ISBN 0-7506-9147-6

Butterworth-Heinemann
80 Montvale Avenue
Stoneham, MA 02180

10 9 8 7 6 5 4 3 2 1

Printed in the United States of America

Contents

Appendix F
Solar Heat Gain Factors 182

Low-E Glazing Design Guide

Preface

Neutral-colored, architecturally acceptable low-e coatings first became available in 1979. By 1984, worldwide production of all classes of low-e glazings was already topping 10 million square meters a year. This marked one of the most rapid acceptances of a new technology by an entire industry, let alone the building industry, which is known for its slow innovation rate. This book explains what all the excitement is about and provides the design methods, examples, and hints for knowledgeably selecting the correct low-e window from today's and tomorrow's products.

The context for these design methods are set in the early chapters. Chapter 1 describes how low-e coatings work and explains why this technology is replacing ordinary glazings. Chapter 2 maps the history of low-e coatings from the beginnings during World War II to the spectacular advances made in the late 1980s. Chapter 3 evaluates a small collection of built examples from Europe and the United States. Both solar-heated residences and commercial buildings that use the solar heat rejecting type of low-e are pictured.

Chapter 4 examines the functional differences between the four types of low-e coatings. The thermal effect of various exotic gas fills and glazing spacing variations on double and triple glazing performance is also quantified.

Chapters 5 through 10 are the applications sections of the book. Chapter 5 classifies each low-e type by its typical performance, including the roll-coated film products for retrofit applications. It lists each coating's benefits and drawbacks and gives new indices for evaluating and selecting various glazings from manufacturers' catalogs.

Chapter 6 introduces several fundamental design methods for determining the minimum window thermal resistance that meets building codes and avoids condensation. In addition, the chapter discusses the solar geometry fundamentals that influence all window designs.

Chapter 7 presents two methods for sizing office windows. The methods take advantage of the latest low-e technology for minimizing the load on the air-conditioner while maximizing daylighting. Typical low-e cooling products are tabulated.

Chapter 8 shows how to design direct-gain, solar-heated spaces that maintain thermal comfort. Several low-e products for solar heating applications are listed.

Chapter 9 covers daylighting and glare reduction in residential and commercial settings. A comprehensive series of charts are presented for predicting daylighting levels in side-lit and top-lit spaces. Finally, several methods are introduced for quickly locating the nearly invisible low-e coated surface in an installed window.

Chapter 10 formally summarizes the book in the form of a guide specification. This guide is intended to aid in the preparation of specifications for particular low-e projects.

Chapter 11 focuses on future expectations. The low-e coatings are rapidly approaching their theoretical performance limits. Higher performance will come with new technologies and a redesign of the window as a whole. Evacuated glazings are examined as the possible next generation window. Some of the emerging edge seal and window frame technologies for combatting thermal bridging at the window's edges are presented. Also, the annual performance of the emerging variable transmission glazings for reducing solar transmission with the flick of an electric switch are compared with the best of the low-e glazings.

This book is the product of many years of research and testing. The work began in 1976 when my students and I built MIT Solar Building No. 5 with U.S. industry to demonstrate the first architecturally acceptable, full-scale, low-e coated glazing.

I wish to acknowledge the efforts of several people who provided me with assistance and advice in preparing this book. I thank Richard Rush, acquisitions editor of Butterworths, for his numerous helpful suggestions and his contributions to the chapter on specifications. Many thanks to Todd Sitrin of Southwall, Glen Chafee of Rolscreen, D. A. Button from Pilkington, and Alex Lohr from Lohr und Lohr for their helpful criticisms. I also wish to compliment my former students Cris Benton, Steve Hale, Ken Gardestad, and William Bartovicks on their impressive thesis projects, which are reproduced in part in the applications sections.

1

Introduction

Low-E Glazings Become an Architectural Standard

Today's low emissivity (low-e) window coatings are quite invisible, but unlike the emperor's new clothes, these layers are remarkably well suited to their job of increasing thermal comfort and controlling solar impact. One is naturally skeptical of any claims credited to an invisible treatment, but low-e coatings are the result of orthodox physics applied beautifully to architecture. The material is usually an ultrathin, yet durable, heat (infrared) reflecting silver coating that has been rendered transparent by the same anti-reflection coatings manufacturers use on camera lenses for admitting more light. A lower emissivity* raises the heat reflection, which, in turn, raises the thermal insulation by up to a factor of two. Any surface with an emissivity at or below 0.20 is considered a low-e surface.

Consider the amazing number of things traditional windows already do: they admit controllable amounts of light and heat, supply fresh air and a view, provide a tantalizing physical and visual connection to the outdoors, insulate interiors from the weather, offer visual privacy, and mirror our world. Windows are an incontrovertibly dramatic building element. Despite these considerable virtues, however, windows are notoriously poor thermal insulators and admit either too much or not enough sun. All previous attempts

"... the cloth is as light and delicate as a spider's web. One might almost think one had nothing on, but that is the very beauty of it"

"The Emperor's New Clothes"
Hans Christian Anderson

---

*Emissivity varies from 0 to 1 and is the complement of reflection for infrared opaque coatings and materials.

(e.g., drapes, tints, thermal shutters) to correct these deficiencies have robbed the window of its intrinsic beauty—until low-e coatings arrived. The usually neutral-colored coating enhances any glazing's thermal resistance without interfering with the window's transparency or optically true reflections. It is, quite simply, an architectural product.

Low-e glazings are a consequence of the 1970s energy crisis, although they are used today as much to increase thermal and visual comfort as to save energy. Neutral-colored low-e coatings were initially devised for residential double glazing. The coating nearly doubled the window's thermal resistance when compared to ordinary double glazing, without added weight or dimension, and without significantly reducing daylight or solar transmission. The move was so successful that the North American triple glazing market dried up nearly overnight because the product's price/performance ratio was better than the heavier triple glazing offering.

A companion product was quickly introduced for the office market and for residences in hot climates. The coating was "tuned" not only to reflect the radiant heat from the surround, but also to reflect most of the near infrared heat contained in sunlight. Essentially, just the sunlight's daylight portion was transmitted through the window, resulting in cool daylight for lighting interiors without exerting the air-conditioner. Some of today's low-e coatings for offices and residences reject as much heat as reflective glass, yet the low-e windows look like ordinary, untinted windows.

Low-e coatings are now available for every type of glazings, from single glass to tinted heat-treated glazing. Low-e coatings are even available on polymer films for upgrading the thermal and solar heat rejecting performance of existing windows.

These high-performance glazings are rapidly becoming the standard choice for windows in the United States where the coating price is low. The area chart in Figure 1-1 compares two types of U.S. low-e production with ordinary double-glazing output over the last 4 years of the 1980s [1]. The figure shows that low emissivity glazing had already taken over a quarter of the U.S. double-glazing market by the end of the decade. Worldwide installed silver-based low-e production capacity reached nearly 60 million m^2 (645 million ft^2) by 1989[2].

The coating is easily formulated during manufacturing to meet the demands of various climates and applications. This fundamentally inexpensive yet flexible product can also make a major impact on world energy consumption.

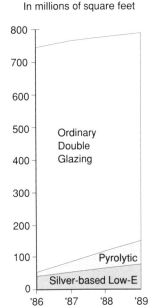

Figure 1-1. U.S. low-e production compared with ordinary double-glazing production over time (Adapted from: *Glass Industry*, May 1988).

Consider the following two choices for netting the same amount of energy:

Alternative 1: *Low-e windows*. According to the American Council for an Energy Efficient Economy,* an $8 million low-e coating plant could produce a minimum of 40 million square feet of residential windows per year for the 10-year nominal life of the coating system. The resulting residential heating savings over ordinary double glazing during the first 10 years of operation is equivalent to 36 million barrels of oil.

Alternative 2: *Off-shore oil.* Invest $300 million in an offshore oil platform, which is capable of producing an identical amount of oil over the 10-year nominal life of the oil field.

How to Navigate This Book

Architects are beleaguered with a nearly unmanageable number of glazing products. Now, along comes a variety of low-e offerings, which are coated on most of the existing glass and polymer glazings. The choices have multiplied into innumerable combinations—how does one travel this maze and make a sound choice, which satisfies the application at hand? This book provides the design methods, examples, and hints for knowledgeably selecting and specifying the correct low-e window from today's and tomorrow's products.

The context for the design methods presented in this book are set in the first four chapters on history and built examples. The remainder of the book deals with principles and applications. Chapter 5 classifies each low-e type by its typical performance. The next three chapters classify low-e products by commercial and residential applications. Chapter 9 deals with the daylighting component, and Chapter 10 formally summarizes the book in the form of a guide specification. The book closes with a chapter on future window technologies.

Graphic navigation aids help the reader locate various forms of information. Separate routes for accessing design, selection, specification, and calculation material are explicitly indicated by tabs at the outside edge of relevant pages, as on this page. The tab labeled *Design* identifies all pages of interest to the designer. The field labeled *Selection* marks the pages that aid in the low-e window selection process. Any reader interested in selecting, for example, a workable

---

*Washington, D.C.

combination of window insulation level and daylight transmission could use the *Selection* tab to find a low-e product that did the job. *Specs* tags the pages that the specification writer requires. *Calculation* marks the various design methods and the material for computing the properties of any low-e window. The interested reader could, for instance, verify a new product's claims using this access route. Each tab occupies a unique vertical position at the edge of a page so the reader can discern any one route in its entirety by glancing at the closed book's unbound edge. Unmarked pages contain introductory and general interest material for the reader interested in how low-e windows work. The book's comprehensive computer-generated index serves as the more conventional means for locating specific information.

Why Use Low-E?

Low-e is not the obvious choice for a glazing treatment in regions where it is still expensive. What are the alternatives, and when is it really required?

The highly insulating low-e window is most useful in residential work with condensation problems and in areas with progressive building codes. Triple glazing is no longer a viable alternative because it almost always costs more than low-e coated double glazing, and it doesn't perform as well. In hot climates, the solar heat rejecting type of low-e window is the only alternative because most home owners will not tolerate reflective or tinted glazings, and many times window shading is difficult.

The situation is not as clear in commercial work. High levels of thermal insulation and solar rejection are not always required, but when they are, low-e windows are a good way to comply with the building codes while keeping the view window areas adequate. For double-glazing jobs, tinted and reflective glazings are still an alternative means of lowering the solar heat gain, but low-e windows do the best job of minimizing solar intake when daylighting is required. Low-e coated sloped glazing is now the cheapest way of controlling the always excessive solar gains in top-lit spaces such as atriums.

The low-e glazings listed in this book are actual products from North America and Europe, but they are not identified by company name. In addition, not every offering is listed in this book because of limited space—only several of the best in each of the four low-e classes are presented. The appendix contains a table of all low-e glazing manufacturers in Japan, North America, and Europe for the reader who wishes to identify further any of the glazings listed.

2

History

Pyrolytics—1940s

The introduction of inexpensive, neutral-colored low-e coatings for windows in the early 1980s marked the fastest acceptance of a new technology by the building industry since England's Pilkington Glass Limited invented float glass in the 1950s. But low-e technology actually predates float glass by almost 10 years.

The coating was invented by PPG (then the Pittsburgh Plate Glass Company) and the Mellon Institute during World War II for draining efficiency-robbing static electricity off the glass face plates of radar screens. Several years would pass before anyone became aware that this same coating could increase the thermal resistance of a window.

One of the first glasses coated with this transparent material worked well as the intended electrical conductor. It was quickly dubbed NESA glass—nonelectrostatic solution A—by its inventors to differentiate the coating from their other experiments. (PPG still markets related coatings under the same name.) Additional applications for the durable coating were quickly introduced. The electrical conductor concept was reversed in 1946 from drawing off electrical charge to pumping in electrical current to generate heat for deicing aircraft cockpit windows. Shortly after that, the coating was put to limited use creating broad electric fields for transparently energizing panel lighting fixtures and wireless neon lights. (It is used more commonly today for similar purposes in digital watch and calculator displays.)

The coatings were made by spraying hot glass in an open atmosphere with a doped solution of stannic chloride, which oxidized immediately to form tin oxide. The process is now known as the pyrolytic process because it is chemically akin to a slow burn. It produced a stable, hard, intermediate emissivity surface, which could not corrode in service, as all possible oxidation took place at the elevated temperatures of the production process.

Engineers did not begin to suggest applications that took advantage of the material's midrange emissivity of 0.40 until the early 1950s. NESA glass was still too expensive to use architecturally, so it was first used nonelectrically as a transparent heat shield in manufacturing plants. Affordable low-e windows would not appear for another 25 years.

Initially, the spraying equipment could coat glass only measuring up to 50 x 76 cm (20 x 30 in) because of the limitations imposed by the equipment's geometry. Unit costs remained high even after larger sizes became feasible because the glass first required reheating to begin the pyrolysis, and then either reannealing to remove the glass's internal stresses or tempering to give it architectural strength. In addition, the material was iridescent in reflected light because of selective reflection and interference effects resulting from slight variations in the coating's thickness.

The price did not drop drastically until the 1970s, when the spray was moved onto the wide-bed float production lines (Figure 2-1) where the glass was still hot from the float process. Color rendition was improved, but not eliminated. It remained a problem until 1989.

Evaporated Monolithic Metallic Coatings—1970s

The nearly true reflections formed by optically flat float glass surfaces made it possible in the 1960s to coat the glass with less expensive metals for reflecting solar heat (and light) away from the glass. Coating the obsolete drawn glass would only emphasize the unevenness of the surfaces resulting from the drawing process.

The metals were literally evaporated in a vacuum chamber by bombarding a metal target with an ionized beam of gas. The metal atoms rocketed off the target and eventually condensed on the glass. This vacuum sputtering method offered exquisite control over the thickness of the deposited metal, which meant color rendition was no longer a problem.

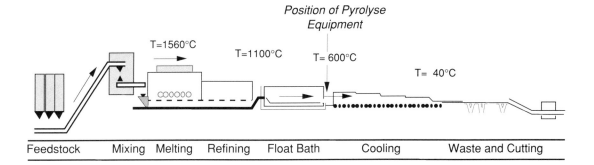

Figure 2-1. Position of the pyrolyse equipment for low-e coatings in the float glass production line (Adapted from: Gläser, H.J., "Coated Heat-Insulating Glasses," *International Journal of Glass Technology*, 1989, vol. 62, pp. 93–99).

Unfortunately, the introduction of metalized glass became a painful experience for building owners and users alike because the product had not been thoroughly tested, and many installations soon discolored. It took several years to correct all the problems, but finally the glass became popular enough to become associated with an older architectural movement known as the International Style—a style that perhaps unfairly became synonymous with glass towers and boxes.

Like all other metals, the aluminum commonly used for reflective glazing also had a very low emissivity, which translated into a higher insulating value than the insulating level offered by the existing pyrolytic coatings. Unfortunately, the aluminum was rendered useless as a heat reflecting mirror by the overcoat used to protect the metal from corrosion. The Europeans searched for a reasonably priced, noncorroding metallic coating that had some transparency as the 1973 energy crisis began to hit Europe the hardest. By the mid 1970s, gold was being deposited in thin enough layers to become reasonably transparent and affordable. It was marketed throughout Europe as the first low-e product that reflected light in a uniform color. Unfortunately, that color was gold, which restricted the product's use to commercial projects because of its obvious color and relatively high expense.

A batch process was necessarily used to coat the glass, as the hard vacuums required for sputtering could be pulled only in perfectly sealable, noncollapsible chambers. Costs were reasonable because the metal sources in the chambers did not require changing with each load of glass. It was known that a multilayer stack composed of an antireflection coating, an ultra thin silver layer, and an antireflection coating deposited on a glass would produce a very low emissivity, transparent coating; but batch processing made the idea decidedly uneconomical.

Continuous Multistack Coatings—1980s

Two independent means of producing complex transparent low-e stacks on a continuous and, therefore, economical basis were under development by the mid 1970s. The first to emerge was the roll-coating process.

Sputtering was the most promising way to coat plastics because it did not require a high temperature, as did the pyrolytic process. 3M in the United States first used the process in 1961 to lay down aluminum on polyester film. Film coating was particularly economical because a whole roll was sealed in a vacuum chamber and spooled past the evaporating metal.

By 1975, roll coaters in the United States and Europe were learning how to unroll polyester film past multiple ion beams in a single vacuum chamber so that the complex silver stack could be made in one pass. The coatings would easily corrode if exposed to damp air, so the coated plastic was sealed inside double glazing. Mounting the film inside two protective lights of glass to form a triple-glazed window proved difficult and labor intensive, but by 1978 Southwall Technologies in the United States and Geilinger AG in

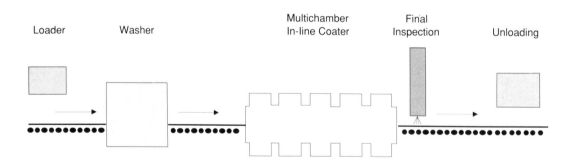

Loader   Washer   Multichamber In-line Coater   Final Inspection   Unloading

Figure 2-2. Schematic of an in-line plant for manufacturing low-e coatings.

Switzerland were demonstrating realistically priced window units. It took several more years for the two companies to shake the bugs out of their proprietary mounting systems. Geilinger went on to make quadruple-glazed units with two interior plastic films to give the highest insulation value of all.

Meanwhile, Airco Coating Technology in the United States, Pilkington in England, and Leybold-Heraeus A.G. in Germany were thinking about how to continuously lay down multilayer low-e coatings on glass. The major problem lay in getting the glass sheet through the seals into the vacuum chamber and pumping the air out of the chamber fast enough to maintain continuous production. The answer was moving the glass through a series of vacuum chambers. Each in-line vacuum chamber (Figure 2-2) reduced the pressure around the advancing glass a little bit more until it reached a hard vacuum in the magnetron coating chamber; then an equal number of chambers were used to ease the glass out to the atmosphere at the other end. In effect, a sheet of glass was quickly jerked through a series of air locks on its way to the coating chamber because any one chamber did not have to remove much air. Thus, the pressure difference over each of the in-line seals was minimal. Any number of coating sections were placed in a row to produce the multilayered stacks. As with the low-e coatings on polymer films, these coatings would also corrode unless the coated glass was sealed in double-glazed units. The companies heavily tested the new coatings for fear of repeating the discoloration debacle of the 1950s. They began shipping the coaters in 1978.

3M had already established a market for retrofitted metalized window films in the 1960s. In 1981, they quickly patented a means of preventing corrosion in a low-e silver stack coated on polyester film. Ultraviolet stabilized polypropylene was used to overcoat the low-e material because the polymer was transparent to impinging infrared radiation. The silver in the low-e stack could continue to work as a reflector to the infrared, which reached it through the polypropylene. The thermal performance was not as good as the performance associated with the uncoated stacks used in double glazing, but the low-e coated film worked wonders when adhered to single glazing.

The timing for the introduction of these products was perfect. From the mid 1970s to the early 1980s, the federal governments in Europe and North America became intent on informing their citizens about the virtues and principles of energy conservation (Figure 2-3), so heating oil and gasoline made precious by the energy crisis would last through another day. Not only did the public become aware of how much energy was lost through conventionally glazed windows, but near the end of the publicity campaigns, the official publications began to educate consumers about the mysteries of low-e windows.

The low-e glass and window companies became the beneficiaries of the free advertising and demand created by the various governments. Except for the triple-glazing industry, the building trades accepted the new technology overnight because the dimensionless, weightless, and neutral-colored coating changed nothing that concerned the in-

Figure 2-3. A collection of consumer-oriented Canadian and U.S. government publications, circa 1983.

dustry: windows were still assembled and installed the same way, margins were protected, and the technology did not step on any building codes. Prices began their inevitable fall as volume increased, until by the end of the decade, some U.S. residential window manufacturers were eliminating choice by standardizing on the low-e coatings at no extra cost to the consumer.

Then the technology began to spill over to other industries. The neutral-colored, low-e, silver-based coating materialized in cars in 1988. Japan introduced a series of high-end cars that used the low-e sandwich in windshields as a transparent electrical conductor for defogging and deicing. The technology had come full circle since its 1946 debut.

The Next Generation of Coatings—1990s

Adding a low-e surface to a double-glazed window means nighttime radiant heat transfer across the air gap is reduced by over 90%. However, heat still moves on the air sealed between the two plates of glass. This remaining traffic, which is normally nearly half of the total heat loss in an uncoated double-glazed window, moves by convection* and conduction.[†] Replacing the trapped air with a more viscous and insulating gas lowers this traffic.

Germany began producing argon-filled, double-glazed windows, which increased the window's insulation level by 25% over an air-filled low-e unit shortly after they introduced low-e windows in the 1970s. Argon is an inert gas that is both more viscous and less heat conducting than air. More important, it is a cheap by-product from the welding industry. Sulfur hexaflouride was also used as an insulating gas because of its noise-deadening qualities and low price. The gas addition raised a double-glazed, low-e window's insulation value by as much as 30%. There was great concern that the window's insulation value would decrease as the argon fill permeated through the organic edge seals over the years. But low insulation values were noticed even after the seals were improved by adding an inner seal. The culprit was improper filling—too much air was still left in the window after the argon injection. Several proprietary filling techniques have since been patented in Europe and North America to overcome the difficulty. There is still some concern over the permeability of edge sealants, but the higher quality double seals used today do an adequate job of containing the above gases over at least a 20-year period [3-5].

Krypton is an even better insulating gas, but it has remained expensive because it is so difficult to wrest from the atmosphere. Nevertheless, Lasituku in Finland was the first to fill insulated glass units with the high performance gas in the early 1980s. The gas fell out of favor

---

*Convection occurs when buoyant, moving molecules of air (or any other fluid) carry heat to or from a surface.

[†]Conduction occurs when heat is transferred through solids or still air (or fluids) by neighboring molecular collisions.

because of its cost. Now interest is turning to krypton gas fills again, as the demand for better insulating windows increases.

The end of 1989 saw three spectacular advances that signaled the next generation of low-e coatings and glazings systems. The announcements heated up the competition and made low-e coatings even more popular.

First, Pilkington and Libby Owens Ford in the United States announced a pyrolytic coating that rivaled the thermal and visual performance of the sputtered silver-based coating. The emissivity was lowered from 0.40 to nearly match the silver coating's low emissivity of 0.10, which meant both coatings produced the same high insulation value when applied to windows. The technology arrived just in time for the English market since the UK Building Regulations were changed in 1989 to define low-e coatings as treatments with an emissivity below 0.20. This time the tin oxide was formed by a chemical vapor deposition system, rather than by a spray. But perhaps more important, all iridescence was suppressed by an additional, proprietary layer, which was also formed by chemical vapor deposition. Economy was improved as well, as the new process allowed for faster production line speeds. Of course the new pyrolytic treatment would not corrode, so single-glazing applications were still quite practical.

Then Airco Coating Technology made it a new horse race when they announced a sputtered silver coating, which significantly lowered both the emissivity (by a factor of 4 over other commercially available sputtered coatings), and the solar heat gain (for air-conditioning applications), while maintaining high daylight transmission. The emissivity drop raised a double-glazed window's bulk insulation value* by 30% when compared with the new pyrolytic coating, and 10% when compared with the usual sputtered silver coatings. The drop in solar heat gain drew the window up even with reflective glazing in heat rejection, but without suffering the high daylight losses that come with reflective glass. Durability was also improved to the point where no special handling was required during production.

The coating performance was improved by adding a second heat-reflecting layer of silver separated by an improved antireflection layer that PPG and Pilkington were also working on independently. The extra layers added a

---

*The bulk insulation value is the thermal resistance at the center of the glass, out of the influence of edge effects caused by thermally conductive edge spacers and frames.

measure of complexity, which increased cost. Ironically, the additional thickness caused a color change from neutral to a uniform, light green with increased viewing angles. However, vacuum-based coating technology is controllable enough to expect this detraction will quickly fade.

The last surprise came from Southwall Technologies at the end of 1989. They became the first North American roll coater to set up volume production of krypton-filled units. They suspended two of their 0.10 emissivity polyester films in a new insulated glass unit to form three krypton gas spaces to yield the lowest bulk U-value* yet for glazing at 0.68 W/°K m² (0.12 Btuh/°F ft²). Normally, uncoated double glazing has a U-value of 2.72 W/°K m² (0.48 Btuh/°F ft²). Daylight transmission was kept at a respectable 62% with a shading coefficient† of 0.52. Krypton was used because its insulation value peaks at a narrow gap dimension near 6 mm (1/4 in). This meant that the overall window thickness could remain nearly the same as ordinary double-glazed units (Southwall uses an uneven gap spacing of 8-3-8 mm (0.312-0.125-0.312 in). Like Geilinger AG in Switzerland, they also designed the unit with a substantial thermal break at the edge seals to prevent any chance of condensation forming at the glass perimeter near the metal edge spacers. The cost for a framed unit was about 50% to 75% more than an ordinary installed double-glazed low-e window and frame (or for the insulated glass unit without the frame, four times more than an air-filled low-e unit), mostly because of the high cost of krypton, which is currently about ten times the price of argon. Both the American and Swiss window units can generate a net seasonal heat gain from just northern light in severe winter climates (see Figure 8-1).

The Airco advance means emissivities are now near their theoretical limit, with solar heat rejection within sight of its theoretical limit. The only path left for heat loss through the bulk of a window is via the conduction and convection path, but this loss has now been minimized by the switch to krypton. Thermal bridging at the edge seals is starting to come under control, but in most cases,

---

*The U-value measures the window heat conductance and is the reciprocal of the thermal resistance R, or U = 1/R.

†The shading coefficient (SC) is the ratio of solar heat gain through a window to the solar heat gain through a single light of 0.125 in (3 mm) clear glass under the same set of conditions.

the bulk glazing loss is still less than through the window's edges and frames. The greatest improvements will now come in the design of the window as a whole, and not in the glazing.

3

Examples

Classifying Buildings

Buildings glazed with low-e windows abound. Low-e production in the United States alone is measured in terms of tens of millions of square meters per month. Applications range from atriums to walkways. The few architect-designed examples pictured in this chapter are not meant to represent all possible uses of low-e windows. Rather, they have been chosen because they attractively typify the two low-e approaches to managing solar gain.

Low-e windows are usually specified because their higher insulation values enhance thermal comfort and conserve energy without noticeably affecting daylighting. But the coating has an extra dimension. It can be tuned at the factory to either maximize solar gain (for solar heating), or to minimize solar gain (for lowering the air-conditioning loads). If the second application is characterized as cool daylighting, then the first becomes the opposite, or warm daylighting.

Warm Daylighting—Solar Heating Examples

Direct-gain solar heating, which is simply accumulating solar energy in the living space via large windows, used to require nighttime thermal shutters or drapes over south-facing windows to produce a net thermal profit. Not only does a south-facing, gas-filled low-e window outperform 2.5

cm (1 in) thick nighttime insulation placed over a similarly oriented clear double-glazed unit, but also the coating is transparent enough on clear double glazing to collect a small seasonal heating profit from many northern orientations as shown at the beginning of Chapter 8. The following examples show how low-e glazing is used in residences to provide significant amounts of solar heat.

New England Residence (Figure 3-1). This two-story living space is an addition to the main house. The trees help ease the solar gain through the extensive glazing dur-

Figure 3-1. Residence, Westboro, Massachusetts, 1983. Interior, looking south. Low-e: Silver based on glass (Architect: Timothy E. Johnson).

ing the winter and shade the elevation during the summer. Normally, this much south-facing low-e glass would overheat the well-insulated space on clear winter days. The problem is diminished by covering the windows' upper reaches on the inside with upside down aluminized louvers to reflect the sunlight to the white ceiling where it bounces diffusely deep into the space. This lights the interior uniformly so that all intrinsic mass of the space participates as thermal storage to protect against wintertime overheating. The louvers also remove the bright pools of sunlight, which would normally bathe the floor in glaring light and locally overheat the occupants.

Northern German Residence (Figure 3-2). Winter time overheating is not as much of a concern in northern Europe as in the United States because totally clear days are uncommon events. This residence opens the majority of its south face to capture the mostly diffuse solar energy, which filters through the clouds. On sunny days there is enough captured solar heat to warm both the sun space and the adjoining living areas when the interior terrace doors at each of the three levels are opened.

The argon-filled low-e windows shown here can even generate a net heating gain in the sun space during cloudy months, as long as the outdoor temperatures average several degrees centigrade above the freezing mark [6]. However, the sun is too low at these latitudes during December and January to force enough diffuse light through the clouds for solar heating purposes. During these few

Figure 3-2. Residence, Cologne, West Germany, 1987. Exterior, south elevation.
Low-e: Silver based on glass (Architects: Gabi Willbold-Lohr, Alex Lohr, Cologne, West Germany).

months, the sun space is isolated from the house by closing the interior terrace doors so that the heavily glazed space acts as a thermal buffer.

The pond helps reflect even more of the low sun's precious heat into the space on sunny winter days. Less of this solar heat is reflected during the summer due to the greatly reduced reflectance of water at high light entry angles. The large roof and terrace overhangs in the ventilated sun space are necessary to shade the majority of the inner glass between the spring and fall equinoxes when the sun and warmer weather would normally combine to create overheating conditions for residences with extravagant areas of south-facing windows. Excess summertime solar heat in the sun space stratifies harmlessly out of the way in the heightened three-story space where it is quickly ventilated to the outside.

Central German Residence (Figure 3-3). This residence predates the previous example by 6 years. It uses

Figure 3-3. Dolmus Haus, West Germany, 1981.
Interior, looking southeast.
Low-e: Silver based on glass
(Architect: Gerhard W.P. Berndt).

the same glazed buffer zone concept, but tucks the sun space under the entire gable end of the house; only two stories are involved instead of three, so the natural convection loops, which carry solar heat to the rest of the house, are not as strong. Argon gas fills were not available for low-e glazing when this house was constructed, so the sun space runs colder than the earlier example in the dead of winter; but the nighttime temperatures never get low enough to threaten the plants. The balconies and the large roof overhang shade the windows on the interior spaces after the end of March, so summertime overheating in the house proper is not an issue, although the sun space does get uncomfortably warm on occasion in the summer.

Much of the solar heat that collects at the sun space peak during winter clear days is blown via ducts through cells in the sunspace's concrete floor, so this relatively low temperature heat stored in the floor can effectively heat the space by radiation during the night. The remaining stratified heat is blown into the house during clear days, but most of the time the temperature of the air at the sun space peak is low enough to make the circulated air feel cool when standing in this air stream.

Cool Daylighting—Commercial Buildings

The commercial buildings pictured below were chosen because of their unusual glazings. Like office buildings, these buildings are vulnerable to excessive solar gains. Low-e glazings were used in all these examples to bring the solar gains under control without sacrificing daylighting.

West Coast Museum (Figure 3-4). This naturally lit 4,645 m² (50,000 ft²) air museum uses low-e coated clear polyester film suspended between two sheets of glass to cut the estimated energy load by 35% and to meet one of the

Figure 3-4. Museum of Flight, Seattle, Washington, 1986. Interior, looking west.
Low-e: Silver based on interior suspended polyester film (Architect: Ibsen Nelsen and Associates, Seattle, Washington). Photograph printed with permission of Southwall Technologies, Inc.

country's toughest energy codes. Three of the four walls and the sloped roof are 100% glazed with different varieties of the suspended low-e film. The neutral-colored wall glazing

Figure 3-5. Princeton University Firestone Library, Princeton, New Jersey, 1988. Interior, looking east. Low-e: Silver based on glass (Architects: Koetter and Kim, Boston, Massachusetts). Photograph: © Jeff Goldberg/Esto, Mamaroneck, New York

has a daylight transmission of 53% to balance the light admitted through the 13% transparent gray-tinted roof. The walls' upper reaches near the eaves are slightly tinted for architectural definition. Solar gain is brought under control by the disproportionately low shading coefficients of 41% for the walls and 18% for the roof. All of the overhead glare is controlled by the heavily tinted roof, while the glare produced by the brighter walls is softened by metal awning-like devices hung off the exterior space frame at three different elevations. Closely spaced, horizontal white-painted tubes form the awnings. The result is an even lighting that does not place the overhead exhibits in silhouette.

Ivy League University Infill Atrium (Figure 3-5). This addition to the Princeton University Firestone Library in New Jersey faces the stone weather wall of the original library. The resulting 20-foot reading space between the two buildings is glazed over with a north-facing shed roof of lightweight, silver-based low-e double glazing to lower the wintertime heat losses through the roof. The lower than normal U-value of 1.8 $W/m^{2\circ}K$ (0.32 Btu/hr $ft^{2\circ}F$) lowers the space's annual heating bill by 16% compared with ordinary double glazing. The graceful steel arches that support the glass are aglow at night from the night lighting concealed in the arches' lower flanges. Wintertime solar heating is not possible due to the higher library to the south. The glazing's 64% daylight transmission (with a 47% shading coefficient to control the summer heat gain) is high enough to daylight the addition's perimeter spaces despite the use of a light green cover plate. Glare from the bright summer sun is minimized with rows of white metal tubing running east-west just below the glass space. They shade over 50% of the transmitted sun while letting through 75% of the transmitted light from the zenith for cloudy day lighting. The tubes are lit from below by the fixtures at the arch bases to give a sense of enclosure at night.

New England Atrium Conversion (Figure 3-6). This space was once a fully exposed well, which only brought light to the central portion of the Aetna Commercial Insurance Division Headquarters Building in Hartford, Connecticut. The architects capitalized on the exceptionally high 16 foot ceilings in this six-story space by opening the long edges of every floor to the converted, fully air-conditioned atrium space. The United States fire codes normally allow only the first three floors to open onto a tall atrium, but the ceilings are high enough here to collect the smoke above the occupant's heads once the robust smoke exhaust fans go into action at the atrium's peak.

The sloped double glazing uses a silver-based low-e coating on a light green cover plate to achieve a shading coefficient of 0.47 and a daylight transmission of 64%. Traditional double glazing would have increased the peak air-conditioning load by 46%. The low-e glazing admits enough light to grow nonflowering plants at the central two thirds of the atrium floor, even during cloudy days in February. Heavy trusses would have cut off too much light in this tall

Figure 3-6. Aetna Commercial Insurance Division Headquarters Building, Hartford, Connecticut, 1989. Interior, looking east. Low-e: Silver based on glass. (Architect: Jung Brannen Associates, Inc., Hartford, Connecticut). Photograph: © 1990 Richard Mandelkorn, Newton, Massachusetts.

atrium, so an airy space frame was used instead to support the glass. Tinted glass would simply not let in enough light to support plant growth, and the peak air-conditioning load would increase by 25% over the existing glazing.

Glare is minimized by fixed vertical louvers positioned in the 2-inch air space between the custom double glazing. The louvers run parallel to the long axis of the atrium, which runs east-west. The louvers main job is to intercept the sun before it reaches the south-facing offices while still allowing at least the spring and summer sun to reach the atrium floor. The railing and spandrel materials use matte finishes to keep the sunlight from reflecting down to the atrium floor and creating hot spots. The west-facing offices do catch some direct sunlight after 4:00 PM between April and August, when the west sun can streak through the east-west lines of louvers.

Swiss Office Building (Figure 3-7). The 1,200 m² (12,916 ft²) of windows in the 7,513 m² (80,877 ft²) open plan Tour Balexert office building are made with two low-e coated clear polyester films suspended between two sheets of glass to achieve a U-value of 0.6 W/m²°K (0.106 Btu/hr ft²°F). The 100 mm (4 in) thick windows have a shading coefficient of 0.46 and a daylight transmission of 56%, which

Figure 3-7. Tour Balexert, Geneva, Switzerland, 1988.
Low-e: Silver based on multiple interior polyester films.
(Architect: Favre Guth et Architectes Associés SA).
Photograph: H. Germond Industrie, Lausanne. Photograph printed with permission of Geilinger Ltd.

is just adequate for daylighting the perimeter spaces. The design exemplifies how equally large, uniform windows can appear on all elevations, with little concern over varying solar impact or excessive heat loss on north-facing orientations.

Nearly all these examples shared a common concern—daylighting with a minimum amount of glare. Low-e glazings make it possible to use larger than normal windows without paying the penalty of increased heating or cooling costs, yet the technology does nothing toward reducing the glare that comes with larger windows. Glare reduction and daylighting still depend on good architectural treatments and a knowledge of light for attractively easing the outdoor brightness into the darker interior. Chapter 9 covers these lighting issues so that the designer can confidently take full advantage of low-e technology.

4

How Low-E Works

Thin Film Principles

There are really four types of low-e treatments for windows, but only one of them is based on the ultrathin, antireflected silver mirror. The see-through silver mirror works as a radiation trap by reflecting thermal radiation* while remaining transparent to daylight, and in some cases, to the incoming solar heat.† The other three types of coatings work on different, but related principles that are explained later in this chapter.

The Greenhouse Effect Myth

Why do we need this high technology radiation trap? Isn't that what ordinary glass does? Don't greenhouses become warm because of the greenhouse effect, where the shortwave solar energy can get in, but the absorbed solar heat that reradiates in the form of longwave infrared radiation is trapped? We need the low-e coatings because ordinary glass does not act as a radiation trap; it only acts as a convection trap.

---

*The infrared radiation we feel as heat radiating from warm objects. Longwave infrared, or far infrared, is emitted from relatively low temperature objects that don't glow red in the dark.

†Most of the solar heat is shortwave infrared. Like light, solar heat can reflect off of many objects. Shortwave infrared is also emitted from high temperature objects that glow red in the dark.

Although the greenhouse effect is indeed responsible for keeping the planet warm, it isn't at work in greenhouses. To understand how the greenhouse effect works in buildings means "seeing" how infrared heat propagates. Infrared heat is really like light—it travels in straight lines, reflects off of shiny surfaces, and is absorbed by most other surfaces. Any object that is warmer than its neighbor will emit this radiation, much like a candle broadcasts light in all directions. But the infrared radiation that emits from any object that doesn't glow with light has a much longer wavelength than light, so if you could see far infrared "light," you would see an unfocused scene with very fuzzy shadows.

Ordinary glass has been incorrectly characterized as a far infrared radiation trap because it is opaque to the infrared radiation emitted from warm building materials. Glass does lose its transparency to wavelengths longer than those contained in the solar spectrum (Figure 4-1),

Figure 4-1. Ideal residential low-e characteristics compared with ordinary glass.

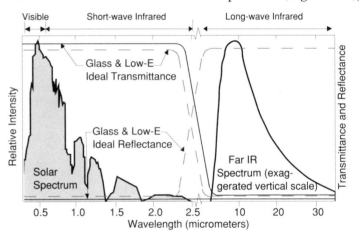

but here infrared opaqueness means black. In fact, all materials (except shiny, unfinished, polished metals and low-e coatings) are a highly absorptive black in the far infrared regime, regardless of their color. The glass necessarily acts as a radiation sponge in the presence of reradiated far infrared, only to reemit and convect the soaked up radiation at the outside surface after the energy readily warms the glass so that the heat can conduct through the dense glass. This long wavelength infrared radiation is formed in greenhouses when the transmitted solar radiation strikes any opaque surface (Figure 4-2). The surface absorbs the short wavelength energy and heats up until the incoming solar energy equals the outgoing energy. Slightly more than half of this outgoing heat is far infrared radiation, and the remainder is energy that is wafted into the air via the convection process. The warm greenhouse air also convects some energy to the glass which, also conducts through the glass to the outside surface.

Thus the far infrared radiation easily leaves the greenhouse via the glass, which absorbs, conducts, and finally reemits it; whereas the solar gain is reduced by the glass's less-than-perfect transmission. The net effect is slightly less heat forming net radiation (solar radiation in minus infrared radiation out) at a plot of ground inside the greenhouse when compared to an equal plot of ground outside in the cold. The greenhouse gets warm because the air warmed at the interior sunlit surfaces wafts its way upward and accumulates in the greenhouse, where outside any warmed air is surely blown away and replaced by more cold air.

High solar transmission low-e glazing is the first true radiation trap—it behaves like ordinary glass was thought to. Its high longwave infrared reflectivity bounces the thermal radiation, which originates in the space, back into the space. Since less radiation gets out, the net radiation goes up, even after accounting for the low-e coated glass's reduced solar transmission, resulting in an even warmer greenhouse.

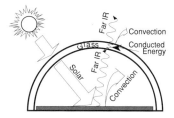

Figure 4-2. The formation and escape of long wavelength infrared radiation in an ordinary glass greenhouse. The infrared escapes to the outside by absorption and reradiation at the glass envelope.

Figure 4-1 shows the entire process. The dark spike is the incoming solar energy, where half the energy lies in the visible region; the gray bump is the reradiated far infrared. The top dark solid curve shows how well ordinary glass transmits solar energy for various wavelengths, and the bottom dark solid curve shows how the glass reflectance remains low for all wavelengths. The gray-colored dashed curves show the behavior for a perfect low-e coated product. Notice how the material acts as a selective reflector—solar transmission is still quite high but solar reflectance is low; then the reflectance increases for the far infrared wavelengths while the transmission goes to zero. Low emissivity in the presence of low transmission means high reflection. Low emissivity also means any energy that is held in the coating has a difficult time leaving as radiation—the energy cannot emit from the surface, hence the name of the product.

It's Done with Mirrors

The interaction of reflection, transmission, and absorption for all materials is given by the relation:

$$100\% = Transmission + Reflection + Absorption,$$

where absorption equals emissivity at any one wavelength. Transmission equals zero for nearly all materials in the far infrared regime, so a low-e (low absorption) surface near 0.10 means the same surface has a high IR* reflection (a low emissivity does not mean a high reflection if the transmission is significantly above zero). Ordinary uncoated glass has a longwave emissivity (absorption) of 0.84, so the IR reflection goes down to 16%. At the solar wavelengths, the low-e coating and the glass carrier have the same high transmission, so everything else must be low.

Sixty percent of the heat lost through ordinary windows is through longwave infrared, so initially paying attention to the infrared traffic makes more sense than going after the other window heat transfer mechanisms—conduction and convection. A low-e window essentially doubles a window's thermal resistance because the low-e coating nearly shuts down the infrared conduit.

A knowledge of how infrared behaves is useful for evaluating manufacturer's claims. Some companies are claiming low-e windows keep heat in during the winter and keep heat out during the summer. This is true only for the longwave infrared version of heat. This means the thermal radiation from radiators, people, and pets is kept in by reflection during the winter, and the reradiated infrared from parking lots, pavements, neighboring buildings and other hot surfaces is kept out by reflection during the summer. But the more energetic shortwave solar radiation gets through all year round. If the low-e window is formulated to keep the solar energy out during the summer, it will necessarily keep the solar radiation out during the winter.

Low-E Coating Modifications for Offices and Hot Climates

Offices generally produce so much heat from people, lights, and equipment that they recover it during the winter to heat the buildings 24 hours a day. Thus the heat contained in solar energy is hardly desirable in most commercial settings, particularly in the summer. Many residences in tropical and subtropical climates suffer from the same problem. Some office and home designers have gone

---

*Infrared.

to great lengths to minimize the heat gain from the sun. External window shading has always been effective. Tinted glazing was once commonly used in offices to reduce solar gain (and sometimes to reduce glare by reducing the daylight transmission), but Figure 4-3 shows that the solar heating reduction for single-tinted glazing is not significant when compared with clear glazing. This is quite understandable when one realizes the tint absorbs enough heat to reach 54°C (130°F) on clear summer days. The glass literally turns into a broiler. There is no escape from this infrared deluge. Closing the blinds only makes the blinds hot enough to emit nearly the same amount of infrared. Double glazing with the tint on the outside pane does a little better (about a 20% to 15% further reduction in the shading coefficient), as the absorbed heat is more readily stripped away by the wind than gained by convecting across the insulating air gap. The trick is to reflect the solar heat away while admitting the worthwhile daylight. Some low-e coatings are formulated to do this very thing.

The office version of Figure 4-1 is shown in Figure 4-4. The two are comparable except that the low-e reflectance curve transition point in Figure 4-1 has been moved into the middle of the solar spectrum, so solar heat is rejected by reflection. (The curve showing the behavior of ordinary glass has been omitted.) Rather than just becoming highly reflective in the far infrared region, this coating also becomes reflective in the near infrared region. Both the residential and office low-e coatings have similar daylight transmission, but the office low-e reflects most of the near IR heat back to the outside rather than admitting it. Figure 4-4 has been idealized to show the changeover from low reflectance to high reflectance clearly—actual coatings

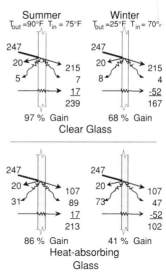

Figure 4-3. Heat gain through clear and tinted single and double glazing on clear summer and winter days (Adapted from: Anderson, B., Riordan, M., *The Solar Home Book,* Brick House Press, Andover, Massachusetts, 1980).

Figure 4-4. Ideal commercial low-e characteristics compared with ordinary glass..

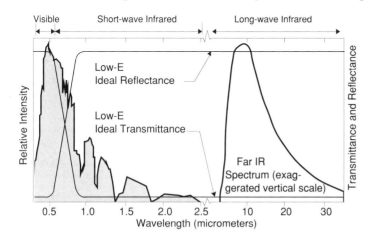

smear this transition. This behavior is usually accomplished by thickening the silver coating in the low-e sandwich. Some daylight transmission is sacrificed, but solar heat rejection is as high as some aluminized glazings, whereas the daylight transmission is as good as triple glazing.

Thick Film Principles

Two of the other three types of low-e glazings are made from semiconductors. Whereas the above films require multiple layers of ultrathin material, transparent semiconductor films can be made in a single, relatively thick layer (several millionths of a meter thick), which avoids the quality control issues associated with thin films. Certain highly doped members of this class exhibit high IR reflectance due to their controlled concentration of charge carriers (a material cannot reflect unless it conducts electricity, i.e. carry a charge). Some of these transparent semiconductors are tin oxide, indium oxide, cadmium tin oxide, and indium tin oxide [7].

The first type of thick film is deposited on warm glass in a vacuum. The second type is sprayed or chemically deposited on hot glass in atmospheric conditions.

Microgrid Principles

The last type of selective reflector is mechanically produced. Metal sheets are etched to create openings of approximately 2.5 µm (a micron, or a millionth of a meter) to allow solar radiation to pass through, but not the longer wave infrared, assuming the widths of the lines are not too narrow to prevent IR reflection (around 0.2 µm) [7]. The technique is sometimes used to improve the performance of thick films such as indium-tin-oxide, but the technique remains a laboratory curiosity because of its cost.

Thin Film Pros and Cons

Each of the four low-e treatments has strengths and weaknesses. The sputtering process used to lay down thin films on glass demands a high degree of control over the various metal deposition rates to maintain the film's thickness at 0.02 µm. On the other hand, this amount of control makes it easy for the operator to change the film's composition with the twist of a dial. A full spectrum of shading coefficients for different climates and applications becomes possible because of this flexibility. The vacuum magnetron

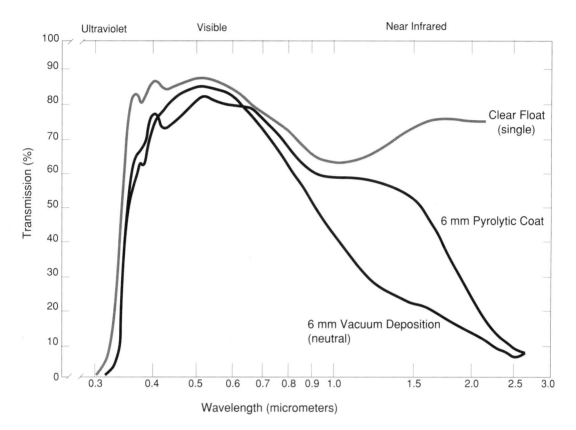

sputtering machinery used to deposit both the metal and the two antireflection coatings is precise enough to guarantee uniformly thick layers, which in turn assures a uniformly colored (or sometimes neutral-colored) coating.

Silver is used as a base because it has the best solar transmission. The antireflection coating has historically been titanium or indium oxide, but now zinc tin oxide is emerging as the material of choice because it more readily resists ultraviolet attack and is much harder (for better abrasion resistance during assembly) [8].

The stack usually reflects 90% of the far infrared, which is enough to nearly double the thermal resistance of a double-glazing assembly. Figure 4-5 compares the typical performance of two different types of low-e double-glazed glass units in the visible and near infrared wavelengths with uncoated, clear, single glazing. The pyrolytic coat curve repre-

Figure 4-5. Spectral transmission curves for two types of low-e double-glazed windows compared with clear single glazing (Adapted from: Pilkington Glass Limited, Low-Emissivity Glasses Catalog, October 1989).

sents a typical residential glazing with a shading coefficient of 0.79 (clear 6 mm double glazing has a shading coefficient of 0.82). The vacuum-deposited thin coat curve shown here is more useful for office applications with its lower shading coefficient of 0.67 due to its increased near IR rejection. The far IR reflection can go as high as 97% (which is the same as a 0.03 emissivity) when a second coating of silver is spaced off the first by an interior antireflection layer. Other low-e coatings and even thick metal mirrors cannot perform better than this.

The antireflection layers are not tough enough to protect the soft silver from corrosion and prolonged abrasion (these thin films are sometimes referred to as *soft coats* because of their delicate metal bases), but future advances are expected to solve this problem. There are three common methods for protecting the coating, each of which has advantages and disadvantages.

Coated on Glass and Sealed in Glass. Double glazing is used to protect the normally one coated light. Coating the facing sides of both panes does not significantly improve the window's thermal resistance because the one low-e surface per gas space arrests nearly all the infrared traffic. However, coating the room side of a double-glazed unit with a corrosion-resistant pyrolytic layer while one of the sealed glass sides is coated does slightly improve the overall thermal performance (by about 10% to 15%). The hollow, perforated metal edge spacer used to attach the two panes is filled with a desiccant, which removes any potentially corrosive water vapor trapped in the unit during manufacture.

The organic seals used to glue the two panes of glass to the edge spacer are now reliable enough to last over 20 years as evidenced by some United States manufacturers' warrantees. These long life seals are actually double seals—most single organic seals are not reliable enough to hold the popular gas fills. Polyisobutylene (Figure 4-6) is used to attach the glass to the metal spacer and to seal in the gas fill while sealing water vapor out. A second seal, usually polysulfide, polyurethane, hot melt butyl, or silicone, is applied along the spacer's outside edge to ensure the structural integrity of the unit. Table 4-1 shows gas leakage rates through different sealants after 20 years as reported by several studies [9,26]. The seals were tested using 12 mm (0.5 in) gaps according to the West German standard DIN 52293, as the United States has no standards on the durability of gas filled units. The data indicate that the conventional dual-seal units are satisfactory. Significantly lower gas leakage rates are listed for sulphur

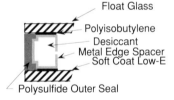

Float Glass
Polyisobutylene
Desiccant
Metal Edge Spacer
Soft Coat Low-E
Polysulfide Outer Seal

Figure 4-6. A typical double organic seal and metal edge spacer assembly.

Low-E Glazing Design Guide

Table 4-1. Percent Gas Loss Through Various Sealants After 20 Years [8]

	Ar/SF$_6$ [21]	Ar* [22}	Ar* [23]	Ar* [24]	SF$_6$* [24]
Single Seal					
Polysulfide	8 to 10	13 to 15		6 to 13	0 to 1
Polyurethane	8 to 10	13 to 15	15 to 20	33 to 45	3 to 5
Silicone			> 45		
Butyl			5 to 7		
Polyisobutylene			4 to 5		
Permapol P-2			5 to 10		
Permapol LPM			1 to 4		
Thikol LP			3 to 9		
Dual Seal					
Polysulfide	5 to 6				
Polyurethane	2 to 5				
Silicone	12 to 15				

*Data extrapolated.

hexafluoride (SF$_6$) and argon/sulphur hexafluoride mixtures than for argon (Ar) alone because of the former's large-sized molecule. No comparable data are available for krypton, but it is expected its permeability is less than argon based on the dimension of its molecule.

The sputtered low-e coating must be stripped off the glass surface that mates with the sealants to avoid corrosion forming at the exposed edge and growing tangentially inward. Most sealants will degrade when immersed for long periods in water, so the bottom glass edge must be lifted above the frame bottom with rubber blocks to avoid contact with any accumulated water. In addition, a few sealants are prone to ultraviolet attack if left uncovered. Always check with the glazing manufacturer for sealant UV resistance if exterior flush glazing or butt-joint glazing applications are under consideration.

The metal edge spacer acts like a significant thermal short circuit when the overall glass R-values approach 0.88 m^2°K/W (5.0 ft^2°F/Btuh). Chapter 6 shows how to account for this effect. The thermal bridging effect is even worse for the relatively thick welded glass edges, but the real reason that glass edges are not used is that the large temperature differences formed over the inside and outside panes in high R-value windows during the winter are enough to crack the glass edge. (The old fashioned double-glazed windows could never develop a large enough temperature difference because they insulated so poorly.) Eventually, as window R-values continue to increase, the metal edge spacers and organic seals will also become limited as newer technologies do a better job of structurally supporting the glass.

The coating is now durable enough to store unsealed for over a year. Special paper packaging can nearly double this shelf life.

Coated on Polyester and Sealed in Glass. One of the advantages of the thin film deposition process is that deposition temperatures are low enough to coat plastics. Polyester film is usually used because of its dimensional stability. Coating plastic is cheaper than coating glass because enormous rolls of film are readily unwound past ion beams in a single vacuum deposition chamber. Unfortunately, the cost of properly mounting and sealing the polyester film outweighs the manufacturing savings. Sealing is still necessary to keep the soft coating from corroding.

The coated plastic is positioned in a double-glazed unit like the middle light in a triple-glazed unit. The extra air gap gives a higher R-value, which only sometimes justifies the increased cost of the unit from an energy savings standpoint, although the increased comfort afforded by the increased R-value usually justifies the approach. The polyester film presents a mounting problem because it undergoes continual plastic deformation, or creep. This can result in a corrugated surface that produces unattractive, distorted reflections. Americans and the Swiss solve the creep problem differently.

Americans adhere a metal edge spacer to each side of the film perimeter using a special double-sided adhesive tape (Figure 4-7). The glass faces are then adhered to the metal edge spacers conventionally, and the entire assembly's edge is potted in polyurethane, which serves as the real plastic restraint. Finally the unit is heated slightly to heat-shrink the plastic. (The silver-based coating is able to withstand the film contraction without cracking.) Heat shrinking preloads the plastic in tension, so the inevitable creep only lessens the tension, without negating it. The unit experiences the same thermal bridging problem at the edge spacers as the all-glass unit. The edge sealants currently used with this unit are not compatible with standard exterior flush glazing or butt-joint glazing applications because of their susceptibility to ultraviolet attack.

The Swiss preload the plastic in tension by mounting it in a metal stretcher frame, much like painting canvasses. The metal frame acts as a permanent spring, which continually pulls the plastic tight as it creeps. The frame can

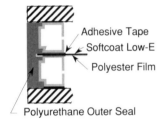

Adhesive Tape

Softcoat Low-E

Polyester Film

Polyurethane Outer Seal

Figure 4-7. Mounting method for coated polyester film.

stretch more than one film layer to form an extra gap. The frame is floated in a thick, ultralow permeability, hard synthetic rubber sleeve, which is adhered to the outboard lights of glass. The design greatly reduces the thermal bridging problem associated with the above approaches.

Figure 4-8 shows how Americans responded to the thermal bridging problem with their krypton-filled units. The metal edge spacers are adhered to the film as before, but since there is an extra film layer, the other sides of the two films are glued to a dense polyvinylchloride foam spacer, which acts as the thermal break. The entire assembly's edge is then potted in polyurethane to structurally tie everything together. Polyurethane is the only economical organic sealant that adheres well to polyester. Normally, the krypton would permeate through the urethane seal, but this difficulty is minimized by covering the insulated glass unit's (IGU) perimeter with a multilayer polymer and metal foil tape. Great care must be taken during framing to keep this barrier wrap intact. Although the thermal break is good enough to prevent condensation at the window's perimeter, it isn't good enough to maintain the window's exceptionally high R-value for small- and moderate-sized units. The thermal bridging at the compound edge spacer for a 1.4 m^2 (16 ft^2) unit, for example, is enough to lower the window's ideal R-value of 1.4 m$^{2\circ}$K/W (8.0 ft$^{2\circ}$F/Btuh) to an average R-value of 1.0 m$^{2\circ}$K/W (5.9 ft$^{2\circ}$F/Btuh).

All the preloading in the world won't prevent creep if the plastic film is found in temperatures above 66°K (150°F)—an admittedly rare occurrence confined to hot climates. The preloading rapidly disappears at these temperatures once the plastic softens and begins to elongate.

A small hole is punched near a corner of the polyester film for equalizing the pressure between the two dead air spaces, so the film does not bow and cause distorted reflections. Both the American and Swiss approaches easily accept more film layers, which create additional dead air spaces (for a higher R-value), with virtually no increase in weight. Creating more than three dead air spaces is not advisable, however, because any extra air volume could expand enough to burst the unit in elevated temperature conditions. In addition, the daylight transmission decreases rapidly with additional layers.

Polyester film is readily attacked by ultraviolet light. UV inhibitors slow down the attack, but do not arrest it. Fortunately, the film is well protected when sealed in glass by both the glass (which reduces UV transmission) and the

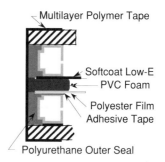

Figure 4-8. An edge mount assembly with a thermal break and an impermeable barrier.

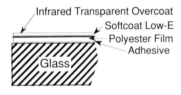

Figure 4-9. The sandwich construction of a low-e retrofit film.

low-e coating itself (which rejects up to 70% of the remaining UV by reflection), assuming the low-e coating is placed on the film side that faces the outdoors.

Low-e coating technology is improving rapidly enough to expect corrosion-proof coatings soon. This will lead to high performance coated plastics for retrofit and agricultural greenhouse applications. Meanwhile, intermediate performance retrofit films are available now.

Coated on Plastic and Sealed with an Overcoat. Transparent plastic films are routinely laminated to the low-e side of coated polyester films for corrosion protection. The typical overall thickness is 38 μm (0.0015 in). The nonlaminated side of the carrier film is adhered to the installed glass to impart low-e properties to the window. The polyester is inexpensively affixed to the glass by a water release adhesive (Figure 4-9) or a pressure-sensitive adhesive with a temporary detackifying overcoat. This method overcomes the high cost of mounting the film between protective panes of glass, but at the expense of lower insulation values.

The overcoat must be transparent to IR, so the low-e coating can reflect the longwave energy. Unfortunately, an inexpensive highly IR transparent material has not yet been identified. Polypropylene plastic is most often used as a protective film because its IR transmission is reasonably high. Even so, the resulting effective emissivity of the sandwich is lowered to a value that lies nearly one third of the way between an unprotected low-e surface and uncoated plastic or glass, which means the U-value is also at a corresponding intermediate value.

Other drawbacks exist. The polypropylene trades in its high IR transparency for UV resistance, so the overcoat begins to yellow and crack from UV attack after 7 to 13 years when installed on the room side of the glass. The service life is decreased to 5 years or less when installed on the weather side. Fortunately, the system is so inexpensive that the savings in heating and air-conditioning bills more than pay for the necessary replacement.

Retrofit low-e film does not work in all settings. The composite film cannot readily reside on the weather side of the window because windblown debris will scratch it in most climates. In cold climates, the film will induce condensation if it is adhered to the inside surface (see Chapter 8 for an explanation of this seemingly contradictory statement) and if the inside humidity is high enough. In this situation, the film should be attached to the inside surface of the storm window. Do not attempt to retrofit sealed double

Low-E Glazing Design Guide

glazing in these conditions. If in doubt, temporarily mount a test piece on the room side of the window during very cold outdoor conditions to test for condensation.

Thick Film Pros and Cons

Thick coats are deposited either by a magnetron cathode vacuum sputtering process or by directly spraying or vapor depositing tin oxides on hot glass. The coatings are relatively thick at 0.5 to 0.1 µm. They are sometimes referred to as hard coats because of their abrasion and corrosion resistance. Edge deletion is not required as is the case for soft coats.

Thick Film on Glass. Doped indium tin oxide or cadmium tin oxide semiconductors are the usual material choices for sputtering on glass because of their exceptional hardness and transparency to daylight. Emissivities range between 0.15 and 0.13. These coatings are good choices for single-glazing applications because they are hard enough to resist all normal sources of abrasion, including window cleanings, and the materials cannot corrode because they are already oxides.

Indium tin oxide has the best selective properties, but unfortunately, indium is very expensive. In addition, these materials are not applicable to polymer films, as they require high substrate temperatures (400°K) during the sputtering process.

Pyrolytics. The more controllable chemical vapor deposition process is rapidly replacing spraying as the preferred method for atmospherically coating tin oxide on hot glass as the plates progress through the production line. The emissivity is lowered to below 0.20 by doping the coating with small amounts of fluorine. The coating is applied while the glass is floating by on a bath of melted tin.

A perforated boom over the tin bath is used to evenly apply the vapors to the moving glass surface. Excess vapors are immediately recovered by a suction apparatus, so the deposition can take place in the open atmosphere. Multiple booms are often used to build up other layers to control color rendition.

Not only does the vapor deposition method produce lower emissivities (0.17 to 0.20, as opposed to 0.40 for sprayed tin oxide), but it essentially eliminates all the vestiges of color iridescence that is associated with the spray process. The multilayer coating does leave a slight haze on the glass, which makes the glass look like it was washed with dirty water when viewed in bright sunlight; but most people won't detect this unless they are looking for it. Some of the emerging coatings have an increased surface roughness which makes them harder to clean.

Like the sputtered thick coats, these corrosion-proof and abrasion-resistant coatings are well suited for single glazing or storm window retrofit applications. These materials are also not applicable to polymer films, as they require high substrate temperatures during the deposition process. Coating hot glass on-line after it emerges from the float tanks is potentially the most economical means of producing low-e glass, as the glass does not have to cool for handling as is the case for the vacuum deposition process.

Microgrid Pros and Cons

The expense of scribing microgrids in metal sheets will most likely relegate this low-e production method to the laboratory. Furthermore, microgrid emissivities are greater than 0.15 unless the method is used for lowering thick coat emissivities. Practicality is limited too, as grease and oils can easily foul the etched surface.

R-value Variation with Gas Fills

Lowering a window's emissivity reduces the radiant infrared traffic, but leaves the convection and conduction paths through the air gap untouched. The most elegant way to reduce the heat loss due to the trapped air layer in a double-glazed low-e unit is to replace the air with a more viscous, insulating gas. This strategy does not work well for uncoated double glazed windows because the high infrared losses would overshadow any reduction in the convection and conduction losses.

Figure 4-10 shows the properties of some candidate gas fills compared with air. The horizontal axis shows gas conductivity, where lower is better. The vertical axis shows viscosity, where higher is better. Low conductivity is the more important of the two variables for the narrow gaps found in double glazing (less than 12 mm [1/2 in]). In addition, viscosity must be greater than a minimum value or convection will degrade the performance. For typical 9 mm (3/8 in) gaps, viscosity must be greater than 0.7 e-5 m^2/s (0.7 e-4 ft^2/s) [9]. Note that although air has the maximum viscosity, it also lies all the way to the right on the graph, which means it also has maximum conductivity. So air is, as expected, less than ideal for minimizing heat flow. The next candidate is argon (Ar), which is the most commonly used gas fill because of its inertness and exceptionally low cost. An

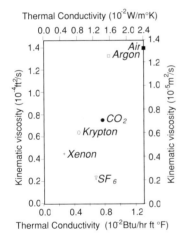

Figure 4-10. Thermal conductivity and kinematic viscosity of gasses suitable for use in gas-filled windows. (Adapted from: Arasteh, D., Selkowitz, S., Wolfe, J.R., "The Design and Testing of a Highly Insulating Glazing System for Use With Conventional Window Systems," *Journal of Solar Engineering, Transactions of the ASME*, 1989, vol. 111).

argon fill will typically raise the R-value of a double-glazed low-e window by 33%. Carbon dioxide (CO_2) has about the same conductivity as argon, but its viscosity is at the borderline. Sulfur hexaflouride (SF_6) is sometimes used in Europe for improved sound insulation, despite its low viscosity. Krypton has an exceptionally low conductivity, but its viscosity is a bit too low. The viscosity is easily raised by mixing in a little argon. Xenon (Xe) is too low in viscosity for most applications. Argon will continue as the most popular fill because of its low cost, at least until a better synthetic gas comes along.

Figure 4-11 shows how important it is to remove the air when filling with argon. The bottom line indicates that a low-e unit filled with half air and half argon has a U-value that is 14% more than a unit totally filled with argon. The top line shows that an argon fill has virtually no effect on an uncoated unit.

Filling double-glazed units is tricky because it's difficult to remove the diluting air. The least advisable method of filling uses two temporary holes drilled in the metal edge spacer, one at the top and one at the bottom. The heavy gas is slowly injected in the bottom hole to minimize mixing. The incoming gas forces the lighter air out the top. Too much air is left in the unit if the process is rushed enough to cause mixing.

A better filling process uses a vacuum chamber to remove positively and quickly all the air through the hole(s) in the edge spacer. Both the chamber and the double-glazed unit are evacuated. The gas is then injected into the double-glazed unit while air is simultaneously bled into the chamber, so the pressure over the glass remains equalized. Some European manufacturers go as far as using robots to fabricate the units in an argon atmosphere. These last two charging methods are far superior to the first.

Use Additional Lights with Caution

Using more than two layers of glazing increases the window R-value, especially if each light has a low-e coating. But the world is rejoicing at the demise of triple-glazed glass windows at the hand of low-e double-glazed windows for a reason; the weight of the third light was excessive, and the windows were too thick to open easily. Using polymer films instead of glass for the inner lights solves the weight problem, but adding too many layers cuts into the daylight transmission. Daylight transmission falls off much

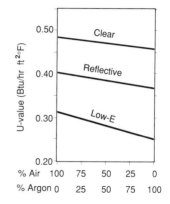

Figure 4-11. U-value vs. argon/air ratio for various glazings (assuming the following emissivities: clear glass = 0.84, reflective glass = 0.40, low-e = 0.08) (Adapted from: Cardinal IG 1990 Architectural Glass Products Catalog, Minneapolis, Minnesota).

faster than the R-value rises when moving past triple-glass glazing while using low-e coated lights (see Chapter 5). This is too much of a price to pay for moderately sized windows whose major function is to bring in daylight. However, the effect is not serious for oversized windows or skylights where daylighting is already excessive.

The Optimal Gap Spacing

If window thickness were not a concern, then one could reason that since air (or argon) is an insulator, more of it

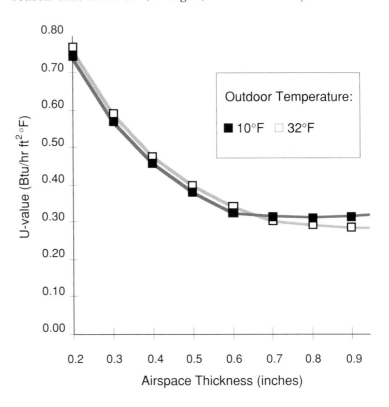

Figure 4-12. U-value vs. air gap separation in a double-glazed window exposed to room temperature on one side and the listed temperatures on the opposite side (Derived from Grashof vs. Reynolds number curves given in: Kreith, F., *Principles of Heat Transfer*, International Textbook Co., Scranton, Pennsylvania).

would insulate better. Unfortunately this is not true. For thin gaps less than 9 mm (3/8 in), friction holds the gas in place, and the insulation value of the gas is solely responsible for holding back the heat flow. The insulation gets better as the gap gets thicker until convection takes over and turns the gap into a chimney. The gas on the warm side is free to rise upward because the opposite light is too far away to constrain it by friction until the buoyant gas reaches the top where it is cooled by the opposite light.

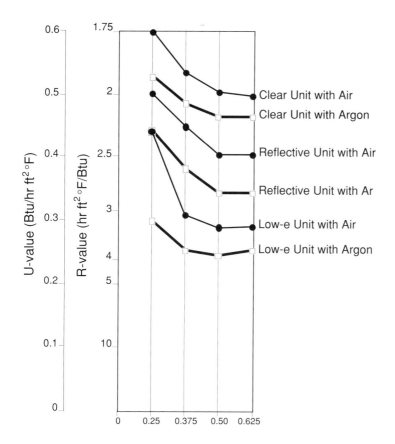

Figure 4-13. Influence of argon on U/R-values (assuming the following emissivities: clear glass = 0.84, reflective glass = 0.40, low-e = 0.08) (Adapted from: Cardinal IG 1990 Architectural Glass Products Catalog, Minneapolis, Minnesota).

Clear Unit with Air

Clear Unit with Argon

Reflective Unit with Air

Reflective Unit with Ar

Low-e Unit with Air

Low-e Unit with Argon

Airspace Thickness (inches)

A large pumping circuit is set up, which easily carries the heat away from the warm light to the cold light. Figure 4-12 shows that there is an optimal separation for a given average air fill temperature before convection takes over. The average temperature of the glass changes throughout the year, so one should choose a gap dimension that works well for the anticipated temperature excursions. Most windows, however, are gapped around 12 mm (1/2 in), which is slightly less than the optimum for air, for easy opening and closing.

Figure 4-13 shows what happens to the center-of-glass U- and R-values for different types of double-glazed windows when argon is used instead of air. Notice that the optimum gap thickness at 12 mm (1/2 in) is slightly less than the gap for air. Krypton's optimum gap is even lower at 6 mm (1/4 in). Krypton is the best gas fill for multiple gap units because ordinary-sized gaps trap too much of a gas volume, which leads to rupture by gas expansion in elevated temperature situations.

Selection

Specs

Cool Daylight with Green Glass

The pyrolytic low-e coatings are used in solar heating applications because their solar transmission is almost as high as clear glass. But many times it is desirable to minimize solar transmission, particularly in office applications where the heat from people, lights, and equipment already is excessive, even during the winter. The solar gain is reduced in two ways: by reflecting more solar heat to the outside with a thicker silver-based coating (see Figure 4-4), and by absorbing more solar heat in the outer layer of the double glazing, where the wind can blow the energy away, all without significantly reducing the daylight transmission. Normal tinted glass does not work well because of the overheating issues discussed in the section titled Low-e Glazings for Offices. Tints also do not work well because the daylight transmission falls off as fast as the solar gain (a 50% tint usually implies a 50% daylight transmission).

The lock-step coupling of solar gain and daylight transmission in tints is favorably overcome by a surprise material—high-iron, or green, glass. Unlike ordinary tints, green glass is a selective absorber—it absorbs more solar energy than daylight energy. An uncoated outer light of green glass in an otherwise clear, double-glazed window transmits almost as much light as triple glazing, yet it rejects as much solar heat as a bronze tint. Coat that same glass with a double layer silver low-e sandwich, and the double glazing solar gain goes down to almost that of reflecting glass, while the daylight transmission remains high, at 60% (about the same as four layers of clear glass). The daylight that filters through this material is termed cool daylight because it contains up to 60% less heat than fluorescent light of an equal brightness, or about the same as light from metal halide lamps. Cool daylight glazing lowers both the daytime air conditioning and the lighting bill because the luminaires are not necessary, and the heat from the daylight is as low as the most efficient lights made.

Growing Plants Under Low-E Glazings

Plants grow fastest in the brightest daylight, so plant growth under glazing slackens according to the glazing's light transmission. Lighting quality also affects plant growth. Photosynthesis, and particularly chlorophyll formation, depend heavily on the blue and red wavelengths at

0.455 and 0.650 μm, respectively. Blue light accelerates chlorophyll production in strong light, whereas red (and even near infrared) radiation is the important lighting component in weak light. Red light is also important for seed germination. Ultraviolet radiation is generally harmful to plants, although some findings suggest that particularly long ultraviolet wavelengths can slightly stimulate photosynthesis if visible light is also present in the correct proportions. Some tinted glazings slow down growth disproportionately, or even harm the plants, because they filter out the important red and blue parts of the solar spectrum.

How do low-e coatings affect plant growth and health? Studies were conducted at the Massachusetts Institute of Technology (MIT) [10] on plant growth under neutral-colored, vacuum-deposited, thin low-e coatings designed for maximizing solar gain. Plant yields were compared with the yields under various other coated and uncoated glazings. The apertures used to admit light through the various test glazings were adjusted so all the daylighting levels were identical. The tests revealed that daylight filtered through low-e coatings on clear and gray laminated sloped glass produced a medium yield of nonflowering plants when compared with uncoated laminated clear glass and polyethylene. Yields were low and unhealthy under low-e coated bronze and green-tinted glass panes.

The vacuum-deposited low-e coatings compensate somewhat for their reduced light transmission by rejecting over two thirds of the damaging ultraviolet radiation, mostly by reflection. The MIT experiments showed that neutral-colored low-e products do not seriously influence yields, plant health, or growth rates if the plants are kept near room temperature.

Plants grow ideally in temperatures between 18°C and 24°C (65°F and 75°F), assuming that night temperatures are 5°C (9°F) lower. Low-e coated glazings can certainly keep plants warmer in the winter, but an excessively glazed growing space can cause higher than normal growing temperatures in the summer due to the added insulation effect of low-e glazings—unless the solar gain is controlled or extra ventilation is used during the summer. The best way to control excess solar gain naturally is to shade the glass externally with a tree canopy that drops its leaves in the fall so that the winter-time solar radiation can heat the growing area.

Excessive shading or insufficient window or skylight opening can lead to the opposite problem of too little light for healthy plant growth. Plant growth does not depend only on light intensity and color, but also on its duration. Very bright light over short durations has the same effect as adequate light over longer durations. For natural lighting durations of 11 to 12 hours, experience shows most common house plant and tree varieties require an average of 800 to 1000 lux (80 to 100 footcandles) throughout the day. Exotic and flowering plants require at least twice these levels.

5

Product Performance

Common Benefits

The major advantages of low-e coatings are their climate adaptability and increased thermal resistance. The coating's shading coefficient and daylight transmission are easily tuned during the deposition process for different climates. This flexibility has inevitably lead to so many offerings and variations that determining the right combination of coating and glazing configuration has become outright daunting. This chapter begins the applications section of this book by comparing the various low-e glazings with conventional windows and classifying the low-e coatings by their type and typical performance ranges. The performance information is based on data published by both European and North American manufacturers.

All types of low-e coatings share the technology's most compelling benefits. These films have optically surpassed the preceding generation of metallic coatings. The color rendition is superb—many coatings appear neutral in color to transmitted light, although technically, transmitted light has the opposite color of reflected light, and some low-e units do slightly color the light reflected off their surfaces. The reflected light appears as a gentle pastel yellow, blue, or purple cast, depending on the product and the coating thickness, but the color is absolutely uniform. Earlier concerns about iridescent, splotchy-colored coatings are now a part of the past. Nonetheless, as is the case with tinted glass, low-e coatings from different manufacturers have different colors and should not mix into the same project.

Specs

All low-e products save energy when compared with similar uncoated products because of the higher insulation value imparted by the coating. Low-e coated double glazing was initially attractive because it minimized condensation problems at the center of the glass and outperformed triple glazing. The initial coatings lowered the winter nighttime U-value of double glazing with a 12 mm (1/2 in) air space to 1.76 W/°K m^2 (0.31 Btuh/°F ft^2), which is about 26% better than triple glazing fabricated with the same air gap dimensions. Today, low-e glazing thermal performance has moved far beyond this, to the point where U-values are low enough to noticeably increase the occupant's thermal comfort in spaces with large windows.

Light and Heat Performance Criteria

Performance is best evaluated against a set of absolute standards. Since low-e products are beginning to reach the limiting laws of physics, it is interesting to measure various products in terms of their ultimate performance bounds.

Figure 5-1 shows the combinations of solar shading coefficients and daylight transmissions that are possible for double-glazed windows. The corresponding total solar transmission, the fraction of solar radiant heat at normal incidence that is transferred through the glazing by both direct transmittance and inward flowing absorbed energy, is given on the opposite axis. The shading coefficient is also given as the total solar transmission divided by 0.87. All insulated glass (IG) units must lie inside the shaded envelope. The upper right hand corner of the envelope represents two panes of high-transmission, 3 mm water-white glass. (Water-white glass does not appear green even at its edges because of its extremely low iron content.) The envelope edge that slopes upward from zero shows the minimum amount of inward flowing solar heat that can possibly accompany a given amount of daylight, assuming all of the near infrared component is rejected. For instance, the graph shows that the lowest possible shading coefficient for a product with 50% daylight transmission is 0.18.

Products used for solar heating should lie near the envelope's top right corner of Figure 5-1. Windows used for light and heat control should lie near the bottom sloped line. The single square near the top right corner shows the performance of ordinary 6 mm double glazing. The circles near the top represent some of the low-e products designed

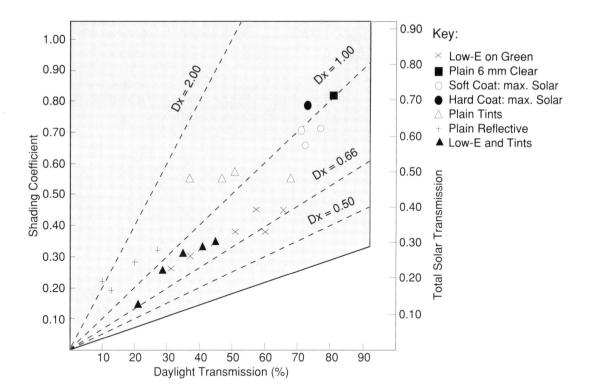

Key:
× Low-E on Green
■ Plain 6 mm Clear
○ Soft Coat: max. Solar
● Hard Coat: max. Solar
△ Plain Tints
+ Plain Reflective
▲ Low-E and Tints

for maximizing solar gain and daylighting in residences. The four triangles in the middle occupy the range covered by ordinary tinted glazings, which is limited and far from the envelope's edges. Reflective office glazing, shown as orthogonal crosses, covers a wider range nearer the bottom edge; but the solar gain is too high for a given daylight transmission. The filled triangles and the crosses show how well the low-e coatings coupled with various tints skirt the envelope's bottom edge.

The ratio of the shading coefficient to the daylight transmission, Dx, is the the transmitted daylight's index of coolness—the lower the number, the cooler the light. Four reference lines—for Dx = 2.00, 1.00, 0.66, and 0.50—are shown as dashed lines radiating from the origin of Figure 5-1. The lowest possible Dx value is 0.36, which forms the bottom edge of the envelope. Figure 5-1 shows that reflective IG generally has the highest Dx values, followed by lowering values for tinted IG units, clear units, and green IG units. A low-e coating added to the inside of the outside light or a low-e film suspended in the airspace lowers Dx dramatically. The lowest Dx value of 0.61 corresponds to the new double silver low-e coating on a light green IG unit.

Figure 5-1. The possible combinations of solar shading coefficients and daylight transmissions for double-glazed windows. The ratio of the shading coefficient to the daylight transmission, Dx, is the transmitted daylight's index of coolness—the lower the number, the cooler the light.

Coolness Index Performance Comparisons

The energy use dependencies on Dx and glazing U-value for offices in both hot and cold climates were assessed by the Windows and Daylighting Group at Lawrence Berkeley Laboratory [11]. Only perimeter offices with a continuous dimming lighting system were modeled.

In cold climates (Madison, Wisconsin), where cooling loads are low, usually a lower window U-value interferes with free cooling via conduction out the windows, particularly on the south and west sides, where solar impact is high. However, the low-e products showed cooling load decreases due to their lower Dx values when compared with their uncoated counterparts. Northern exposures depended little on Dx or U-values. The study also found incremental energy savings diminish as Dx lowers; that is, changing from a bronze tint to a low-e coated bronze tint is much more effective than going from a green tint with an already low Dx to a green tint with a low-e coating. For heating applications, a higher Dx indicates warmer daylight, which means more solar heating. Surprisingly, the study found that a lower U-value saves more energy than a higher Dx.

The same general trends for cooling loads evidenced in a cold climate were found in a hot climate (Lake Charles, Louisiana). The largest savings in cooling energy are attained by changing from a glazing with a high Dx (2.0) to fenestration with a moderate Dx (1.0); however, greater savings are possible at low Dx values when using large apertures.

U-value Measures

The last germane measure is the window's ultimate U-value. A U-value of 0.0 is theoretically obtained by evacuating a double-glazed low-e unit—assuming the coating's emissivity is zero. Several realities increase the U-value: real emissivities do not fall below 0.03, real window edges must be sealed, and practical double glazing must resist the atmosphere's formidable pressure with internal compression supports. The sealed edges and supports will always cause thermal bridging. The supports must become either slimmer as they become more numerous, or thicker as they become less populous. The resulting thermal short circuits suggest a limiting U-value of approximately 0.19

W/°K m² (0.033 Btuh/°F ft²) over a normal double glazing thickness, assuming the supports slim down to granular microcells. The ultrahigh performance low-e windows with four glazings, two low-e coatings, and krypton gas fills have reached U-values as low as 0.68 W/°K m² (0.125 Btuh/°F ft²). The highest U-value for a low-e unit, at 1.82 W/°K m² (0.32 Btuh/°F ft²), is for a double-glazed air-filled window.

U-value Variations with IG Unit Design

A window's U-value is altered by more than the low-e treatment. The following graphs show how various treatments and geometries determine the window's resistance to heat flow. Chapter 4 explains the principles behind these effects.

Emissivity Effects. Figure 5-2 shows how emissivity alters the U-value for single-, double-, and triple-glazed windows, when the 4 mm lights are spaced 12 mm apart. The curves do not extend all the way to the right because uncoated glass has an emissivity of 0.84. Low-e coatings change single glazing's U-values the most, but only in climates where condensation is not a problem (water clinging to a low-e surface cancels out its low emissivity due to the water's high emissivity). Note that the U-value for single glazing nearly matches the U-value for uncoated double glazing when the single glazing's emissivity is 0.02. Reducing the already low emissivity from 0.15 to 0.02 lowers the U-value for double glazing by about 23%.

Gas Fill Effects. Filling double-glazed units with exotic gases significantly lowers the U-value. Figure 5-3 shows

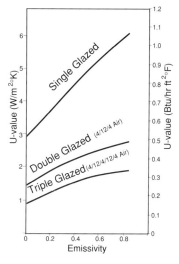

Figure 5-2. U-value variation with emissivity for single-, double-, and triple-glazed windows with 12 mm air gaps (Adapted from: Button, D.A., Dunning, R., *Fenestration 2000*, July 1989, Pilkington Glass Limited, and 3M Sun Control Tech notes DSI909 Sept 21, 1979).

Figure 5-3. U-value variation with gas conductivity in double and triple glazing (emissivity = 0.10) (Adapted from: Button, D.A., Dunning, R., *Fenestration 2000*, July 1989, Pilkington Glass Limited [25]).

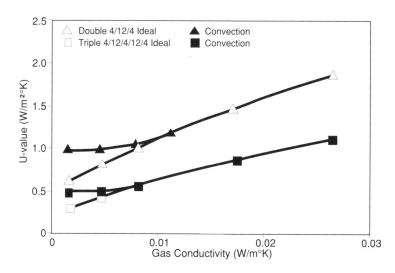

the effect of gas conductivity on the heat flow through double and triple glazing. The curves marked with unfilled data points show idealized behavior when there is no convection. In reality, convection is always present. The extension lines with solid data points show how convection losses overshadow a low conduction gas's inconsequential heat flow and raises the idealized U-value in 12 mm gapped IG units. For reference, air's conductivity is 0.024 W/m°K, argon's is 0.016, and krypton's is 0.0085.

Multiple Gap Effects. Adding more panes creates more dead air spaces for an added insulation effect, but at the ultimate expense of light transmission. Figure 5-4 shows how the wintertime U-value decreases with the number of ordinary and low-e coated panes for air-, krypton-, and argon-filled units. Each additional pane is spaced 12 mm (0.5 in.) away from its neighbor. The thick gray curve shows how the low-e daylight transmission falls at a faster rate than the U-value after the third pane is added (the thinner gray curve represents the noncoated panes.) The shading coefficients are also shown as dashed curves for the same materials. Extra panes usually increase the volume of trapped gas, which can cause ruptured seals when the gas expands due to ordinary summer warming, or

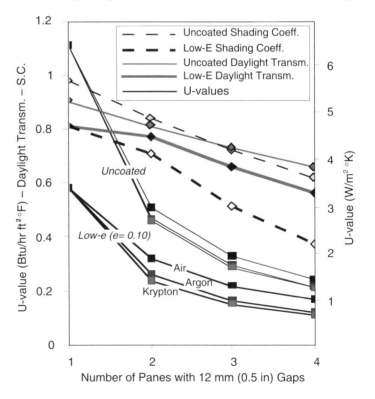

Figure 5-4. U-value vs. the number of panes for low-e and uncoated glazings with various gas fills.

reduced atmospheric pressure at a site that is significantly higher than the manufacturing site. Using krypton minimizes this problem since the gas gives the best insulation values when the gap dimensions are the narrowest.

Edge Geometry Effects. The last variable that significantly affects a window's thermal performance is the edge geometry. The metal edge spacers used to seal most IG units can seriously raise a window's effective overall U-value, depending on the window's size and nominal U-value. The amount of heat lost through the highly conductive metal edge spacer is not significant when compared with the amount lost through the central portions of ordinary double glazing. The situation is reversed for R-values near 0.88 °K m^2/W (5°F ft^2/Btuh) to the point where 25% more heat is lost through the edges than through the bulk of the IG unit. Chapter 6 outlines a procedure for predicting the effective U-value for a window with metal edge spacers and a given glazing U-value and area.

Given these effects, how does one choose a window that does the job properly? Chapters 6 through 9 introduce several design methods for determining the trade-offs between daylight, shading coefficient, and U-value, depending on the application.

Comparisons by Product

Glazing performance comparisons can also take place among representative products, rather than across variables. Tables 5-1 through 5-4 classify the popular low-e coatings by their five types of manufacture. Comparisons are also made with similar products without the low-e treatment. Noncoated entries are identified in the tables by their emissivity of 0.84. Products are labeled as either North American or European to indicate their manufacturing sources and marketing regions. The daylighting index for coolness, Dx, is given for each entry to quantify the ratio of the listed shading coefficient to the given daylight transmission. As with the shading coefficient, the lower the Dx, the lower the solar gain; but unlike the shading coefficient, a low Dx can also indicate high daylight transmission.

Where applicable, manufacturer's U-values are given for air, krypton, and argon fills. The U-values are at a window's center; the edge effects and window framing system effects are not considered, although they can significantly affect the overall unit U-value when an argon or krypton filling is used. Most manufacturers only publish center-of-glass U-values; overall U-values for given window sizes are only beginning to be published on a voluntary basis. All the remaining information in the following tables, except the emissivity column, is identical to the information published by the manufacturers listed in Appendix A, so the reader can compare the listed products with offerings from multiple sources.

Thin Depositions on Glass

Pros. Glass coaters can easily create a variety of metal-based coatings for different window applications because a thin coating's composition is easily controlled during the vacuum deposition process. The typical combinations of solar transmission and U-values listed at the end of this section are sufficient to produce a heating season profit for even north-facing windows at many midlatitude locations. There is always heat in light, even north light. The better gas-filled low-e windows can capture this heat because their solar transmission is still high, and the U-value is low enough to prevent overshadowing back losses through the window. At the other end of the spectrum, some low-e coatings can reject as much heat as reflective glazing, but without sacrificing much in daylight transmission. Between these two extremes are all the combinations for dealing productively with specific climates and locations.

The other advantages of thin coating low-e depositions are as follows:

- high—200°C (392°F)—operating temperatures (for solar collectors or industrial uses such as windows for high temperature manufacturing areas)

- ultralow emissivities, as low as 0.03 (which produces the lowest double-glazed U-values, typically 1.31 W/m^2°K [0.23 Btu/hr°F ft^2] with argon gas fills)

- up to two-thirds less UV transmission than ordinary double glazing due to the high UV reflection (for lengthening the life of fabrics and art works)

- simple installation (the coated glass handles and glazes like noncoated glass)

- low cost (only the pyrolytics are less expensive)

- wide ranging shading coefficients (varying from 0.38 to 0.74, depending on the coating composition)

Cons. The drawbacks of the so-called *soft coat* product arise from the need to package the coating as a double-glazed unit to prevent the coating from corroding. This adds significantly to the cost of a window unless double glazing is required anyway. Many manufacturers are offering up to 20-year warrantees on the glass coatings and edge seals to dispel any consumer uneasiness over the coating's durability.

Other disadvantages include the following:

- limited (6 months to a year) shelf life when unsealed, depending on storage conditions

- longer glazing times (proper sealing requires stripping the coating back from the glass edges)

Table 5-1. Performance Comparison Between Thin (Soft) Coatings and Conventional Treatments Using 6 mm Double Glazing with a 12 mm Gap (0.5 in)

	Emissivity (uncoated =0.84)	Glass	Daylight %Transmittance	Shading Coefficient	Coolness Index Dx	Wintertime U-value W/sq m °K air	argon	Btuh/sq ft °F air	argon
	0.84	Clear	80	0.82	1.03	2.72	2.55	0.48	0.45
	0.10	Clear	77	0.71	0.92	1.76	1.42	0.31	0.25
	0.03	Clear	69	0.49	0.71	1.65	1.31	0.29	0.23
	0.10	Clear	43	0.40	0.93	1.76	1.48	0.31	0.26
	0.84	Green	68	0.55	0.81	2.72	2.55	0.48	0.45
	0.10	Green	67	0.49	0.73	1.76	1.42	0.31	0.25
North	0.03	Green	60	0.38	0.63	1.65	1.31	0.29	0.23
	0.10	Green	37	0.30	0.81	1.76	1.48	0.31	0.26
America	0.84	Gray	37	0.55	1.49	2.72	2.55	0.48	0.45
	0.10	Gray	36	0.45	1.25	1.76	1.42	0.31	0.25
	0.03	Gray	35	0.31	0.89	1.65	1.31	0.29	0.23
	0.10	Gray	21	0.26	1.24	1.76	1.48	0.31	0.26
	0.84	Bronze	47	0.55	1.17	2.72	2.55	0.48	0.45
	0.10	Bronze	46	0.47	1.02	1.76	1.42	0.31	0.25
	0.03	Bronze	41	0.33	0.80	1.65	1.31	0.29	0.23
	0.10	Bronze	26	0.28	1.08	1.76	1.48	0.31	0.26
	0.50	Pewter	20	0.30	1.50	2.44	2.21	0.43	0.39
	0.50	Stainless	13	0.19	1.46	2.33	2.16	0.41	0.38
	0.84	Clear	80	0.82	1.03	2.72	2.55	0.48	0.45
	0.10	Clear	74	0.72	0.97	1.80	1.43	0.32	0.25
	0.04	Clear	69	0.67	0.97	1.68	1.33	0.30	0.23
	0.10	Green	61	0.47	0.77	1.80	1.43	0.32	0.25
Europe	0.04	Green	57	0.45	0.79	1.68	1.33	0.30	0.23
	0.10	Gray	36	0.44	1.22	1.80	1.43	0.32	0.25
	0.04	Gray	33	0.42	1.27	1.68	1.33	0.30	0.23
	0.10	Bronze	43	0.47	1.09	1.80	1.43	0.32	0.25
	0.04	Bronze	40	0.45	1.13	1.68	1.33	0.30	0.23
	0.04	Pewter	20	0.28	1.40	1.65		0.29	
	0.04	Stainless	26	0.29	1.12	1.65		0.29	

- no posttempering—the glass must be pretempered
- slightly colored reflections

Performance Figures. Various tinted cover plates are listed on the previous page in Table 5-1 along with clear cover plates for the various coated and uncoated products. The interior plates are always clear glass. All U-values are at the glazing center.

Thin Depositions on Suspended Polyester Film

Pros. Roll coaters can easily create a variety of low-e coatings on polyester film for different window applications because the low-temperature vacuum deposition process is easily controlled. The extra gas space(s) formed by the suspended film(s) produces a lower U-value than any of the other approaches. The overall thickness of the unit is nearly the same as an ordinary double-glazed unit when krypton is used as the gas fill. In addition, the polymer carrier also produces the second lowest shading coefficient among all the low-e alternatives because of its reduced solar transmission.

The other advantages of thin low-e coatings on suspended plastic are as follows:

- lightweight construction (gives the lowest U-value at normal dimensions)

- best noise control (because of the extra air space[s])

- lowest center-of-glass U-value at 0.68 $W/m^{2}°K$ (0.125 $Btu/hr°F\ ft^2$) when using two suspended films and krypton gas fills

- lowest UV transmission (less than 0.5%, or 0.01 the transmission of ordinary clear double glazing) due to the high UV reflection at the multiple low-e coatings and the moderate UV absorption within the polyester films (for lengthening the life of fabrics and art works)

- second lowest shading coefficient due to the high light absorption in the suspended plastic

- simple installation (the unit handles and glazes like noncoated double glazing)

Cons. The drawbacks arise from the need to protect the suspended film in a double-glazed unit to prevent the low-e coating from corroding. The polyester film mounting system adds significantly to the cost of the window, so the manufacturing cost advantage of roll-coated plastic is more than negated.

Other disadvantages include the following:

- low operating temperatures—less than 66 °C (150°F)

- distorted light reflections off the suspended plastic in very hot climates due to creeping

- reduced daylight transmission due to the light absorption in the suspended plastic

- slightly colored reflections

- higher than normal daylight reflections off the outside surface

Table 5-2. Thin Coat on Suspended Plastic with 6 mm Cover Plates and Two 12 mm Air Gaps (0.5 in) Compared with Conventional Double Glazing

	Emissivity (uncoated = 0.84)	Glass	Daylight %Transmittance	Shading Coefficient	Coolness Index Dx	Wintertime U-value			
						W/sq m °K air	krypton	Btuh/sq ft °F air	krypton
	0.84	Clear	80	0.82	1.03	2.72		0.48	
	0.10	Clear	68	0.61	0.90	1.36		0.24	
	0.10	Clear	61	0.49	0.80	1.25		0.22	
	0.07	Clear	53	0.41	0.77	1.25		0.22	
	0.05	Clear	45	0.35	0.78	1.25		0.22	
	0.05	Clear	28	0.23	0.82	1.25		0.22	
	0.10	Clear	62	0.52	0.84		0.68		0.12
	0.84	Green	68	0.55	0.81	2.72		0.48	
	0.07	Green	51	0.38	0.75	1.25		0.22	
North	0.07	Green	45	0.33	0.73	1.25		0.22	
	0.07	Green	38	0.30	0.79	1.25		0.22	
	0.84	Gray	37	0.55	1.49	2.72		0.48	
America	0.05	Gray	29	0.33	1.14	1.25		0.22	
	0.05	Gray	25	0.28	1.12	1.25		0.22	
	0.05	Gray	17	0.22	1.29	1.25		0.22	
	0.84	Bronze	47	0.55	1.17	2.72		0.48	
	0.05	Bronze	35	0.34	0.97	1.25		0.22	
	0.05	Bronze	21	0.23	1.10	1.25		0.22	
	0.05	Bronze	16	0.18	1.13	1.19		0.21	
	0.05	Pewter	13	0.18	1.38	1.19		0.21	
	0.84	Clear	80	0.82	1.03	2.72		0.48	
Europe	0.10 *	Clear	56	0.46	0.82	0.60		0.11	
	0.10 *	Clear	63	0.58	0.92	0.75		0.13	

* Overall glazing thickness is 100 mm (4 in) using 3 argon gaps.

Performance Figures. Various tinted cover plates are listed in Table 5-2 along with clear cover plates for the various suspended films. The performance figures for the same glass cover plates are listed without suspended films for comparison. The interior plates are always clear glass. All U-values are at the glazing center.

Thin Depositions on Retrofit Plastic Films

Pros. Roll coaters can easily create a variety of low-e coatings on polyester films for different window retrofit applications because the low temperature vacuum deposition process is easily controlled. The coating is usually protected by a lamination of polypropylene film. Any window retrofitted with the film sandwich adopts the low-e characteristics of the film. The film reduces the U-value by 35% for single glazing , and by 22% for double glazing.

The advantages of retrofit thin low-e coatings are as follows:

- increased insulation levels, with no increase in weight or volume

- no need for seals or special construction

- inexpensive and cost effective over the product's lifetime

- low UV transmission (up to 90% less transmitted UV than ordinary double glazing due to the low-e coating's high UV reflection and the plastic carrier's high UV absorption, resulting in lengthened fabric and artwork life)

- second lowest shading coefficient due to the extra layers of light absorbing plastics

Cons. The drawbacks arise from the need to regularly replace the exposed film, which inevitably succumbs to corrosion and ultraviolet attack.

Other disadvantages include the following:

- limited to low temperature applications—less than 66 °C (150 °F)

- limited life of 9 to 15 years when installed inside, less than 5 years when installed outside because of ultraviolet attack

- reduced daylight transmission due to the adhered polyester film

- highest emissivity (emissivities as high as 0.25 give the highest U-values of all the low-e approaches).

Performance Figures. Retrofitted tinted and clear glass panes are listed in Table 5-3, along with the performance figures for retrofitted double-glass glazed units with either clear or tinted cover plates. The figures for the same units without the adhered films are listed for comparison. All U-values are at the glazing center.

Table 5-3. Performance Comparison Between Thin Coat on Retrofit Film and Conventional Treatment Using 6 mm Glass

	Emissivity (uncoated = 0.84)	Glass	Daylight %Transmittance	Shading Coefficient	Coolness Index Dx	Wintertime U-value W/sq m °K air	argon	Btuh/sq ft °F air	argon
North America	0.84	Clear	90	0.98	1.09	6.30		1.11	
	0.25	Clear	50	0.43	0.86	3.92		0.69	
	0.23	Clear	34	0.42	1.24	3.92		0.69	
	0.29	Clear*	20	0.29	1.45	4.37		0.77	
	0.25	Tinted	26	0.35	1.35	3.92		0.69	
	0.23	Tinted	18	0.31	1.72	3.92		0.69	
	0.84	Clear	80	0.82	1.03	2.72		0.48	
	0.25	Clear	45	0.42	0.93	2.21		0.39	
	0.23	Clear	31	0.43	1.39	2.21		0.39	
	0.25	Tinted	26	0.31	1.19	2.21		0.39	
	0.23	Tinted	17	0.31	1.82	2.21		0.39	

Denotes double glazing.

* Does not use a polypropylene overcoat.

Pyrolytic Coatings

Pros. A pyrolytic treatment is a virtually colorless, thick coating, which is usually produced by enveloping hot glass with inorganic vapors. The latest process produces a stable, hard, surface without iridescence. The other advantages of pyrolytic low-e coatings are as follows:

- ultrahigh, over 300°C (572°F), operating temperatures (for solar collectors or industrial uses such as windows that overlook high temperature manufacturing areas)

- highest double-glazing shading coefficient at 0.79 (for solar heating applications), with the same daylight transmission as thin coatings

- theoretically, most economical low-e product to manufacture

- corrosion proof (this is necessary for single glazing and vented, double-glazed units)

- abrasion proof (for easy cleaning and long life)

- simple installation (the coated glass handles and glazes like noncoated glass because edge stripping is not necessary)

- posttempering possible

- good color rendition

Cons. The so-called *hard coat* product offers inherently less variety since the deposition process gives less control over the coating's thermal and optical characteristics than the vacuum sputtering process used for depositing thin coatings.

Other disadvantages include the following:

- intermediate emissivities of 0.17 to 0.20 produce slightly higher U-values than the thin coatings

- slight surface haze (this effect becomes visible in bright sunlight)

Performance Figures. Various tinted cover plates are listed in Table 5-4 along with clear cover plates for the various coated and uncoated products. The interior plates are always clear glass. All U-values are at the glazing center. The first two lines in the table are for clear, single glazing.

Table 5-4. Performance Comparison Between Pyrolytic Coatings and Conventional Treatments on 6 mm Single Glazing and Double Glazing with a12 mm Gap

	Emissivity (uncoated = 0.84)	Glass	Daylight %Transmittance	Shading Coefficient	Coolness Index Dx	Wintertime U-value W/sq m °C		Btuh/sq ft °F	
						air	argon	air	argon
North America	0.84	Single	90	0.98	1.09	6.30		1.11	
	0.18	Single	82	0.95	1.13	3.52		0.62	
	0.84	Clear	80	0.82	1.03	2.72		0.48	
	0.18	Clear	74	0.80	1.12	1.87		0.33	
Europe	0.84	Single	90	0.98	1.09	6.30		1.11	
	0.18	Single	84	0.95	1.13	3.52		0.62	
	0.84	Clear	80	0.82	1.03	2.72		0.48	
	0.18	Clear	73	0.79	1.08	1.90		0.33	
	0.84	Green	68	0.55	0.81	2.72		0.48	
	0.18	Green	60	0.52	0.87	1.90		0.33	
	0.84	Gray	37	0.55	1.49	2.72		0.48	
	0.18	Gray	35	0.49	1.40	1.90		0.33	
	0.84	Bronze	47	0.55	1.17	2.72		0.48	
	0.18	Bronze	42	0.52	1.24	1.68	1.33	0.30	0.23

Thick Coating on Glass

Pros. A thick coating is a transparent semiconductor, usually indium oxide, cadmium tin oxide, or indium tin oxide, which is deposited at high temperature on glass as a single, relatively thick layer (several millionths of a meter thick). The thick layer avoids the quality control issues associated with thin coatings and pyrolytics, but actually ends up costing more than even the multilayered thin coatings because the semiconductor material is expensive, and relatively large amounts of material are required. Nevertheless, the material is worth waiting for because of the following advantages:

- corrosion proof (for single glazing and vented, double-glazed units)

- abrasion proof (for easy cleaning and long life)

- ultrahigh operating temperatures—over 300°C (572 °F)

- handles and glazes like noncoated glass

- lower emissivities than the pyrolytics

Cons. Thick coatings are not in common use yet because they are expensive. Some coatings add a slight color to the glass.

Selection

Specs

Performance Figures. No figures are tabulated because of the coating's current unavailability. Typical emissivities are between 0.13 and 0.15 (which produce a U-value of 1.80 W/m²°K (0.32 Btuh/ft²°F). The shading coefficient for a double-glazed unit is relatively high at 75%.

Tables classifying all products by application are found at the end of Chapters 7 and 8. Information on daylight and solar reflectivity is also listed in these same tables so that the reader can evaluate the coating's visual appearance. In addition, values for solar absorption and transmission are given to further aid the reader in corresponding the listed products with offerings from the multiple sources listed in Appendix A.

Basic Design Choices

The Right Glazing for the Job

The previous chapter ranks a rainbow of low-e glazings by their thermal and optical characteristics. Of course there is more to choosing a glazing material than successfully navigating tables of performance figures. Design decisions, such as the following, quickly come into play:

- choosing the correct R-value for the job
- sizing the fenestration opening
- choosing the correct color and aesthetics
- finding reliable (and many times, multiple) suppliers

The first two issues are settled objectively in this chapter, while the last two issues depend on experience.

Determining the correct glazing R-value has become a fundamental issue common to both commercial and residential jobs now that low-e glazings can insulate so well. This chapter presents several design methods for selecting the maximum R-value depending on the application. In addition, the solar geometry fundamentals that influence all window designs are presented. Sizing a window to save energy without sacrificing daylighting, view, or visual comfort also depends on the application; but the procedures are involved enough to require the subsequent separate chapters on residential and commercial applications.

How Much R-value Is Enough?

Low-e glazing assemblies span R-values from triple glazing to the equivalent of 5 cm (2 in) of Styrofoam®. Given

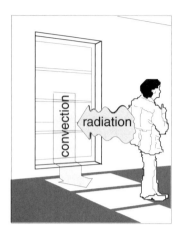

Figure 6-1. How windows affect thermal comfort. Radiation can travel across the room, whereas cold drafts are usually located only near the windows.

that more R-value costs more, how much of a good thing is enough? The answer, of course, depends on the climate and location and, most of all, on whether the application is commercial or residential.

Residential. Home owners and tenants alike are more concerned with thermal comfort than energy conservation, even when energy costs are dear. In moderate to cold climates such as Northern Europe, large conventionally glazed windows always adversely affect comfort during the seasonal extremes because the glazing acts either as a radiant sink, or in the summer, as a radiant source. In the winter, the cold glazing literally draws heat from the occupants as infrared energy. Figure 6-1 illustrates how this infrared heat loss path can beam all the way across a room, whereas the cold drafts off the window are confined to the floor near the cold glass. In these cases, the designer should use a higher window R-value than called for by the building codes or condensation avoidance curves that follow. The infrared draw is not important for conventionally glazed windows when the window areas are small compared with the room's floor area, usually less than 10%, or when the occupants are not expected to sit near the windows for long periods of time.

The least expensive means of achieving an elevated R-value in a sealed low-e unit is with a gas fill. Creating extra air, or gas spaces with suspended low-e coated films, or even glass, gives the highest R-values, if one can afford it. More than three gaps are not recommended because the added layers severely cut into the daylight transmission.

The R-values dictated by the building codes and the condensation curves that follow are sufficient in most climates, particularly since the newer codes reflect the current thinking on energy conservation. Life-cycle costing is rarely used to evaluate glazing alternatives.

Commercial. Elevated window R-values are not necessarily better for most offices. The high density of warm bodies, the office computers and peripherals, and of course the extra lighting already generate a heat surplus during most of the year. The windows can help in removing some of this unwanted heat by not insulating too well. Condensation isn't a problem either when the humidity is controlled by an air conditioner. Even thermal comfort is ensured during the winter months in perimeter offices with sill-mounted forced air heaters, which direct an air flow over the windows. The warm air brings the otherwise cold glass surface temperature to room air temperature before the air flows on to heat the room. One achieves summertime comfort in

Low-E Glazing Design Guide

a similar fashion by blowing the cool air from the air-conditioner outlets over the windows rather than directly onto the occupants. The practice isn't recommended when annealed glass is used, however, for any uneven flow over the glass can cause enough thermal stressing to break the window. In addition, washing windows with conditioned air wastes energy in underheated or overheated climates, especially when the windows are single glazed. A double-glazed low-e window overcomes the problem because it insulates well enough to maintain the inside pane to within 6°C (10°F) of room temperature when it is a frigid -18°C (0°F) outside.

The fenestration must insulate well enough to conserve a reasonable amount of energy during the peak months. The building codes indirectly name this reasonable amount by dictating maximum window U-values. In most cases, the worst low-e U-values are sufficient to meet the newer codes. Gas fills are overkill unless the majority of the wall is glazed, in which case a lower U-value is required to meet the code requirements that prescribe a maximum aggregate wall U-value. The next section shows how to compute this trade-off using the English and American building codes as examples.

The exception is the low-rise, low-density office which really resembles the energy use patterns of a residence more than an office. Here, the code should be bettered to ensure thermal comfort when large window areas are used near seating areas.

Large air-conditioning operating costs are associated not with an office window's U-value, but rather with the window's area, shading coefficient, and daylight transmission. The next chapter describes two design methods for choosing the right combination of these three fenestration variables.

Low U-value windows also come into play commercially in certain performance building codes. A performance code outlines performance trade-offs among different building components for meeting an overall thermal figure, rather than just independently meeting a minimum prescriptive standard for each building element. It is rather like robbing Peter to pay Paul. For example, if the opaque section of an office wall cannot meet the maximum U-value listed in a prescriptive code, then an alternative performance code is often used to show how a low U-value window can offset the deficit, providing that the area-weighted average of the fenestration and wall U-values meet a prescribed limit. Most countries now offer a performance code alternative. The next section shows some examples of early 1990 performance building codes from the United States and England.

Computing the U-value

U-value Determination by Building Code. Performance building codes often are based on the concept of an average U-value for a wall (or roof). This value, U_{walls}, is an area-weighted average of each wall component's U-value as given by:

$$U_{walls} = \frac{U_{opaquewall} \times A_{opaquewall} \times U_{window} \times A_{window} + etc.}{A_{wall}}$$

where A_{wall} includes the areas of all vertical exposed surfaces (walls, windows, doors, etc.). A_{wall} is really the sum of all the areas appearing in the numerator of the preceding relation.

Table 6-1. English Insulation Requirements for Walls, Roofs, and Floors in W/sq m°K

Building Type	Exposed Wall	Ground Floor, Exposed Floors	Roofs	Semiexposed Walls and Floors
Houses, Flats	0.45	0.45	0.25	0.6
All Others	0.45	0.45	0.45	0.6

In England, this concept is embodied in the performance code published by Building Regulations in Document L1, *Conservation of Fuel and Energy*. It is an alternative cal-

Table 6-2. English Maximum Single Glazed Areas for Various Buiilding Types

Building Type	Windows	Rooflights
Houses, Flats, Maisonettes	15% of total floor area	
Other Residential, Hospitals, Hotels	25% of exposed wall	20% of roof area
Places of Assembly, Offices, Shops (except for ground floors)	35% of exposed wall	
Factories, Similar Buildings	15% of exposed wall	

culation procedure for modifying the attendant prescriptive codes as reproduced in Tables 6-1 and 6-2.

The total heat loss as computed by the performance code for the alternative building must be equal to or less than the loss of a single glazed reference building of the same size, which complies with Tables 6-1 and 6-2. The procedure shows, in effect, that using low-e windows in dwellings increases the permitted window area up from 15% to approximately 45% of the floor area (double glazing increases the area up to 30%).

In the United States, ASHRAE/IES Standard 90.1-1989 is used to determine a wall's average U-value and the percent glazing. This standard is frequently updated and must be consulted regularly. The code applies to all new buildings except for buildings used in manufacturing or single and multiple family dwellings of three or fewer stories above grade.

The alternative performance code is complex enough to demand the use of computers. A program for MS-DOS machines is supplied with this code. The performance code must be used to go beyond the fairly restrictive glazing areas dictated by the prescriptive code. The simpler prescriptive code depends on so many variables that for all intents and purposes, it outlines performance trade-offs among different building components as does a performance code.

The prescriptive code uses tables that characterize various United States locations by their average daily western solar intake and their heating and cooling degree days. A season's degree days are the sum of each day's mean temperature subtracted from a base temperature (which is related to the thermostat setting). Monthly and annual heating and cooling degree day records are published by the weather bureau and by ASHRAE.

Figure 6-2 shows a typical table (called an Alternative Component Package) from the code for determining the maximum allowable percent of fenestration (as a percentage of the total exterior wall area) and the maximum wall U-value. Some of the cities to which Figure 6-2 applies are found at the top of the table. The characteristic heating degree days are shown in the upper left corner as HDD50, the cooling degree days as CDD65, and the average vertical western solar gain as VSEW (in Btu/ft^2 day). The table uses the following variables as input:

- the lighting and equipment power density
- the exterior shading coverage

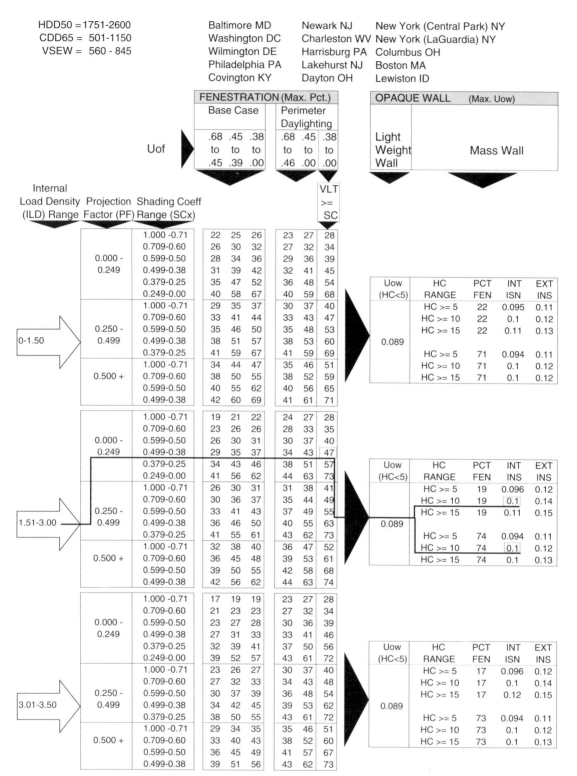

Figure 6-2. Table 8A-25 from ASHRAE/IES Standard 90.1-1989 for determining the maximum wall U-value and the permissible amount of glazing (as a percentage of the total exterior wall area) (Reprinted by permission from ASHRAE Standard 90.1-1989, Energy Efficient Design of New Buildings Except Low-Rise Residential Buildings, published by the American Society of Heating, Refrigerating and Air-Conditioning Engineers, Inc.)

- the glazing shading coefficient

- a choice between daylighting (which must include lighting with automatic dimmers) or artificial lighting

- the window U-value

- the wall heat capacity

The following shows how the table is used to fix the envelope design. To find the maximum allowable percent fenestration:

Step 1: Enter the table from the left with the internal load density—the average of the lighting power within 15 feet of each exterior wall, plus the expected average receptacle power density for all areas within 15 feet of each exterior wall (the receptacle power density is usually between 0.50 and 0.75 Btu/ft^2).

Step 2: Choose one of the three classes of projection factor for the corresponding internal load density. The external shading projection factor, PF, is given as:

$$PF = \text{Overhang Depth} / (\text{Window Height} + \text{Distance}),$$

where Distance is the distance from the top of the fenestration to the bottom of the external shading projection. Select the projection factor range of 0.000–0.249 if there is no external shading.

Step 3: Choose a row corresponding to the window's shading coefficient.

Step 4: Choose a column class corresponding to either no daylighting or perimeter daylighting.

Step 5: Choose a column within the lighting class according to the window's U-value, U_{of}. Note that all double-glazed low-e windows fall within the column labeled 0.38 to 0. This column also implies that the visible light transmittance is greater than the shading coefficient (VLT >= SC).

Step 6: The intersection of the chosen row and column gives the maximum allowable percent fenestration as a percentage of the total exterior wall area.

All the glazing percentages listed for low-e windows are significantly higher than for ordinary windows (only a minority of other climates list small increases).

To find the maximum allowable attendant U-value, U_{ow}, for the opaque wall assembly, perform the following steps:

Step 7: Determine the heat capacity, HC, of the opaque section of the envelope in Btu/ft^{2}°F.

Step 8: Using the same alternative component package table, select the subtable to the right of the allowed percent fenestration given in Step 6 and determine its column class corresponding to the wall's heat capacity. For a lightweight wall assembly, where HC < 5, use the U-value listed in this column class, which is the same for all loading conditions. For a mass wall, select the two rows corresponding to the wall's heat capacity. The maximum allowable range of U-values is given at the intersection of these rows and the column labeling the insulation position. If the wall insulation is placed internal to or integral with the wall mass, use the column headed INT INS; if not, use the exterior insulation column labeled as EXT INS.

The two U-values, which represent the range of allowable U-values, are keyed to a small or large percent fenestration. The maximum allowable U-value is found by straight line interpolation over these fenestration percentages according to the fenestration percentage found in Step 6.

Example 6-1. Determine the maximum allowable percent fenestration for unshaded windows and the corresponding U-value for the remaining section of office wall in New York City. The office wall is insulated integrally and has an interior heat capacity (HC) of 10 Btu/ft^{2}°F. Assume the artificial lighting draws 1.5 W/ft^{2}, but the office is normally daylit. The low-e windows have a shading coefficient of 0.39 and a U-value of 0.29 Btu/hr°F ft^{2}.

Solution:

The path to the solution is shown as a heavy underline in Figure 6-2. Assuming the receptacle power density is 0.75 W/ft^{2}, the internal load density becomes 2.25 W/ft^{2}, which puts the entry point to the figure at the middle table on the page.

No exterior shading and a shading coefficient of 0.39 selects the middle row of the top class in the middle table.

The low-e U-value of 0.29 Btu/hr°F ft^{2} for the daylit scheme selects the column labeled *Perimeter Daylighting, 0.38 to 0.*

The intersection of this column and the selected row gives a maximum allowable percent low-e fenestration of 47, twice as much window as is allowed using clear double glazing.

Low-E Glazing Design Guide

Following the horizontal solution line to the right gives the maximum allowable U-value range of 0.10 to 0.10 Btu/hr°F ft^2 for an interior insulated wall with an HC range >= 10. No interpolation is necessary.

U-value Determination by Condensation Charts. A lower window U-value means a warmer inner glass surface during the winter. Damaging window condensation on the bulk of the glazing area is altogether avoidable if the correct U-value is chosen for the glazing. A low-e window product probably exists for warding off condensation in a given climate condition. The next section shows how to identify that low-e window.

Although the low-e glazings are up to the job of stopping condensation in the central viewing area, most edge assemblies used to mount the glazings are not. There is enough thermal bridging through the commonly used metal edge spacers to induce condensation at the window perimeter during high humidity conditions or cold outdoor temperatures. Usually this band of condensation is narrow enough—less than 3 cm (1.25 in) in most cases—to avoid the formation of damaging water rivulets. It is tempting to solve the problem by burying the window edge deeper into the frame, particularly if the frame is a good insulating material, but one should avoid this practice because it shadows too much of the glass from the sun. The shadowing could lead to high thermal stresses and could, under extremely severe weather conditions (high solar load combined with low outdoor temperatures), increase the potential for glass breakage. The best solution to the perimeter fogging problem so far is the thermally broken edge seal, as exemplified by companies that produce the multiple polyester film glazings.

The onset of water vapor condensation at the center of the glass depends on four factors: the indoor relative humidity, the window's U-value, the indoor air temperature, and the outdoor air temperature.

The relative humidity in a residence varies with the living conditions. Heavy cooking, showering, or a large number of plants can raise the relative humidity to over 60% when there is little natural ventilation. On the other hand, microwave cooking and quick baths will create very dry indoor conditions. One way to determine the relative humidity without the benefit of a weather forecaster's sling psychrometer is to record the indoor and outdoor temperatures when condensation forms on an existing window, and to use the following chart to look up the relative humidity. The relative humidity in an air-conditioned office

Calculation

Basic Design Choices

Figure 6-3. Condensation Prediction Chart for Vertical Windows with Heat Flow Outwards. Copyright © Pilkington Glass Ltd., 1989.

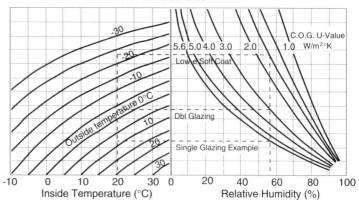

Vertical Window Heat Flow Outwards

simply runs at wherever the air-conditioner is set, typically 50%.

Once armed with the expected relative humidity and minimum outdoor temperature, the required U-value for condensation avoidance over the bulk of the glass is determined by intersecting two lines on the condensation prediction chart (Figure 6-3) for vertical windows. The U-values are also labeled by window type to aid in the selection process.

The chart is used by first selecting a point on the left graph that corresponds to the outdoor and indoor air temperatures. A horizontal line is then drawn from that point to the right until it intersects a second vertical line at the expected relative humidity on the second graph. This intersection marks the U-value for avoiding condensation. Interpolation over the U-value curves is usually required to pinpoint the exact U-value.

Calculating the Real U-value. The window U-value determined by the above condensation avoidance criteria is the U-value for the window's center. Any low-e glazing assembly that has a U-value less than this value will remain free of condensation at the center. On the other hand, the U-value determined by a performance code calculation does not necessarily specify the low-e glazing U-value because the code is usually referring to the U-value for the entire window, not just the glazing. The following section shows how to calculate the effective U-value for windows with thermally unbroken metal edge spacers. The method explicitly accounts for the added heat loss through the spacers and the window frame itself.

Figure 6-4 shows how the metal edge spacer used in 0.91 x 1.21 m (3 x 4 ft) double-glazed unit acts as a noticeable

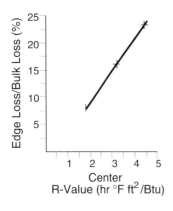

Figure 6-4. Losses at the metal edge spacer in a 3 x 4 foot window as a percentage of the total window heat loss rate for various R-values.

Low-E Glazing Design Guide

thermal bridge when the glazing's center-of-glass R-value rises above 0.70 m²°K/W (4.0 °F ft² hr/Btu). Ordinary double-glazed units lose only 7% of the bulk heat flow through the edge spacers. This figure doubles when a low-e coating is added and rises to a significant 23% when an argon gas fill is used. The organic sealants used to adhere the glass faces to the spacer are too thin to impede the heat flow through the highly conductive metal spacer. Low-e windows call attention to this problem since all gas-filled low-e units have center-of-glass U-values (U_{cog}) below 1.4 W/m²°K (0.25 Btuh/°F ft²). The spacer, in effect, degrades the manufacturer's published center-of-glass U-value for the double glazed assembly. The effective U-value for the window, U_{eff}, also depends on the size of the window in relation to the edges. U_{eff} is estimated by using area-weighted U-values for each contribution according to the following relation:

$$U_{eff} = \frac{U_{cog} \times (A_{igu} - A_{edge}) + (U_{edge} \times A_{edge})}{A_{igu}}$$

where U_{edge} as a function of U_{cog} is given by Figure 6-5, and A_{igu} is the area of the insulated glass unit, not counting the window frame.

A_{edge}, the area where heat transfer is along the glass into the edge spacer rather than perpendicular to the glass, for aluminum spacers is a 60 mm (2.375 in) wide band around the perimeter of the glazing unit.

Example 6-2. Calculate the effective U-value for the insulated glass unit diagramed in Figure 6-6. Assume the low-e window measures 1.2 m x 1.8 m (3.85 x 5.77 ft), and has a center-of-glass U-value of 1.4 W/m²°K (0.25 Btu/hr°F ft²).

Solution:

$$A_{edge} = 1.2 \times 1.8 - 1.08 \times 1.68 = .346 \text{ m}$$

$$U_{eff} = \frac{1.4 \times (2.16 - 0.346) + (2.2 \times 0.346)}{2.16} = 1.52 \text{ W/m}^2°C$$

Of course some thermal bridging also occurs in the window frame. The overall U-value for the window and the

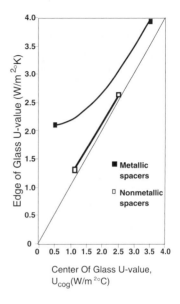

Figure 6-5. Edge of glass U-value vs. Center of Glass U-value. (Reprinted by permission from the 1989 ASHRAE *Handbook—Fundamentals* published by the American Society of Heating, Refrigeration and Air-Conditioning Engineers, Inc.)

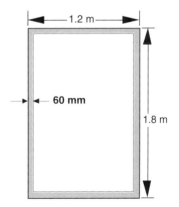

Figure 6-6. The IGU for Example 6-2.

frame, $U_{overall}$, is given in terms of the frame manufacturer's U-value, U_{frame}, and U_{eff} as:

$$U_{overall} = \frac{U_{eff} \times A_{igu} + U_{frame} \times A_{frame}}{A_{igu} + A_{frame}}$$

where A_{frame} is the projected area of the frame, and A_{igu} is the area of the insulated glass unit. The previous relationship assumes the frame covers just the edge spacer where the glass is supported by the frame.

Window Rating Labels. Windows have often been compared with home appliances—the poorer ones consume as much energy as appliances, and the larger ones certainly cost as much as refrigerators. In the interest of energy conservation, many countries require energy rating labels on all residential appliances so energy-conscious buyers can make informed comparisons. Canada [12], the United States,* and some European countries are now readying similar labeling legislation for residential windows.

The labels rate the overall performance of the insulated glass unit, the edge spacer, and the frame. The performance metric is based on a combination of thermal test data and computer simulations. The metric differs for each country, but all of them at least account for the overall U-value, and some of them indirectly account for the inward flowing energy contained in daylight.

U-values from Material Properties. Inevitably, the center-of-glass U-values listed in Chapter 5 for various low-e products will become outdated as low-e window technology advances. Keeping current isn't difficult though, because the center-of-glass U-value for any window assembly is always calculable given the surface emissivities and the gas fill properties. In fact, most manufacturers' published U-values are not measured, but calculated based on the simplified procedure presented in Appendix E, *U-Value Calculation*.

In 1989 all U.S. glass manufacturers agreed to standardize on a U-value determination method based on the U.S. Department of Energy's WINDOW 3.1 computer program for predicting U-values (see Appendix B). These calculations apply for the center of the insulating glass units, although the computer program is capable of calculating the

---

* National Fenestration Rating Council, Silver Spring, Maryland.

actual U-value based on the edge effects from the spacers and frames. Appendix B also describes how to obtain a free copy of the program.

Calculating the Shading Coefficient

Another way of defining the shading coefficient is the ratio of a glazing's solar heat gain to the incident solar radiation divided by 0.87. (The 0.87 is the ratio of the solar heat gain through 3 mm [0.125 in] clear glass to the incident solar radiation in summer conditions.) The measurement assumes the sun strikes the window at right angles. It also accounts not only for the directly transmitted solar radiation, but also for the solar heat absorbed in the glazing, which eventually flows inward. Figure 6-7 shows that the eye is notoriously bad at judging the shading coefficient, which is to be expected, for over half of the solar radiation is invisible near infrared energy.

The shading coefficient for single glazing is found from:

$$SC = (\text{Solar Transmission} + \eta \times \text{Absorption})/0.87,$$

where the quantity in the parentheses is the Solar Heat Gain Coefficient,* or the ratio of a glazing's solar heat gain to the incident solar radiation.

The fraction η of the absorbed solar energy that flows inward is:

$$\eta = h_i/(h_e + h_i)$$

where η is normally 0.45 for a non-low-e glazing, and 0.36 for a pyrolytically coated glass (see Appendix E for general values of h_e and h_i).

The solar transmission and solar absorption are not always listed by the manufacturer, but the information is usually available on request. Sometimes the manufacturer lists the solar reflectance and either the solar transmission or the solar absorption. The missing quantity is equal to 100% minus the two given values because transmission, reflection, and absorption must always add up to 100%. Chapters 7 and 8 list solar transmission, reflection, and absorption values for typical low-e products.

Figure 6-7. Which glass sample has the lower shading coefficient? The larger sample on the left with the higher daylight transmission has the lowest shading coefficient because of its "cool daylight" low-e coating. (The other sample has a traditional 50% tint for a coating.)

ASHRAE 1981 Handbook of Fundamentals, ASHRAE, Atlanta, Ga. p. 27.1

Calculation

Finding the shading coefficient for double glazing is more complex. Like the overall daylight transmission for double glazing, the shading coefficients are found for each light and then multiplied together to form the overall co-efficient. But the calculation for each light's shading co-efficient is not based on the same η. One side of each light faces a sealed gap, so the corresponding h_e or h_i adopt values according to the position of the low-e coating as shown in Appendix E. The shading coefficient for multiple glazings is calculated similarly.

Determining the Window U-value in the Field

Of more immediate concern than predicting a window's U-value is determining if an installed window is living up to the manufacturer's claimed U-value. None of the properties that fix a low-e window's center-of-glass U-value are visible to the eye: any gas fill is of course transparent, and a surface with a 0.40 emissivity looks the same as a surface with a 0.03 emissivity. No simple method gives accurate results, but the following outlines a relatively easy (and inexpensive) field procedure for finding out if the window is performing close to specification.

The method is based on comparing temperature drops across the center of a window and a material of known U-value that is adhered to the room side of the window. At least three remote thermometers with small sensor dimensions are required (the inexpensive thermistor-based electronic thermometers are recommended for their small sensor size and ease of use). The method only works for:

- windows that have a U-value comparable to the reference material, and

- windows that do not have the low emissivity surface on the outside

Thus the U-value for single-glazed pyrolytically coated glass is not obtainable by this method. The reference material is usually a foam board thick enough to withstand handling, so uncoated single glazing is ruled out because of its high U-value compared with, say, an inch of Styrofoam®.

Any insulating board material with a known insulation value is appropriate. Unfortunately, finding such a product is harder than it sounds. Any material's U-value varies with temperature and age. It varies with age because most foam boards are not foamed with air, but with some other blowing agent. The trapped gas is eventually replaced by air as the blowing agent permeates through the material over a 5- to 10- year period. The best way to overcome the aging problem is to locate fresh stock from a major dealer along with the manufacturer's performance figures. For example, Figure 6-8 shows the U-value versus the material's average temperature for 1-inch thick new extruded polystyrene (EPS) of various densities.

The method is based on the principle that heat flow through adjacent materials is the same. Since the heat flow per unit area through the two materials is the U-value times the temperature drop through the material, or,

Heat flow = $U_{EPS} \Delta T_{EPS} = U_{window} \Delta T_{window}$,

knowing the temperature drop through the known material establishes the U-value of the unknown material, given its temperature drop, or

$U_{window} = U_{EPS} \Delta T_{EPS} / \Delta T_{window}$.

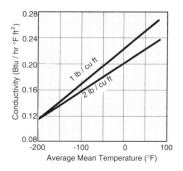

Figure 6-8. U-value vs. average temperature of new 1-inch thick extruded polystyrene (Adapted from the Foamular™ Manufacturer's Fact Sheet, United States Gypsum Company, Chicago, Illinois).

The window is first instrumented by taping a temperature sensor to the center of each side of the installed window. The board is then firmly glued to the room side of the window over the inside temperature sensor. The approximately 1-inch thick board must be at least 30 cm (12 in) on a side to keep the heat that is flowing tangentially through the glass from reaching the central thermometer. The third thermometer sensor is then taped at the center of the room side of the board. The window is sealed shut, and the simultaneous temperature measurements are then taken at night to avoid any solar heating effects. The sensors should stabilize after a 15 minute wait. The two sensor readings on either side of the known material are averaged to determine the average temperature of the insulation for use in Figure 6-8. The U-value from Figure 6-8 is read according to the product's listed density. The formula is used to calculate the bulk U-value of the window according to the temperature drops over the window and the known insulation. *This U-value does not include the thermal resistance of the two air films that normally cling to the window.* Manufacturer's listed center-of-glass U-values always include the effect of these two films, which is still significant for low-e windows. Appendix E lists the figures most manufacturers have adopted for these two films. According to the equations listed in Appendix E, the window's actual center-of-glass U-value based on the measured U-value, U_{window}, becomes:

Center-of-glass U-value$=1/(1/U_{window} + 0.599 + 0.068)$ W/m²°K,

Center-of-glass U-value$=1/(1/U_{window} + 0.25 + 0.40)$ Btu/hr ft²°F.

Solar Geometry

Knowing where the sun is means knowing how buildings are discerned and experienced. The sun's position relative to a window also determines the daylight availability, solar impact, and shadow lines cast by the window's edges. The amount of incident solar radiation for various window orientations at various latitudes is most conveniently given in tabular form (Table 7-3 and Appendix F). Shadow line positions depend both on the sun's absolute position and the window's relative position.

α, solar altitude;

ø, solar azimuth;

ƒ, solar azimuth angle relative to the window;

Ω, local window azimuth relative to south;

Δ, angle of incidence.

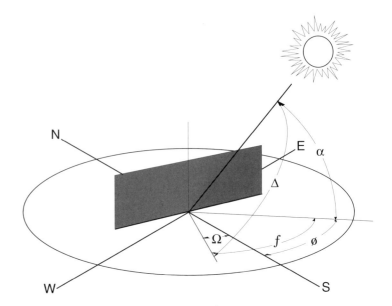

Figure 6-9. The various angles for specifying the sun's position.

The sun's position is expressed absolutely as two measures, the solar altitude, α, above the horizontal, and the solar azimuth, ø, measured from the south (Figure 6-9).

The time corresponding to any given solar position is given as either solar or watch time. Solar time, as told by a sundial, varies from watch time throughout the year due to the earth's varying orbital velocity. The difference between solar time and the time at the center of a time zone is known as the equation of time (ET) when graphed as a function of the calendar date (Figure 6-10). The local watch time, LST for local standard time, also varies from solar time by the position of the observer relative to the center of the observer's local time zone as given by the observer's longitude, LON (the sun rises earlier for people to the east in a given time zone). The following relates watch time to solar time:

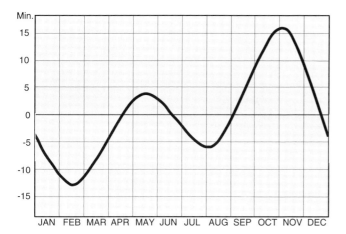

Solar Time = LST + ET + 4 min/° x (SM - LON),

where SM is the standard meridian (longitude) for the local time zone as given in Table 6-4. The watch time for solar noon, for example, is found by rearranging the previous equation and plugging in 12:00 for the solar time to give:

LST = 12:00 - ET - 4 x (SM - LON).

Note that the solar time may differ as much as 47 minutes from the watch time. Daylight savings time adds 1 hour to LST.

The solar altitude and azimuth variations with time and longitude are presented below graphically, for quick estimates, and trigonometrically in Appendix C, for accurate computer-based work. The trigonometric equations are also useful for predicting solar positions not covered by the graphical presentations.

Graphical Solar Positions. The sun's movements as observed at various latitudes are readily depicted with projections as shown by the sun path diagrams in Figure 6-11. The sun's path is projected onto a horizontal plane as a series of heavy elliptical curves, where the horizon is shown as the outer circle, assuming the observer is at the center. True south is at the bottom of the diagram, as shown by the outer ring of compass points. The inner concentric circles mark the sun's altitude in 10° increments. The radial lines mark the sun's azimuth relative to south.

Each elliptical curve is the projection of the sun's path on the twenty-first day of the month, as designated by the Roman numerals. The heavy curves that intersect the sun path curves at right angles show the solar time in Arabic numerals.

Table 6-4. Standard Meridians for Various Time Zones		
Zone	Position	Standard Meridian (Longitude)
-1	European	15°E (-)
0	Greenwich	0°
4	Atlantic	60°W (+)
5	Eastern	75°W (+)
6	Central	90°W (+)
7	Mountain	105°W (+)
8	Pacific	120°W (+)

Calculation

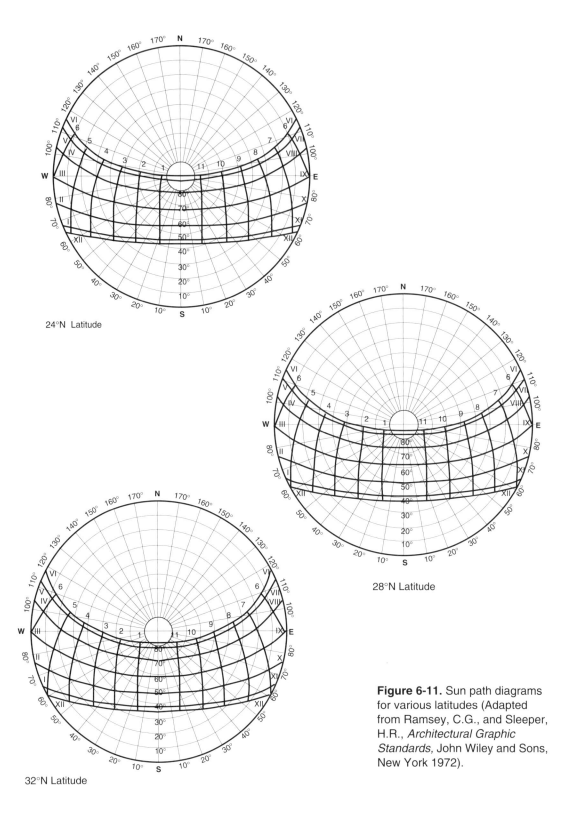

24°N Latitude

28°N Latitude

32°N Latitude

Figure 6-11. Sun path diagrams for various latitudes (Adapted from Ramsey, C.G., and Sleeper, H.R., *Architectural Graphic Standards,* John Wiley and Sons, New York 1972).

Low-E Glazing Design Guide

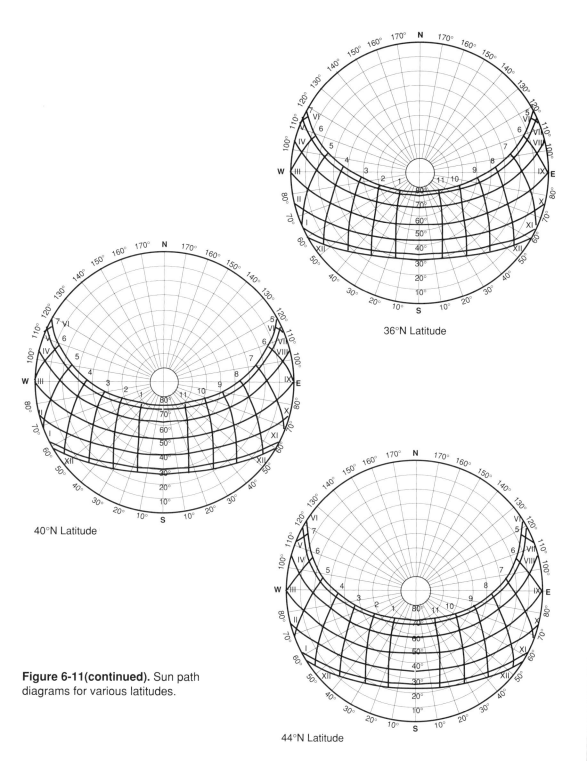

36°N Latitude

40°N Latitude

44°N Latitude

Figure 6-11(continued). Sun path diagrams for various latitudes.

Calculation

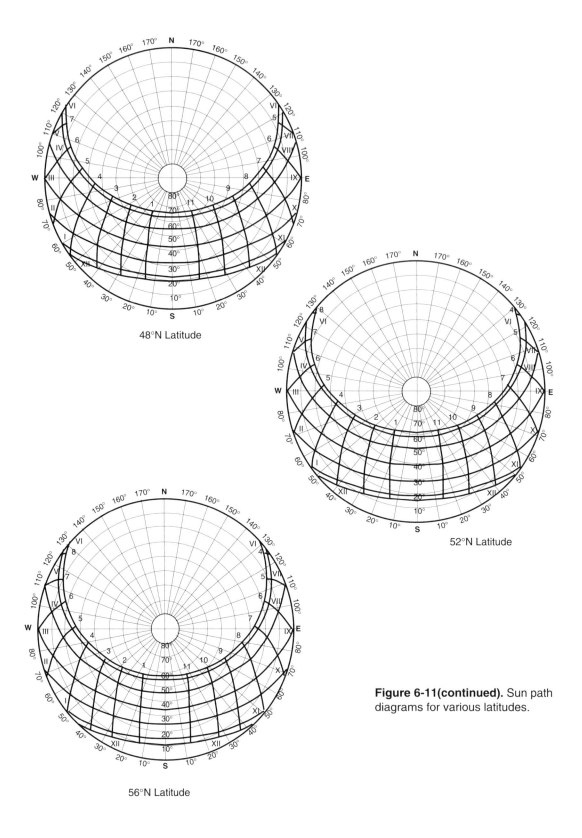

48°N Latitude

52°N Latitude

56°N Latitude

Figure 6-11(continued). Sun path diagrams for various latitudes.

The solar altitude and azimuth for a given time are found by doing the following:

- choosing the sun path diagram closest to the site's latitude

- sketching in the given day's sun path by interpolation

- positioning the sun on this path by interpolating between the hour curves

- corresponding the sun's position on the sun path with a point on the lighter curves to determine the altitude (interpolated over the concentric curves) and the azimuth (interpolated over the radial lines)

For example, the sun's position at 40°N latitude at 10:00 A.M. on December 21 is altitude 20°, azimuth -30°. The times given on these charts are solar times, not local times. The relationships for LST given previously must be used to convert solar time to watch time.

The Angle of Incidence. The angle of incidence for any surface is the angle that the sun's rays make with a perpendicular to the surface (Figure 6-9). This angle greatly influences the solar gain through a window. Figure 6-12 shows the solar transmittance versus the angle of incidence for various double glazings. The solar transmission is virtually unchanged for angles of incidence below 55°, and is negligible for angles of incidence above 75°. Thus windows situated at low latitudes (below 34°, or below Los Angeles, California) become self-shading in the summer when the sun is at high altitudes. Conversely, solar gain remains high and does not vary much for several hours before and after noon during the winter at higher latitudes when the sun is low and the angle of incidence is essentially equal to the sun's azimuth. The angle of incidence is mathematically defined in Appendix C.

The Profile Angle. The final important measure of the sun's position is the profile angle, the angle the sun's rays make with the horizon when projected onto a plane parallel to a given section (usually a section taken perpendicular to a facade) as shown in Figure 6-13. The angle is useful for determining shadow lines in sections showing window openings or overhangs.

The profile angle for a given window can be determined graphically by using a transparency of Figure 6-14—the profile angle and shadow mask—in conjunction with the sun path diagrams shown in Figure 6-11. The profile angles are shown on the mask as the elliptical curves that terminate at the two 90° points. Each curve is labeled with its corresponding angle. To determine the profile angle, the

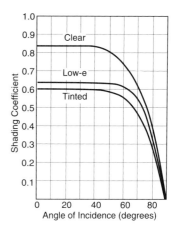

Figure 6-12. The shading coefficient vs. the angle of incidence (Adapted from *Windows and Environment*, Pilkington Environmental Advisors Service, McCorquidale and Co., Newton-Le-Willows, England, 1971).

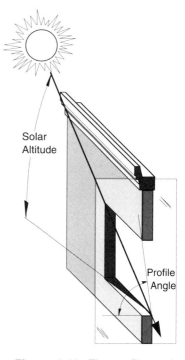

Figure 6-13. The profile angle is the angle that the sun's rays make with the horizon when projected onto a plane parallel to a given section.

Figure 6-14. The profile angle and shadow mask for use with Figure 6-11 (Adapted from Ramsey, C.G., Sleeper, H.R., *Architectural Graphic Standards*, John Wiley and Sons, New York, 1972).

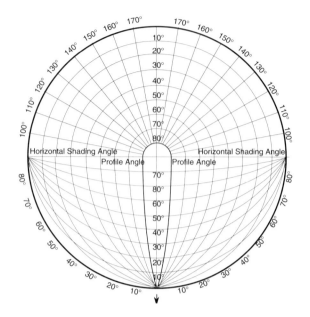

transparency should be centered on the site's sun path diagram so that the arrow at the base of the transparency is parallel to the section taken through the window, as indicated by the compass points on the sun path diagram. The sun's position on the sun path diagram should be projected through the transparency for interpolation between the two nearest profile angle curves. The sun is behind the window (and therefore creating shade) if the sun's position projects on the upper half of the mask.

The profile angle behaves wonderfully for south-facing windows. By rotating the mask so that it points south on any sun path diagram, one will notice that the profile angle

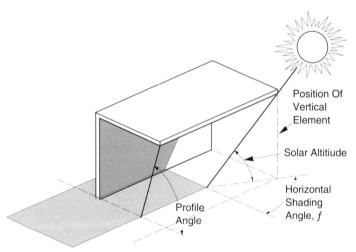

Figure 6-15. Using the profile angle to determine the extent of a shadow cast by an overhang.

does not vary more than 5° on any given day. This means that a fixed overhang can easily provide shade throughout the day. During the equinoxes, the profile angle remains constant all day for south-facing windows. Shading becomes difficult with fixed architectural elements as soon as the window points more than 20° off of south. This is easily seen by rotating the profile angle mask 20° and noting how many profile angle curves are crossed by a single sun path.

Figure 6-15 shows how the profile angle is used to determine how far the sun penetrates through a window or where a window overhang's shadow line falls. The figure shows the shadow position is also determined by a second angle, the horizontal shading angle, which defines the leading edge of a shadow cast by a vertical element. This angle is the plan angle the sun makes relative to the window's perpendicular and is the same as the solar azimuth when the window is facing south (shown as angle f in Figures 6-9 and 6-15). The horizontal shading angle is plotted in the upper half of Figure 6-14.

Figure 6-17 shows how the shading mask from Figure 6-14 is superimposed over a sun path diagram to determine the amount of time a window is shaded to some specified percentage. Assume we want to know how many hours the window in Figure 6-16 is at least 50% shaded, and also assume this window is facing the southeast. The corresponding profile angle for 50% shading is shown in the same figure. The shading mask has been rotated to the southeast in Figure 6-17 to align the arrow at the base of

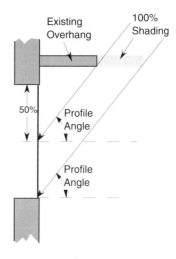

Figure 6-16. The profile angle, which shades half of the existing window section with an infinitely long overhang.

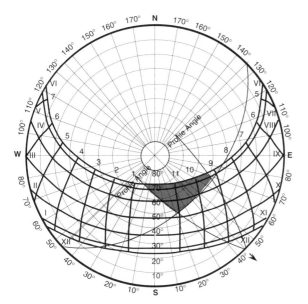

Figure 6-17. A typical shading mask for a finite horizontal overhang shown superimposed on a sun path diagram. The mask uses the profile angle from Figure 6-16 to provide 50% shading for the entire width of the window. The hours this occurs are determined by the intersection of the mask perimeter with the date/hour lines of the sun path diagram.

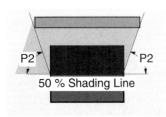

Figure 6-18. The profile angle P2, which shades half the window in elevation.

the transparency with a perpendicular to the outside of the window opening. The profile angle from Figure 6-16 is traced out as a dark semiellipse on the shading mask. All sun positions that lie above this profile angle (shown as the light shading) will create more than 50% shading, but only if the overhang is infinitely long.

The cutoff times for each end of the overhang are also determined using the profile angle concept. Figure 6-18 shows the same window in elevation with a finite overhang. The 50% shadow line has been drawn halfway down the window. The line drawn from the intersection of the shadow line with the window jamb to the edge of the overhang defines the profile angle for the overhang ends, shown as angle P2 in Figure 6-18. The profile angle P2 can be determined in Figure 6-17 only by overlaying a second and third shadow mask for angle P2 at 90° orientations relative to the first shadow mask. The 90° rotation is necessary because the plane of projection in Figure 6-18 is perpendicular to the window section plane shown in Figure 6-16. (The profile angle always lies in the plane of projection.) These 90° overlays have already been plotted as elliptical curves terminating at the south edge of Figure 6-14. The two curves corresponding to profile angle P2 are plotted in Figure 6-17. All sun positions that lie above this profile angle will shade the window in elevation more than 50% of the time. The union (shown as darker shading) of this area and the area for a infinite overhang show the times that the window is at least 50% shaded in both projections.

Cooling Applications

Design Methods for Cooling

The sun's heat is generally unwanted for the majority of the year in recently built (well-insulated) offices, whether or not they are air-conditioned, because of the high internal gains from people and equipment. But the light in that heat is always appreciated because it saves energy and furnishes a psychological lift. Spaces with sloped glazing, large skylit areas, and even well-insulated residences with excessive south- or west-facing glazing also need light with little heat content, particularly residences in southern climates. The following sections show how to achieve these apparently contradictory goals.

Maximize Daylight While Minimizing The Shading Coefficient. This obvious dictum rules out tinted glazing; yet it has historically been the most commonly used glazing for minimizing solar gain. Figure 4-1 illustrates the tint's lack luster thermal performance when compared with clear glazing, and anyone who has worked behind the material on a cloudy day knows how gloomy the world appears. Figure 5-1 nicely points to the glazings that do the job right. All the products that lie near the bottom sloped edge of the graph do nearly an ideal job of maximizing light while minimizing the solar gain. The best performers in this group are the newest thin film low-e coatings on green glass. Unlike tinted glazing, the outer green glass selectively absorbs much of the incoming solar heat without greatly diminishing the light transmission. Then the inside low-e coating selectively chokes off the inward-flowing absorbed heat and any remaining solar energy that made it past the green

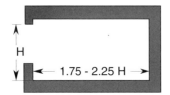

Figure 7-1. The recommended depth of a mostly white office in relation to the window header height for adequate daylighting on cloudy days using windows with over 50% daylight transmission. The deeper dimension is used if the daylight is bounced off the ceiling.

glass by arresting the infrared flow of heat, while still admitting most of the daylight.

Other products along the bottom edge of Figure 5-1 also do the job, particularly if the pale green color is not visually acceptable. Generally, any glazing product lying along this edge that transmits over 50% daylight will work in an off-white office, assuming the bare windows are carried all the way up to the ceiling, and the far wall is less than 1.75 to 2.25 times the window header height away from the windows (Figure 7-1). The larger factor is used if the daylight is bounced off the white ceiling with highly reflective louvers or lightshelves (the louvers also work on cloudy days). The daylighting section in Chapter 9 shows how to predict room daylighting levels behind an arbitrary window or skylight when greater detail is required.

Residences do not require as much light, so smaller windows or slightly deeper rooms are possible. Nevertheless, the glazing daylight transmission should remain greater than 50% to avoid the feeling of gloom.

On the other hand, sloped glazing admits at least three times as much light (and heat) as vertical glazing because of its exposure to either the brighter zenith on cloudy days, or the sun on clear days. Low slung (low aspect ratio) atria with large skylights using low-e glazings with 50% daylight transmission will admit an overabundance of light, which means too much heat, even when the heat-rejecting effects of some low-e coatings are considered. Either glazings that lie closer to the origin along the bottom edge of Figure 5-1 (a lower daylight transmission) or smaller openings are required to control the solar heat gain. For atrium designs, generally the low-e product with the lowest daylight transmission that meets the lighting task requirement is best. The reader can easily predict the daylighting levels in a given atrium by consulting the figures on top-lighting in the daylight section found at the end of Chapter 9. The cool daylight low-e coatings make it possible to totally glaze the top of an atrium without incurring unacceptable seasonal air-conditioning operating costs.

Some low-e coatings increase the outdoor daylight reflectance. Architects concerned about the shininess of the windows as seen from the outside should specify low outdoor reflectances (see Table 7-4 for typical values). An ordinary double-glazed unit with clear, float glass has an outdoor reflectance of 14%.

Orient the Glazing Properly. The cool daylight low-e coatings are not perfectly selective—they absorb noticeable amounts of solar energy. In double-glazed units, the low-e coating should be placed on surface number two,* so most of the absorbed energy is conducted along the easier path to the outside and stripped away by the inevitable breezes.

Green or tinted glass should always be placed on the outside of a double-glazed unit for the same reason. Some tints absorb enough solar energy on a hot day to fry an egg. This heat creates high thermal stress when part of the glass is shadowed by a glazing bar or by the building itself. Tinted outside plates should be heat strengthened to reduce the breakage potential of these unavoidable stresses. Luckily, most low-e coatings, or even clear low-e retrofit films do not absorb enough solar energy by themselves to justify tempering their glass bases.

The coating never belongs on surface number 3 of a double-glazed unit used in a cooling application because the unwanted solar energy absorbed in the coating would have an easier time of it conducting through the glass into the room, rather than back across the air gap to the outside. The position of the coating does not affect the window's R-value, only the shading coefficient.

Where does one place a low-e coating on a single-glazed window to dissipate the absorbed solar heat? The coating never belongs on the outside because the wind overpowers the insulating effect of the low-e coating. A low-e coating placed on the inside is fortuitously thermally self-regulating. The heat absorbed in the coating leaves along the easiest path, which is still to the outside whenever there is any wind.

To understand how heat leaves a low-e window, one must recall from Chapter 4 that a low-e coating is simultaneously both a good reflector and a low emitter of infrared heat. So although the single glazing is warmed by the solar energy absorbed in the glass and the low-e coating on the room side of the glass, the heat cannot easily leap into the room as radiation. The easiest route for the heat is through the relatively conductive glass to the outside where the wind strips most of it away (the rest is reradiated to the environment). This path is much easier for heat flow than the convection path into the still air on the inside. Of course nothing is perfect, so some of the absorbed heat does end up flowing inward by convection, but only a small fraction. This principle is very effectively applied when-

---

*The industry has standardized the surface numbering nomenclature by numbering from the outside in.

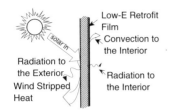

Figure 7-2. How retrofitted low-e film reduces the solar gain through tinted glazing by reducing inward-flowing radiant heat.

ever low-e film is retrofitted on tinted single glazing (Figure 7-2). Tinted single glazing in the sun is an infrared broiler that roasts anyone working behind it. Sticking on a good low-e retrofit film turns off the broiler by choking off the infrared emission.

Simplified Cooling Load Design Method for Perimeter Spaces

Light is always accompanied by heat. This simple fact is used as the basis for the design method presented here to size office windows. The method guarantees that the heat of fluorescent lights is replaced by the heat of daylighting while maintaining or raising the lighting levels. A second method is presented to calculate quickly the total air-conditioning load on a perimeter office. Both methods are designed to substitute for the usual methods based solely on load calculations.

Window Sizing Method. Daylighting an office does not always save energy or reduce the load on the air-conditioner, particularly when using ordinary clear glazing. To be sure, using daylight saves on lighting electricity, but the solar heat that accompanies the daylight can easily put a greater load on the air-conditioner than the fluorescent lighting it replaces, especially when the daylight is distributed unevenly. In addition, the demand for a view tends to oversize the windows. The following method sizes the windows in an office with one exposure so that the air-conditioning load is maintained. It assumes that a lightshelf or other light redirecting device is used to move sunlight up to the ceiling so that the lighting (and the solar energy) levels are evened out.

The efficiency of any lighting source is termed its efficacy and is expressed as the number of lighting units it delivers (lumens) per watt. The efficacy of today's most efficient fluorescent lighting is essentially the same as the light provided by sunlight (119 lm/W). This ratio is virtually unchanged for transmitted daylight through clear glazing and becomes as much as 60% more efficient for the best cool-daylight low-e glazings.

The window size is found by dividing the heat produced by the fluorescent lighting by the peak solar heat gained per square meter (foot) of glass. Although this calculation assures that the load on the air-conditioner is not exceeded during peak hours, it also provides for brighter conditions behind the low-e glazings because of their increased efficacy. The computed window area can either stand as is to raise daylighting levels during nonpeak and cloudy times, or reduced by multiplying the area by the Dx coefficient (the inverse of the efficacy) found in Tables 5-1 and 5-2 and Table 7-4 for a particular coated product. This will, of course, reduce the air-conditioning load due to lighting proportionately. The following discusses the calculation procedure.

The fluorescent lighting load is given in Figure 7-3, which relates lighting load to illumination levels for different artificial lighting sources. The chart is most accurate for rooms between 46 and 84 m^2 (between 500 and 900 ft^2). Lighting levels for air-conditioned offices today vary from 215 to 538 lux (20 to 50 footcandles). The average lighting level for an example office is measured by averaging several sample light meter readings if a figure is not available. Figure 7-3 is entered at the desired illumination level to de-

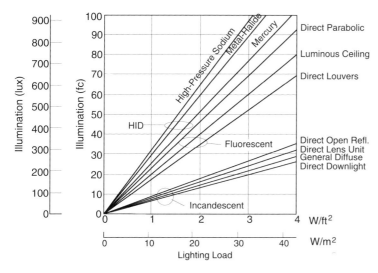

Figure 7-3. Estimating chart for lighting load and related illumination levels for different sources. The chart was calculated for a classroom size room. Although the figures are necessarily approximate because of the variables involved, the chart gives figures close enough for a first approximation (Adapted from Stein/Reynolds/McGuiness, *Mechanical and Electrical Equipment for Buildings,* 7th ed., John Wiley & Sons, New York, 1986).

termine the corresponding W/area for direct parabolic (the most efficient) fluorescent fixtures. This result is multiplied by the office area and divided by the maximum transmitted solar energy per unit area during the air-conditioning season for the given window orientation and glazing. The transmitted solar energy figure is formed by taking 87% of the entry in Table 7-3 corresponding to the window orientation and multiplying it by the glazings' shading coefficient (see Table 7-4 for typical values).

Example 7-1. Determine the appropriate unshaded south window area for daylighting a one-person 13.9 m^2 (150 ft^2) office in Munich during August. (Assume the current artificial lighting level is 538 lux (50 fc) and the low-e glazing has a shading coefficient of 0.38.) Munich is at north latitude 48°.

Cooling Applications

Solution:
The lighting load
From Figure 7-3, the corresponding load is 24 W/m² (7.6 Btuh/ft²). The total load is 24 W/m² x 13.9 m² = 334 W (1138 Btuh).

The maximum transmitted solar energy
From Table 7-3
676 W/m² x .87 x .38 = 215 W/m²
(214 Btuh/ft² x .87 x .38 = 68 Btuh/ft²).

The corresponding window area
334 W/215 W/m² = 1.6 m²
(1138 Btuh/68 Btuh/ft² = 18 ft²).

This method does not work directly with sloped glazing such as found in atrium spaces. Generally, atriums require selective air-conditioning at the pedestrian circulation levels. The cloudy day lighting prediction method given in Chapter 9 for sloped glazing will give a warning of excessive clear day solar gains if the predicted cloudy lighting levels exceed 538 lux (50 fc).

Total Air-conditioning Load. Air-conditioning units are usually sized for the peak load. Summertime worst-hour heat gain calculations for individual spaces with windows are at best intricate. The difference in temperature between indoors and outdoors is not as important as the solar gain through the windows and walls, the internal gains from people and equipment, and the ventilation requirement. To make things worse, the peak hour does not necessarily occur when the sun is in front of the window if the building's thermal mass is significant. However, most offices built in the last 30 years are really lightweight structures because they use thin exterior veneers on steel (or concrete) frames and lightweight materials for the internal walls and partitions. The following streamlined heat gain method recognizes this by assuming the worst-hour heat gain does indeed occur when the sun is in front of the window. The method will result in oversized equipment if the office is not built with lightweight materials. A further simplification is introduced by assuming the office space only gains solar energy through a single wall (including the windows), and not through the ceiling. This assumption holds for well-insulated roofs and for noncorner offices in multistory buildings.

The method is based on the Sol-air temperature concept for predicting the heat gain through walls and other opaque elements. The Sol-air temperature is an equivalent outdoor temperature derived from the conversion of solar radiation effects and the daytime outdoor air temperature into a combined temperature. The method assumes that the equivalent air temperature, T_e, is transferring heat to the opaque element solely by convection. The following relationship for T_e holds only for vertical surfaces and assumes the presence of a slight breeze.

In degrees Centigrade:

$$T_e = T_{outside} + \frac{Absorption \times (Incident\ Solar\ Energy)}{17}$$

where the Incident Solar Energy is in W/m^2,
or in degrees Fahrenheit:

$$T_e = T_{outside} + \frac{Absorption \times (Incident\ Solar\ Energy)}{3}$$

where the Incident Solar Energy is in Btuh/ft^2, and $T_{outside}$ is the summer design temperature (essentially the weather bureau's average peak outdoor temperature) for the site.

Table 7-1 lists some typical absorptions for various colors as listed in the PPG Design-a-Color™ System paint chip catalog. Common light-colored, weathered walls generally have an absorptions near 0.45.

Table 7-3 tabulates the maximum incident solar energy for various window exposures at various latitudes. (Appendix F gives the hourly and monthly data for the same conditions when nonmaximum conditions are required.) Urban locations should use 80% of these figures because of atmospheric pollution. The air-conditioning season is assumed to occur between June 21 and October 21.

The air-conditioning load for the worst hour is computed by summing the heat gains, q, due to the following items:

Gains through the walls. The sensible heat gain through each opaque wall section of area A is calculated with the equation

$$q = U \times A \times (T_e - T_{indoors})$$

Table 7-1. Color vs. Absorption

Color	Absorption
Gypsum	.14
Rose morn	.24
Mission beige	.25
Polar sky	.28
Sun yellow	.30
Orange-glow	.38
Wisteria blue	.47
Mint green	.78
Slate	.85
Slate brown	.86
Really rust	.88
Ultramarine blue	.89
Deep red	.91
Ebony black	.95

(Adapted from: PPG Design-a-Color™ System.)

Calculation

where the U-value is the manufacturer's listed wall thermal conductance per unit area, and $T_{indoors}$ is the thermostat setting.

Gains through the glass. The sensible heat gain through the glass of area A is calculated with the equation

$$q = A \times SC \times SHGF_{peak} +$$
$$U \times A \times (T_{outside} - T_{indoors})$$

where A is the window's area, and the U-value in the second term is the manufacturer's listed window thermal conductance per unit area (see Table 7-4 for typical values). The center-of-glass U-value should be adjusted downward for gas-filled windows that are less than 1.9 m^2 (20 ft^2) in area to account for the heat loss through the edge spacers. The second line in the equation accounts for the heat gained through the window by conduction. The first term, $A \times SC \times SHGF_{peak}$, accounts for the solar energy transmitted and reradiated through the window. $SHGF_{peak}$, the peak solar heat gain factor, is the solar gain through clear 3 mm (0.125 in) glass and is found by taking 87% of the maximum incident solar energy used from Table 7-3 to calculate the peak Sol-air temperature. Eighty-seven percent of the northern exposure in Table 7-3 for $SHGF_{peak}$ should be used if the window is 100% externally shaded, regardless of orientation. SC is the window's shading coefficient (see Table 7-4 for typical low-e glazing values). The shading coefficient is the ratio of the solar energy admitted through a window over the solar energy admitted through a clear 3 mm glass window. This coefficient is multiplied by the shading coefficient of any window dressing that is present (Table 7-2).

Gains from outdoor air. The sensible and latent heat gain from the ventilation air is given as

$$q = 1.232 \times L/s \times (T_{outside} - T_{indoors}) \times LF$$
$$[q = 1.08 \times cfm \times (T_{outside} - T_{indoors}) \times LF\,]$$

where LF is a factor used to estimate the latent heat gain from the ventilation air. LF is taken as 1.2 for dry climates, and 1.3 for humid climates. L/s (cfm), the ventilation rate, is determined by local codes; but a value of 7 L/s (15 cfm) per person is suggested for estimating purposes.

Gains from people. The sensible and latent heat gain from a seated person doing light office work is given as

Table 7-2. Shading Coefficients for Typical Window Dressings.

Type of Shading	SC
Indoors:	
Venetian blinds (light)	0.67
Venetian blinds (medium)	0.74
Roller shade (opaque,dark)	0.81
Roller shade (opaque,light)	0.39
Roller shade (transl.,light)	0.44
Open Weave Drapes (light)	0.71
Med. Weave Drapes (light)	0.59
Tight Weave Drapes (light)	0.48
Between double glazing:	
Venetian blinds (light)	0.37
Venetian blinds (medium)	0.41
Louvered sun screen	0.48

(Adapted from *1989 ASHRAE Fundamentals*, ASHRAE, Atlanta, Georgia)

Low-E Glazing Design Guide

q = 140 W/person x No. of occupants

[q = 480 Btuh/person x No. of occupants]

Gains from equipment (and lights). This is the most difficult category to estimate because of the impact of the personal computer and its peripherals. Computers tend to consume more electrical power as they become more capable because of the increased chip density. Power consumption can range any where from 9.5 to 500 W/m² (3 to 160 Btuh/ft²) of office space. Offices without computers tend to run around 9.5 to 12.5 W/m² (3 to 4 Btuh/ft²). The

Table 7-3. The Maximum Incident Solar Energy for Various Window Exposures at Various Latitudes

Latitude (North)	Date		Solar Position		Incident Solar Radiation		
	Month	Solar Time	Altitude	Azimuth	Orientation	W/sq m	(Btuh/sq ft)
16	21-Jun	8	33.4	-107.9	NE	729	231
	21-Sep	8	28.7	-81.0	E	852	270
	21-Oct	9	38.2	-62.2	SE	845	268
	21-Oct	12	63.5	0.0	S	564	179
	21-Aug	12	86.3	0.0	S	173	55
	21-Oct	15	38.2	62.2	SW	845	268
	21-Sep	16	28.7	81.0	W	852	270
	21-Jun	16	33.4	107.9	NW	729	231
	21-Jun	16	33.4	107.9	N	248	79
24	21-Jun	8	35.5	-102.6	NE	692	219
	21-Sep	8	27.2	-76.8	E	833	264
	21-Oct	9	34.1	-57.1	SE	882	280
	21-Oct	12	55.5	0.0	S	701	222
	21-Aug	12	78.3	0.0	S	273	86
	21-Oct	15	34.1	57.1	SW	882	280
	21-Sep	16	27.2	76.8	W	833	264
	21-Jun	16	35.5	102.6	NW	692	219
	21-Jun	17	22.3	106.8	N	207	66
32	21-Jun	7	24.3	-103.4	NE	661	210
	21-Aug	8	31.8	-84.7	E	823	261
	21-Oct	10	38.7	-39.1	SE	898	285
	21-Oct	12	47.5	0.0	S	805	255
	21-Aug	12	70.3	0.0	S	417	132
	21-Oct	14	38.7	39.1	SW	898	285
	21-Aug	16	31.8	84.7	W	823	261
	21-Jun	17	24.3	103.4	NW	661	210
	21-Jun	17	24.3	103.4	N	176	56

Dark areas are not maximum values. (Adapted from *1989 ASHRAE Fundamentals,* ASHRAE, Atlanta, Georgia)

Calculation

Table 7-3 (continued)

Latitude	Date		Solar Position		Incident Solar Radiation		
(North)	Month	Solar Time	Altitude	Azimuth	Orientation	W/sq m	(Btuh/sq ft)
40	21-Jun	7	26.0	-99.7	NE	646	205
	21-Aug	8	30.7	-79.9	E	811	257
	21-Oct	10	32.4	-35.6	SE	894	284
	21-Oct	12	39.5	0.0	S	877	278
	21-Aug	12	62.3	0.0	S	558	177
	21-Oct	14	32.4	35.6	SW	894	284
	21-Aug	16	30.7	79.9	W	811	257
	21-Jun	17	26.0	99.7	NW	646	205
	21-Jun	18	14.8	108.4	N	179	57
48	21-Jun	7	27.0	-95.8	NE	620	197
	21-Aug	8	29.0	-75.4	E	793	251
	21-Oct	10	25.7	-33.1	SE	875	278
	21-Oct	12	31.5	0.0	S	910	288
	21-Aug	12	54.3	0.0	S	676	214
	21-Oct	14	25.7	33.1	SW	875	278
	21-Aug	16	29.0	75.4	W	793	251
	21-Jun	17	27.0	95.8	NW	620	197
	21-Jun	18	17.2	106.2	N	173	55
56	21-Jun	6	19.3	-103.6	NE	601	191
	21-Jul	8	33.6	-76.7	E	793	251
	21-Sep	9	23.3	-50.3	SE	825	262
	21-Oct	12	23.5	0.0	S	879	279
	21-Aug	12	46.3	0.0	S	762	242
	21-Sep	15	23.3	50.3	SW	825	262
	21-Jul	16	33.6	76.7	W	793	251
	21-Jun	18	19.3	103.6	NW	601	191
	21-Jun	19	11.4	115.3	N	199	63
64	21-Jun	6	21.0	-100.8	NE	608	193
	21-Jun	7	27.5	-87.5	E	800	254
	21-Aug	9	29.6	-52.6	SE	815	259
	21-Sep	12	26.0	0.0	S	852	270
	21-Aug	12	38.3	0.0	S	815	259
	21-Aug	15	29.6	52.6	SW	815	259
	21-Jun	17	27.5	87.5	W	800	254
	21-Jun	18	21.0	100.8	NW	608	193
	21-Jun	19	14.8	108.0	N	233	74

Dark areas are not maximum values.

loads from artificial lighting are added in if the daylighting is inadequate.

Example 7-2. A one-person, 13.9 m^2 (150 ft^2) west-facing office in Munich has 2.8 m^2 (30 ft^2) of cool daylight low-e window with a shading coefficient of .38 and a U-value of 1.3 W/m^2°K (0.23 Btuh/ ft^2°F). The remaining 4.65 m^2 (50 ft^2) of insulated wall (U-value of .68 W/m^2°K (0.12 Btuh/ ft^2°F)) is covered with dark stone. The thermostat is set at 24°C (75°F). Find the peak heat gain assuming the lights are off and no computer is present.

Solution:

Munich is at north latitude 48° and has a design temperature of 30°C (86 °F).

Sol-air temperature
T$_e$ = 30°C + 0.85 (793/17) = 69.7°C
[86 °F + 0.85 (251/3) = 157.1°F]

(a) Gains through the walls.
q = 0.68 x 4.65 m^2 x (69.7 °C - 24°C) =	144.5 W
[0.12 x 50 ft^2 x (157.1 °F - 75°F) =	492.6 Btu/hr]

(b) Gains through the glass.
q = 2.8 m^2 x 0.38 x 793 x 0.87 +	
1.3 x 2.8 m^2 x (30°C - 24°C) =	
708.8 + 21.8 =	730.6 W
[30 ft^2 x 0.38 x 251 x 0.87) +	
0.23 x 30 ft^2 x (86°F - 75°F) =	
2403.6 + 75.9 =	2479.5 Btu/hr]

(c) Gains from outdoor air.
q = 1.232 x 7 x (30°C - 24°C) x 1.2 =	62.1 W
[1.08 x 15 x (86°F - 75°F) x 1.2 =	213.8 Btu/hr]

(d) Gains from people.
q = (as given above) =	140.W
	[480.0 Btu/hr]

(e) Gains from equipment (and lights).
q = 12.5 x 13.9 m^2 =	173.8 W
[4 x 150 ft^2 =	600.0 Btu/hr]

TOTALS	1251.0 W
	[4,265.9 Btu/hr]

The glass gains 58% of the total energy in this example, which is a danger sign that the window is too large or needs additional shading. The best way to evaluate the air-conditioning load is to ratio the solar gain to the floor area and compare it with normal artificial lighting densities as shown in the next paragraph.

The term showing the solar gain through the window, A x SC x $SHGF_{peak}$, is 708.8 W (2403.6 Btu/hr), or in terms of office floor space, 51 W/m^2 (16 Btuh/ft^2). This is quite a bit higher than the maximum lighting (538 lux or 50 fc) criteria of 24 W/m^2 (7.6 Btuh/ft^2), based on equating fluorescent efficacies with daylight efficacy as shown in the first design method. Even using a cool daylight low-e window on the western exposure in this example does not do the job: externally shading 60% of the window, or reducing the glass area by 50% would make the situation acceptable.

Typical Low-E Values for Cooling

Table 7-4 lists typical commercially available low-e products for cooling applications. The cited figures are from European and North American glazing manufacturers. The table is broken into two parts: the top lists representative products with daylight transmissions greater than 50% and lower than normal shading coefficients; the bottom shaded section lists tinted products with daylight transmissions greater than 30%. All the thin film units are 2.54 cm (1 in) thick, air-filled double glazing. The interpane gaps for the suspended film units are reduced so the overall thickness is still 2.54 cm. The units filled with argon or krypton are footnoted. Some manufacturers offer thicker units, which insulate better when filled with argon or krypton. These higher insulating products are listed in Table 5-2, which shows the insulated glass units with suspended low-e films.

The unshaded listings at the top of Table 7-4 are for daylighting applications such as offices. Only clear or green cover plates are used in these listings because all tinted outer glazings lower the daylight transmission below 50%. (It is nearly impossible to daylight normal-sized offices with window daylight transmissions below 50%.) The products with the lower daylight and solar transmission figures found in the shaded section are desirable for some low aspect ratio atria or other excessively glazed light wells.

The figures are further classified by low-e type. Any one row can serve as the basis for a glazing specification. Sam-

Table 7-4. Typical Commercially Available Low-e Products for Cooling Applications (all units are 2.54 cm [1 in] Thick).

Low-E Type (e, tint)*	Cooling Descriptors				Solar (%)			Summer U-value (air filled)	
	Outdoor Reflt.(%)	Daylight Trans.(%)	S.C.	Dx	Absorp.	Trans.	Reflection	W/m²°K	Btuh/ft²°F
Thin film (.10,c)	11	77	0.71	0.92	27	52	21	1.68	0.30
Thin film (.03,c)	12	69	0.49	0.71	44	35	21	1.53	0.27
Thin film (.10,g)	10	66	0.45	0.68	59	30	11	1.76	0.31
Thin film (.03,g)	10	60	0.38	0.63	65	25	10	1.31	0.23
Thin film (.10,g)	11	57	0.45	0.79	63	27	10	1.68	0.30
Pyrolytic (.17,g)	12	60	0.52	0.87	61	32	7	1.90	0.33
Suspended(.10,c)†	NA	56	0.46	0.82	NA	NA	NA	0.60	0.11
Suspended(.10,c)‡	21	62	0.52	0.84	23	34	43	0.68	0.12
Suspended(.05,c)	31	53	0.41	0.77	35	26	39	1.99	0.35
Suspended(.07,g)	18	51	0.38	0.75	59	24	17	2.04	0.36
Thin film (.10,b)	7	49	0.44	0.90	63	29	8	1.76	0.31
Thin film (.03,b)	8	45	0.35	0.78	64	22	14	1.65	0.29
Thin film (.10,y)	7	35	0.45	1.29	59	30	11	1.76	0.31
Thin film (.03,y)	6	35	0.31	0.89	67	19	14	1.65	0.29
Thin film (.10,z)	7	45	0.45	1.00	57	32	11	1.76	0.31
Thin film (.03,z)	8	41	0.33	0.80	65	21	14	1.65	0.29
Pyrolytic (.17,b)	8	45	0.52	1.16	61	32	7	1.90	0.33
Pyrolytic (.17,z)	8	42	0.52	1.24	61	32	7	1.90	0.33
Pyrolytic (.17,y)	7	35	0.49	1.40	64	29	7	1.90	0.33
Suspended (.05,b)	16	34	0.30	0.88	67	16	17	2.04	0.36
Suspended(.10,z)	13	30	0.29	0.97	68	15	17	2.04	0.36
Suspended(.07,y)	10	30	0.33	1.10	68	18	14	2.04	0.36

*The letter code in column 1 indicates the cover plate: clear (c), green (g), bronze(z), blue(b), gray(y).

†Argon unit with 3 gaps

‡Krypton unit with 3 gaps

30% < Daylight Transmission   50% < Daylight Transmission

ples should always be evaluated outdoors on both sunny and cloudy days for their color appearance. The consistently best performers are the products with a 0.03 emissivity. All listed U-values are for the center of the glass.

8

Design

Heating Applications

A Design Method for Solar Heating

In the United States low-e market, more low-e glazing has been sold for residential applications than for commercial buildings. This trend has developed for the most part because the reduced U-value leads to savings on heating costs, increased comfort, and reduced indoor condensation—issues that are not paramount in commercial design.

The heat-rejecting variety of residential low-e window is commonly used in overheated climates to lower the air-conditioning bill. For housing in underheated climates, solar heating becomes affordable and attractive when using the low-e technology designed to maximize solar gain.

At first glance, selecting a low-e glazing for residential solar heating seems simple—just maximize the R-value, the shading coefficient (for maximum solar gain), and the daylight transmission (while using the daylighting methods shown in Chapter 9). Although this approach is true for northern exposures, it isn't always true for other orientations.

Northern Exposures. Figure 8-1 shows that some north-facing low-e windows generate a net seasonal heat gain during the winter in a severe, but clear climate when the window's U-value is below 0.9 W/m^2°K (0.16 Btu/hr °F ft^2). This window's performance is not highly dependent on the glazing's shading coefficient as long as it is above 0.50. Windows must have U-value and shading coefficient combinations that place them to the right of the zero net heat transfer line if they are to provide a net energy benefit. Even though European locations are warmer than the U.S. location shown in Figure 8-1, the days are shorter because

Specs

99

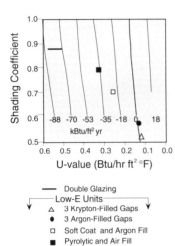

Figure 8-1. The net annual useful flux in Madison, Wisconsin through a north window area of 66 sq ft expressed as a function of the window U-value and shading coefficient. A window is represented by a data point on the graph (Adapted from: Arasteh, D., Selkowitz, S., J. R., Wolfe, "The Design and Testing of a Highly Insulating Glazing System for Use With Conventional Window Systems." *Journal of Solar Engineering, Transactions of the ASME*, 1989, vol. 111).

of the higher latitudes, so essentially the same graph applies to Europe. The graph plots the net annual heating energy captured by 6.1 m² (66 ft²) of north facing glazing.

Solar heating with northern light works because there is always heat in daylight, even during an average cloudy day. The amount of solar heat in north light on the equinox at mid latitudes is about 15% of the heat falling on a south-facing window at the same location on a clear day. The better low-e glazings have nearly 2.5 times the thermal resistance of clear double glazing, at nearly the same solar transmission, so losses are more than halved while solar gains remain nearly the same. This leverage is enough to draw a slight heating profit from north light in benign winter climates considering that a clear south-facing double-glazed window normally gains about twice as much solar heat as it needs to compensate for its 24-hour wintertime losses. Unfortunately, the heating profit from the north-facing windows isn't enough to compensate for all of a typical home's heating losses (such as the heat lost to the outside by air seeping through joints in the wall), so some south-facing windows are usually required to accomplish 100% solar heating. Admittedly, even the newest low-e technology fails at garnering a solar heating profit on rainy days due to the excessive cloudy cover.

Another way to comprehend the performance leverage of low-e windows is to compare an insulated wall with a double-glazed, gas-filled low-e window in a moderate winter climate. A north-facing insulated wall always loses heat in the winter, no matter how much insulation is used. But a north-facing low-e window with a high shading coefficient can replace much of that lost heat with the heat gained through the window as diffuse light. A 24-hour accounting of all the heat losses and gains through the low-e window would reveal that the window's average U-value is always significantly lower than the published U-value (manufacturers list winter time U-values for night conditions). For instance, the average winter U-value for a north-facing, argon-filled low-e unit with a shading coefficient of 0.71 in Cleveland, Ohio (the average outdoor temperature is -2°C or 29°F) is 0.91 W/m²°K (0.16 Btuh/ft²°F) compared with the published nighttime U-value of 1.42 W/m²°K (.25 Btuh/ft2°F) [13]. The average U-value is comparable with an opaque wall insulated with 5 cm (2 in) of beadboard foam insulation.

Southern Exposures. Solar heating used to depend on covering the windows every night with insulation to trap the day's solar gains through ordinary double glazing. The idea proved thermally efficient, but people lost interest in baby-sitting their south-facing windows. Figures 8-2 and 8-3 compare the average daily southern solar heating energy captured in Boston and Seattle by one square foot of argon-filled soft-coat low-e double glazing with one square foot of clear double glazing, and with one square foot of clear double glazing covered with 5 cm (2 in) of nighttime board insulation. The charts also give the corresponding annual net solar intake through each glazing. Figure 8-2 reveals that ordinary double glazing barely operates at a profit during the months of December and January in Boston. Figure 8-3 shows the same window loses heat in a mostly cloudy Seattle during the same months. The movable insulation vastly improves the situation in both climates. The soft coat low-e window comes in a close second to the moveable insulation

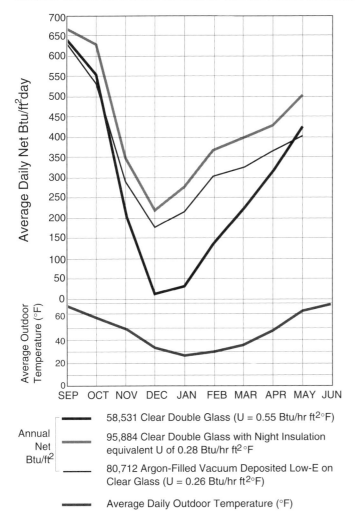

Figure 8-2. Average daily net heating energy per square foot of window for three different glazing systems in Boston, Massachusetts (Adapted from: Johnson, T., *Solar Architecture: The Direct Gain Approach*, McGraw Hill, New York, 1981).

Annual Net Btu/ft^2

58,531 Clear Double Glass (U = 0.55 Btu/hr ft^2°F)

95,884 Clear Double Glass with Night Insulation equivalent U of 0.28 Btu/hr ft^2°F

80,712 Argon-Filled Vacuum Deposited Low-E on Clear Glass (U = 0.26 Btu/hr ft^2°F)

Average Daily Outdoor Temperature (°F)

system due to its lower solar transmission, even though the low-e window has a lower U-value than the 24-hour average U-value for the movable insulation system.

Although Figures 8-2 and 8-3 show how efficient gas-filled low-e windows are for solar heating, they are misleading when considering thermal comfort. Low-e's nominal 2.5 to 1 insulating leverage over clear double glazing can quickly cause winter daytime overheating if the southern windows are too large, particularly for superinsulated homes. (Traditional large double-glazed windows helped keep a solar heated space cool because they lost so much heat.) Who cares if a solar heating design saves 80% of the homeowner's fuel bill if most of the home is unlivable during the sunny hours? The wintertime overheating problem is quite real now because of today's increasing insulation

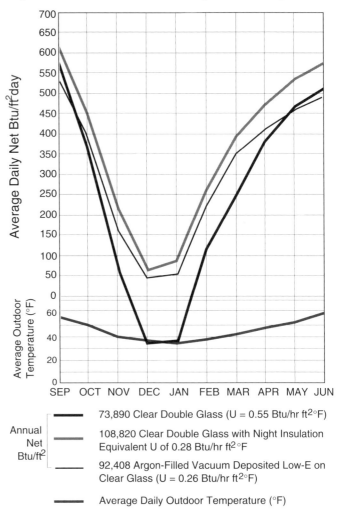

Figure 8-3. Average daily net heating energy per square foot of window for three different glazing systems in Seattle, Washington (Adapted from: Johnson, T., *Solar Architecture: The Direct Gain Approach*, McGraw Hill, New York, 1981).

Low-E Glazing Design Guide

standards. The south-facing window sizing method found near the end of this chapter rigorously addresses this increasingly common problem. It directly addresses the thermal comfort issue by accounting for the latest low-e technology, the house's insulation levels, the window size, the room geometry, and the presence of any internal mass for minimizing the room air temperature swings.

The overheating problem caused by excessive southern glazing is overcome either by reducing the glazing size, adding exterior shading, or by using a window with a lower shading coefficient. The first approach usually isn't popular because the window area is probably large for a good reason—to enjoy a view, or to maintain the facade proportions. The second alternative, exterior shading, is expensive and almost always interferes with the view if the device is supposed to work with the low winter sun. The third alternative, which draws on low-e office glazing technology, substitutes a low shading coefficient, yet clear-looking low-e unit for the southern glazing. Mostly likely, just the right shading coefficient is available for canceling out the extra gains from the larger than recommended window area.

Western and Eastern Exposures. Eastern exposures are rarely a problem, even in the summer, because cool morning air is usually available to wash away any interior solar gains. On the other hand, unshaded western exposures become acutely uncomfortable after the spring equinox. (Very little sun reaches a western window during the winter at midlatitudes.) The low afternoon sun can quickly overheat a room, even when conservative window areas are used. Generally, the same clear, low-shading coefficient low-e windows recommended for overglazed southern exposures also work on a western exposure. Although the design method at the end of this chapter only works accurately for south-facing glazing, the same method is usable as an approximate check on overheating conditions in a west-facing room during late spring and early summer by assuming that the west window faces south and the solar intake is given by the March solar figures.

Low-E Coating Orientation

The best glazing surface (out of the four possible surfaces in a double-glazed unit) to coat for an office application is not necessarily the best for a solar heating design. In the solar heating case, nearly one third of the 4% to 6%

solar heat absorbed by the low-e coating should find its way to the adjacent room, so the low-e coating is best located on a surface that is closest to the room. This implies that either surface number 3 or 4 are coated, but comfort criteria dictates that only surface number 3 gets the coating.

The window will run colder at night if the coating is placed on surface number 4 rather than surface number 3, yet either placement results in nearly the same R-value. This counterintuitive statement is best understood by realizing that a low-e surface not only reflects infrared energy, but also barely emits infrared energy.

When the coating is on surface number 4, any infrared energy trying to leave the room through the window is reflected back in. The infrared heat that normally would go into heating the window does not get absorbed by the glass, so the window runs colder—cold enough to create drafts and induce condensation at the center of the window in conditions that might not even see condensation on ordinary double-glazed units.

When the coating is on surface number 3, the room side of the window easily absorbs the room's infrared since ordinary glass has a high emissivity (emissivity equals absorption at the same wavelength). The heat warms the glass as it conducts to the other side, where it cannot leave via radiation because the low emissivity surface chokes off the radiation transfer. Some heat does get across the double glazing gap via convection and conduction because the glass is warmer than normal. In either case, the R-value is almost unaffected by the surface choice because over 90% of the normal infrared radiation traffic is arrested.

The low-e coating is usually not placed on surface number 2 of a double-glazed unit used for solar heating because the wind would strip away most of the useful solar energy absorbed in the low-e coating. However, glass breakage has been known to occur when surface number 3 is coated and exposed to the sun. The heat buildup at this coated surface is less easily dissipated than when the coating is on surface 2, so local glass stresses can develop. Some window manufacturers are no longer offering low-e coatings on surface number 3 in order to avoid the potential breakage problem. The R-value is not influenced by the coated surface choice only the shading coefficient is potentially affected.

The new, highly transparent pyrolytic coatings have effectively done away the surface 3 versus surface 2 question for solar heating applications. The coating's high solar transmission avoids the possibility of absorption heat-buildup inside the double-glazed unit, and the correspondingly high shading coefficient isn't affected by the position of the coating, so surface number 2 becomes the safe and sure bet. Furthermore, lifting the solar transmission always increases the solar gain more than an equal increase in solar absorption lifts the solar gain at surface number 3.

Nighttime thermal comfort is also noticeably reduced, and condensation probability is readily enhanced in cold climates when the inside of a single-glazed unit is coated. For this reason, pyrolytically treated single glazing and low-e retrofit film are not appropriate in cold climates when thermal comfort is an issue. The corrosion-resistant pyrolytic surface is best placed on an interior storm window with the pyrolytic treatment facing the original window.

Windows with a suspended low-e film are built with the low-e surface facing toward the outside for the best performance. The effect is the same—the low-e film keeps the infrared energy from crossing the glazing gap closest to the outside.

Tints must be avoided in residential solar heating applications. It is best to keep the solar heat in the form of light as long as possible on its way to thermal storage. In addition, most home owners prefer clear windows for aesthetic reasons.

Distribute the Solar Heat as Light

Potential wintertime overheating can occur in a well insulated space any time the south-facing window area is greater than about 7% to 10% of the floor area that "sees" the window. One way of minimizing the attendant temperature fluctuations is to add thermal mass to the room, usually as a cementitious material. The window-sizing method near the end of this chapter assumes that the solar energy admitted through these windows is distributed evenly over the room thermal storage masses, so all this storage material participates equally. In most cases, the amount of mass necessary to tone down the fluctuations occupies a larger area than the sun can directly illuminate. The only way to reach all this material is to keep the sunlight moving deeper into the room by bouncing it off light-colored floors and walls. Lightshelves or upside down reflectorized louvers (Figure 8-4) redirect the light to the ceiling.

The heat-absorbing and temperature-leveling capacity of a room is not affected by light colors once the sunlight

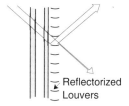

Figure 8-4. Upside down reflectorized louvers used on the room side of double glazing to bounce daylight to the ceiling. The louver's convex surfaces must have a matte finish to avoid glare.

bounces off the first light-colored surfaces. Seventy percent of the transmitted solar radiation is absorbed in an all-white room when one of the long walls is half glass and facing south [14]. White paint is not a perfect reflector; it absorbs 10% of the solar radiation that strikes it. A solar ray entering such a room will undergo many multiple reflections and absorptions before it reaches the window again. An off-white room will absorb more than 90% of the entering solar energy if the window wall is less than 50% glazed. Light colors are also preferred for daylighting because daylighting distribution is enhanced by the same multiple reflection mechanism.

Shading

Summer solar heat is ideally intercepted with shading devices at the outside rather than the inside of a window because once the sun's rays pass through the glazing, they are in the building for good. The sun spends very little time in front of a south-facing window during the summer. Its south passage is at high altitudes, so window shading with eyebrow-like devices becomes relatively easy.

Space heating loads are not synchronous with the sun's springtime climb in altitude. The sun is nearly at its maximum altitude late in May, but solar heating is still necessary at this time in northern climates. In September the sun has lowered to half its maximum altitude, yet solar heating is rarely required in this month. Solar heating requirements are significant in March when the sun is at the same midaltitude. Any fixed overhang device that gives maximum shading in June while permitting the March sun to sneak underneath would admit unwanted sun in September. The most elegant way to get in phase with the seasons is to shade naturally with vegetation. Leaves bud at the right moment in May to filter the sunlight, and they continue their work as shading devices through September and October.

Nevertheless, trees are not a perfect solution. A bare canopy of branches can still shade up to half of the sun's rays during the winter when maximum intake is required. Many species of trees (oak, ash), however, will transmit 70% to 80% of the wintertime solar energy [15]. One way to overcome the branch shading problem is to place trees so close to the windows that the sun's rays strike the window by passing underneath the tree canopy between September 21 and March 21 (Figure 8-5).

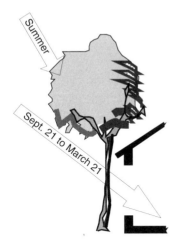

Figure 8-5. The house should be close enough to the tree to allow the winter sun to continue underneath the occluding bare branches on its way to the south-facing glazing.

Trees are not always available in the required position and planting takes time to mature. In addition, some multiple family units are completely out of scale with the trees. Mechanical devices are usually used as shades in these cases. The devices must admit diffuse daylight to prevent inside gloominess during the summer. Exterior louvers fill the bill, but they are expensive. An alternative, more festive look is achieved with retractable awnings, particularly the lateral arm type, which keep the translucent fabric taut in all positions. A nice combination of natural and artificial shading is achieved with a latticework eyebrow covered with deciduous vines. Like the tree canopy that hugs a building, this device's horizontal dimension is short enough to admit the sun underneath the eyebrow in October, and the vines provide shading in the summer.

The geometric extent of the shadow coverage for a given month is determined by the profile angle variation as shown in Figure 6-17. The end of Chapter 9 shows how to use a sun path diagram to reveal when a window is protected.

Auxiliary Heating

Choosing the correct auxiliary heat system for a solar heated home is always challenging. Economics, distribution, and fuel availability are always primary concerns, but radiant heating should always be considered in addition to the usual choices when using low-e windows because radiant heat and low-e coated windows work synergistically together.

Large area radiant heating systems deliver heat as infrared energy—independent of distance and orientation. Any room surface will emit infrared when it becomes warmer than its neighbors. Typically hot water pipes or electrical resistance circuits are buried in half of a drywall ceiling or rugless wood floor to lift its surface temperature to about 32°C (90°F). If the room is well insulated, the radiant energy will bounce around the room and heat everything uniformly. Uncomfortable and wasteful thermal stratification does not build up in rooms with cathedral ceilings, as is the case with convective heaters. Energy is conserved when compared with conventional heating systems because the heating thermostat must be set back many degrees to compensate for the elevated radiant temperature. The cooler room air loses less heat to the outside, as the air inevitably leaks through the building's innumerable joints.

Low-e windows arrest infrared loss and raise thermal comfort in a radiantly heated building. Whereas normal windows would absorb great quantities of infrared only to conduct this heat outside, low-e windows choke off the infrared beam as it tries to leap the gap in a double-glazed window. In fact, the room-side surface of a low-e coated window in a radiantly heated room runs warmer in the winter than its R-value would suggest. The inside light must heat up noticeably, as it is deluged with artificially supplied infrared energy that cannot continue on its path. A warmer window surface means a higher degree of thermal comfort, particularly when the window areas are large.

Radiant heat makes particular sense in a solar-heated building because the heat is delivered by the same means in both cases. Large, open-plan spaces become effective distribution conduits for the infrared emissions. Convective heat is not distributed well in large spaces, as the heated air wants to float to the ceiling. In addition, convective heaters frequently set up air currents that run counter to the air currents generated by the sun.

Convective heaters are normally placed underneath windows in conventional buildings to counteract the adverse convection currents set up by the windows in the wintertime. The rising hot air from the heater reverses the normal downward flow of cold air, which would naturally run along the floor and chill people's legs. The better low-e windows insulate so well that cold air drafts are avoided altogether. Low-e technology finally breaks the window's iron grip on the heater so that now the heater can hide out in any architecturally convenient location.

A Graphic Method for Predicting Solar Heating Thermal Comfort

Energy is saved as a by-product whenever south-facing windows in well-insulated solar-heated spaces are sized to preserve thermal and visual comfort. Conversely, focusing on maximizing energy savings will certainly lead to loss of comfort and an unpleasant, useless space.

The next chapter addresses the visual comfort problem. This section presents a graphic design method [16] for predicting a room's thermal comfort on a clear day in terms of the room's air temperature swings. Wintertime overheating can unexpectedly ruin thermal comfort when the sun is pouring in through oversized windows. The method accounts for today's and tomorrow's low-e technology, the space's insulation levels and geometry, the solar exposure, the outdoor temperature, the window size, and the presence of any internal mass for minimizing the room air temperature swings. The procedure only works for open-plan spaces with south-facing, vertical-glazing, and internal-thermal masses, which are nearly uniform in temperature. Furthermore, no auxiliary heating system, or intermittent ventilation is allowed.

Clearly, this is a large set of assumptions, and many buildings will not fit them all. However, the following graphs are very useful given their design-aid nature for quickly predicting overheating. These graphs are most appropriate for buildings that are largely solar heated on a clear day, because the method assumes there is no auxiliary heating.

The single thermal zone restriction is not always difficult to accommodate. An entire residence can be modeled as one zone when most of the spaces are part of an open plan. The method cannot be used for rooms that are out of radiation contact with south-facing glass. Small, individual south-facing rooms must be modeled as separate zones. The hourly heat loss rate used to model a zone must not include losses experienced by separate zones. The assumption about nearly isothermal mass works for spaces that use thin (less than 15 cm [6 in]) slabs of massive material.

It is possible to approximate the effect of auxiliary heating in the modeled zone by artificially raising the outdoor air temperature. The average outdoor air temperature used in the model is raised until the average indoor temperature is in the comfort zone. The effect of internal heat gains from appliances is simulated by raising the average outdoor air temperature by the following amount:

$$\frac{\text{Daily Heat Gain}}{\text{UA}_{total} \times 24 \text{ hr/day}}$$

where UA_{total} is discussed in Step 2.

The subsequent graphs give room air temperature swings for thermal storage masses that are either convectively or radiatively coupled. The differences between the two cases are shown schematically in Figures 8-6 and 8-7. In convective coupling, the sun is assumed to strike a perfect insulator, which instantly convects the absorbed energy to the room air. Therefore, any heat that makes its way to a thermal storage mass gets there via the room air. This would happen if all the incoming sunlight were to

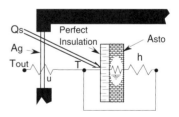

Figure 8-6. The convectively coupled case for direct gain solar heating in a single zone space. The south-facing window is shown in section. The nomenclature is summarized in Table 8-5.

Calculation

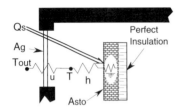

Figure 8-7. The radiatively coupled case for direct gain solar heating in a single zone space. The south-facing window is shown in section. The nomenclature is summarized in Table 8-5.

strike dark rugs, furniture, and other lightweight surfaces, which heat up and convect most of the absorbed energy into the air. In radiative coupling (Figure 8-7), the sun is assumed to directly strike the surface of the thermal storage masses (usually heavy concrete or masonry floors or walls), which are free to radiate their stored energy directly into the living space. Actual situations will lie somewhere between these two extremes, so it is up to the designer to decide which one predominates. In most cases, radiative coupling is desirable, if not essential for thermal comfort. The design method is set up to quickly test each alternative.

A solar building may overheat on clear days when the outdoor temperature is warm, but indoor temperatures can be lowered by merely opening the windows. The same space could overheat on a cold clear day, but venting becomes undesirable in the winter because it wastes energy.

It is too time-consuming to use this method to test for overheating on every clear day of every month so it becomes necessary to choose weather data to represent typical days in the heating season. A clear day in March works well. In March, the average monthly outdoor temperature usually equals the average for the entire heating season, and the sun is at its average altitudes for the heating sea-

Table 8-1. Daylong Solar Heat Gain Factors for Vertical, South-Facing, Double-Strength Glass for the 21st Day of the Month (W/m² [Btuh/ft²])

Latitude	2 4		3 2		3 6		4 0		4 4		4 8		5 6	
January	5295	1680	5377	1706	5251	1666	5125	1626	4772	1514	4419	1402	3070	974
February	4406	1398	4917	1560	5046	1601	5176	1642	5150	1634	5125	1626	4646	1474
March	2887	916	3713	1178	4044	1283	4375	1388	4605	1461	4835	1534	5043	1600
April	1538	488	2269	720	2673	848	3076	976	3445	1093	3814	1210	4406	1398
May	1179	374	1576	500	1916	608	2257	716	2651	841	3045	966	3808	1208
June	1179	374	1418	450	1702	540	1986	630	2367	751	2749	872	3543	1124
July	1204	382	1563	496	1891	600	2219	704	2604	826	2988	948	3738	1186
August	1532	486	2219	704	2604	826	2988	948	3344	1061	3700	1174	4274	1356
September	2843	902	3618	1148	3927	1246	4236	1344	4441	1409	4646	1474	4797	1522
October	4255	1350	4747	1506	4867	1544	4986	1582	4949	1570	4911	1558	4425	1404
November	5201	1650	5283	1676	5157	1636	5031	1596	4678	1484	4325	1372	2994	950
December	5472	1736	5371	1704	5128	1627	4886	1550	4384	1391	3883	1232	2162	686

Note: These figures were obtained by linear interpolation of tables from the *1989 ASHRAE Handbook of Fundamentals*, ASHRAE, Atlanta, Georgia. They assume 20% ground reflectance and an atmospheric clearness of 1. Reduce these figures by 15% to 20% to account for lower atmospheric clearness in urban locations. Snow would increase these figures by 10% to 15% due to increased ground reflectance.

Low-E Glazing Design Guide

son. The interior temperature excursions for March are only slightly higher than for January or, for that matter, for all the other heating months except September and October.

Given representative weather data, the first steps in the method are concerned with reducing the data to usable form:

Step 1: *Calculate the average hourly clear day solar heat gain (Qs).* The daylong clear day solar heat gain must be determined and then divided by 24 to yield the average hourly value. Table 8-1 is used for the daylong clear day solar heat gain in the absence of measured data. March data will conservatively represent most days of the heating season. In this case the average hourly clear day solar heat gain, Q_s, is given by :

Q_s = Daylong clear day solar heat gain x SC/24 hours.

The numerator represents the solar heat admitted over a clear day, through one layer of vertical, south-facing, clear, 3 mm (0.125 in) window glass. The values include both transmitted solar energy and inward-flowing energy due to absorption, conduction, convection, and reradiated infrared radiation.

The shading coefficient is given for several types of low-e glazing in Tables 5-1 and 8-6. For comparison purposes, the shading coefficient is 1.0 for a single sheet of 3 mm (.125 in) thick clear glass, and 0.87 for clear double glass.

Step 2: *Determine the Equilibrium Temperature (A_g, T_e)* This step is used to calculate the equilibrium temperature resulting from the solar intake through a known amount of south-facing glass. The equilibrium temperature equals the average daily room temperature due to solar heating and is not related to the thermostat setting. Note that a south glass area and equilibrium temperature consistent with this step are used in all the following steps. The equilibrium temperature is given as:

$$T_e = T_{out} + \frac{A_g \times Q_s}{UA_{total}}$$

where:

T_e = equilibrium temperature °C (°F)
T_{out} = average daily outdoor temperature °C (°F)
A_g = south glass area m^2 (ft^2)
Q_s = clear day solar heat gain W/m^2 (Btu/hr ft^2)
UA_{total} = total zone heat loss per hour W/°K (Btu/hr°F)

Calculation

UA$_{total}$ is a measure of how much heat leaves the zone by conduction through the building skin and air leakage through cracks in the building. Infrared traffic through the window forms part of this loss, but this loss is included in the U-value figures given for windows in the previous chapters.

Just as a window has a U-value, every other building skin component also has a U-value, usually determined by code as shown in Chapter 6. The heat loss rate through each component is its total area times its U-value so, the heat loss through the building skin is given as:

$$UA_{total} = U_{windows} \times A_{windows} + U_{ceiling} \times A_{ceiling} + U_{doors} \times A_{doors} + U_{walls} \times A_{walls} + U_{floor} \times A_{floor} + \text{Heat loss rate by air exchange}$$

The heat loss by air exchange to the outside is easy to compute for offices: it is the fan-forced ventilation rate to the outside times the heat capacity of air. Building codes give ventilation rates in terms of a unit area of office floor or per occupant. A typical value is 7 L/s (15 cfm) per person. Coupling this with the heat capacity of air gives:

Heat loss rate by air exchange (W/°K) =
    1200 J s/m^3 °K h x 7 L/s x no. of people

Heat loss rate by air exchange (Btu/hr °F) =
    0.018 Btu/ft^{3}°F x 15 ft^3/min x 60 min/hr x
    no. of people

The heat loss by air exchange to the outside for homes without fans is not as easy to compute. The leakage, known as infiltration, increases almost linearly with temperature difference, but no correlation is evident yet for wind speed variations. Infiltration is usually determined empirically because most attempts to quantify it are too complicated to use in estimating. One way of characterizing the infiltration rate is to quantify the air change rates for various construction types. Table 8-2 gives average air change rates for structures that have at least two exposed walls. The listed rates occur when there is an approximately 11°C (20°F) temperature drop to the outside and when the wind speed averages 11.3 kph (7 mph). Of course any given structure will vary from these average figures, but the figures are intended as estimates for design purposes. These figures were determined by the author using tracer gas measurements.

Table 8-2. Average Air Change Rates for Various Residential Construction Systems

For average indoor-outdoor temperature difference of 14°C (25°F) and near calm	
1. Stick built with no vapor barrier	1.5 - 2.0 ac/hr
2. Masonry or stick built with filled wall cavities	0.8 - 0.9 ac/hr
3. Continuous vapor barrier	0.3 - 0.5 ac/hr

Air change rates below 0.4 ac/hr are not recommended because odor and humidity accumulation becomes a problem. Sometimes air-to-air heat exchanges are used to economically ventilate homes that have tighter construction.

The following equation is used to find the heat loss rate for each degree temperature drop to the outside given an estimated air change rate:

Heat loss rate by air exchange = ac/hr x 1 hr/3600 sec x
        Zone volume x 1200 J s/m^3 °Kh ,

or in imperial units:
Heat loss rate by air exchange = ac/hr x Zone volume x
        0.018 Btu/ hr ft^3°F

Step 3: *Calculate the outdoor air temperature amplitude (ITI).* The outdoor temperature amplitude is defined as one-half the outdoor daily temperature swing as given by the formula:

$$ITI = \frac{T_{max} - T_{min}}{2}$$

where:
ITI = the outdoor temperature amplitude °C (°F)
T_{max} = normal maximum daily temperature °C (°F)
T_{min} = normal minimum daily temperature °C (°F)

Step 4: *Find the zero mass amplitude (IZI).* The zero mass amplitude is a required intermediate value. It is a fictitious worst case value defined as one-half the temperature swing that would result if the building contained no thermal mass. The value is determined from Figure 8-8 using the difference between the average indoor and outdoor air temperatures (T_e - T_{out}), and the value from Step 3 as indices to the figure.

Calculation

Figure 8-8. Temperature amplitude with zero mass (Adapted from "A Simple Direct Gain Passive House Performance Prediction Model", Niles, P.W.B., *Passive Solar: State of the Art, Proceedings. of the 2nd National Passive Solar Conference*, Philadelphia, ISES, March 1978).

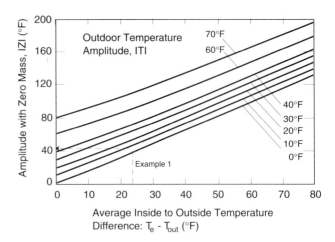

Step 5: *Look up the effective storage mass heat capacity (MCsto).* The graphs used to compute the temperature swings assume that the storage mass behaves isothermally; that is, the heat is distributed evenly and instantly through the entire mass. Though this is a fair assumption for water, it is not accurate for masonry thicknesses over 7 to 10 cm (3 to 4 in). Because masonry has a relatively low conductivity, the outer portion of the mass will store more heat than the inner portions. To compensate for this phenomenon and to model storage surface temperatures accurately, an effective heat capacity lower than the volumetric heat capacity is used.

The effective heat capacity is the isothermal equivalent of various storage materials and is used to compensate for the temperature gradients that will form in most thermal storage materials. It represents the heat capacity of a thermal storage material in direct sunlight over a daily cycle, thus making it the diurnal heat capacity for radiant coupling. Values of effective storage mass heat capacity for various masonry materials (and pine wood) are listed in Table 8-3.

This effective heat capacity is greatly reduced for convective coupling. The heat capacity value for a material greater than 3 inches thick becomes approximately equal to the effective heat capacity of 3-inch material that is radiantly coupled to the room. The effective heat capacity for convectively coupled material is equal to the heat capacity for radiantly couple mass of equal thickness when the thickness is less than 3 inches.

This method is not restricted to a one-side insulated storage mass when water is the thermal storage medium. It can also model freestanding water barrels, tubes, and tanks. Water storage is always assumed to behave iso-

Properties	Concrete	Limestone	Brick	Pine	Dry Sand	Adobe	Dry Wall
Density							
kg/cu. m	2291	2451	1794	497	1522	1922	801
lb/cu ft	143	153	112	31	95	120	50
Specific Heat							
kJ/kg°K	0.88	0.92	0.92	2.80	0.79	0.84	0.84
Btu/lb °F	0.21	0.22	0.22	0.67	0.19	0.20	0.20
Conductivity							
W/m°K	1.73	0.93	0.69	0.16	0.33	0.57	0.16
Btu/hr ft °F	1.00	0.54	0.40	0.09	0.19	0.33	0.09
Thickness							
2.54 cm	52.69	59.02	43.21	36.04	31.83	42.16	17.71
1.0 inch	2.50	2.80	2.05	1.71	1.51	2.00	0.84
5.08 cm	105.18	116.35	85.15	62.39	61.13	82.62	33.72
2.0 inch	4.99	5.52	4.04	2.96	2.90	3.92	1.60
7.62 cm	155.34	164.62	120.78	66.18	81.36	114.66	43.00
3.0 inch	7.37	7.81	5.73	3.14	3.86	5.44	2.04
10.16 cm	199.61	193.28	142.06	61.76	87.26	130.68	44.47
4.0 inch	9.47	9.17	6.74	2.93	4.14	6.20	2.11
15.24 cm	251.67	196.02	144.59	58.17	80.52	127.52	40.47
6.0 inch	11.94	9.30	6.86	2.76	3.82	6.05	1.92
20.32 cm	255.88	181.90	134.05	58.39	76.30	118.46	38.78
8.0 inch	12.14	8.63	6.36	2.77	3.62	5.62	1.84
30.48 cm	231.64	174.73	128.57	58.39	76.09	115.72	38.99
12.0 inch	10.99	8.29	6.10	2.77	3.61	5.49	1.85
40.64 cm	224.48	175.58	129.21	58.39	76.30	116.35	38.99
16.0 inch	10.65	8.33	6.13	2.77	3.62	5.52	1.85

	Wh/sq m °K		Btu/sq ft °F

thermally because convective currents in the water evenly distribute the heat through the fluid. Thus, one can model two-sided storage by properly forming the heat storage capacity per exposed surface area.

If freestanding water containers are used, they may be imagined as spread out and flattened into the one-sided insulated storage mass. The surface area of the storage (A_s) will be the containers' area exposed to room air. This is the heat transfer area of the storage. The storage mass heat capacity (MC_{sto}) will be the volumetric heat capacity per surface area of heat transfer. This heat capacity does not have to be reduced to an effective heat capacity because thermal gradients will not occur in the water storage. For freestanding water storage:

Calculation

$$MC_{sto} = \frac{\text{Specific Heat of Water} \times \text{Total Volume}}{\text{Exposed Surface Area of Container}}$$

where the Specific heat of water is
$261 \text{ KJ/m}^3 \text{ }^\circ\text{K}$ ($62.4 \text{ Btu/ ft}^3 \text{ }^\circ\text{F}$)

Step 6: *Determine the storage surface film conductance (h).* This factor represents the convective heat transfer coefficient from the storage mass surface to the room air. Room air is heated directly by convection between the surface of the mass and the air. In addition, it is heated indirectly when radiation from the mass surface strikes the room walls. The walls then heat the air by convection. This radiant heating effect is included in the design curve.

Table 8-4. Surface Film Conductance (h)

Orientation	h (W/m² °K)	h (Btu/hr ft² °F)
Vertical Wall	4.5	0.8
Horizontal Floor	5.7	1.0
Horizontal Ceiling	3.4	0.6

The exact value of the convective heat transfer coefficient depends on the geometric relationships in a room. Table 8-4 lists these values for various surface orientations. The figures account for the mixing induced by infiltrating air and assume that the surfaces are always warmer than the room air, as would occur for radiant coupling. For the convectively coupled case, the figures for the floor and ceiling are interchanged.

Step 7: *Find the convective temperature swings (ICI).* To determine the temperature swings in the case of convective coupling, first find the ratio of the convectively coupled case to the zero mass indoor temperature amplitude (ICI/IZI) from Figure 8-9, using the following value to select the appropriate curve on the graph:

$$\frac{(T_e - T_{out}) \times h \times A_{sto}}{Q_s \times A_g}$$

and the value of MC_{sto}/h to enter the graph on the horizontal axis. A_{sto} is the mass area illuminated by the sun. When the sun is diffused, A_{sto} is the entire exposed area of mass. When the sun sweeps the mass with beam energy, A_{sto} is approximately 80% of the swept area.

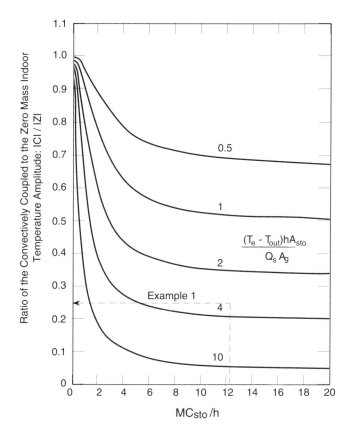

Figure 8-9. Convectively coupled temperature amplitude ICI (Adapated from: "A Simple Direct Gain Passive House Performance Prediction Model", Niles, P.W.B., *Passive Solar: State of the Art, Proceedings of the 2nd National Passive Solar Conference*, Philadelphia, ISES, March 1978).

Calculate the maximum and minimum air temperatures for the convective case from the following formulas using the value for (ICI / IZI) from Figure 8-9:

ICI = IZI x (ICI / IZI)

Maximum interior air temperature = T_e + ICI

Minimum interior air temperature = T_e - ICI

where:

ICI = one-half the air temperature swing for the convectively coupled case °C (°F).

IZI = one-half the air temperature swing with zero mass, from Step 4 °C (°F).

T_e = the equilibrium temperature °C (°F).

Calculation

Step 8: *Find the radiative temperature swings (IRI).* To determine the temperature swings in the radiative case, first find the ratio of the radiantly coupled air temperature amplitudes to the convectively coupled air temperature amplitudes (IRI / ICI) from Figure 8-10. Use the value for $(T_e - T_{out})$/ ITI to select the appropriate curve on the graph. Then calculate the maximum and minimum temperatures for the radiative case from the following formulas:

IRI = ICI x (IRI / ICI)
Maximum interior air temperature = T_e + IRI

Minimum interior air temperature = T_e - IRI

where:
IRI = one-half temperature swing (amplitude) with radiatively coupled mass °C (°F).

ICI = one-half temperature swing (amplitude) in convectively coupled case °C (°F).

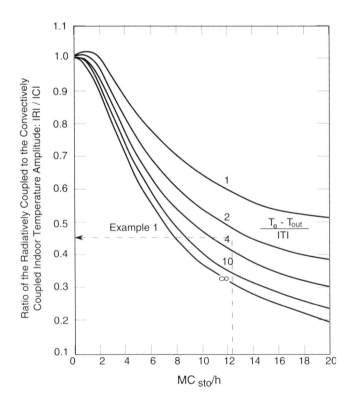

Figure 8-10. Radiatively coupled temperature amplitude (IRI) (Adapted from "A Simple Direct Gain Passive House Performance Prediction Model", Niles, P.W.B., *Passive Solar: State of the Art, Proceedings. of the 2nd National Passive Solar Conference,* Philadelphia, ISES, March 1978).

Table 8-5. Thermal Comfort Nomenclature

Term	Definition	Units (SI)	Units (Imperial)
A_g	South glass area	m^2	ft^2
A_{sto}	Surface area of thermal storage mass	m^2	ft^2
ICI	One-half temperature swing with convectively coupled mass	°C	°F
DSHGF	Daylong solar heat gain factor	Wh/m^2day	Btu/ft^2day
h	Storage surface film conductance	$W/m^2°K$	$Btu/hr°Fft^2$
MC_{sto}	Effective storage mass heat capacity per thickness specified	$Wh/m^2°K$	$Btu/ft^2°F$
Q_s	Average clear day solar heat gain	W/m^2	$Btu/hr\ ft^2$
IRI	One-half temperature swing with radiatively coupled mass	°C	°F
SC	Shading coefficient		
ITI	One-half outdoor temperature swing	°C	°F
T_e	Average daily room air temperature (equilibrium temperature)	°C	°F
T_{out}	Average daily outdoor temperature	°C	°F
T_{max}	Normal daily maximum outdoor air temperature	°C	°F
T_{min}	Normal daily minimum outdoor air temperature	°C	°F
T_e	Average daily room air temperature (equilibrium temperature)	°C	°F
IZI	One-half temperature swing with zero mass	°C	°F
U_g	South glass heat transfer coefficient (equilibrium temperature)	$W/m^2°K$	$Btu/hr°Fft^2$
UA_{total}	Total zone heat loss coefficient (including south-facing glass)	$W/°K$	$Btu/hr°F$
UA_{ns}	Heat loss coefficient without south glass (UA_{total} - U_g)	$W/°K$	$Btu/hr°F$

Calculation

This method does not account for the broiler effect where high surface temperatures can lead to thermal discomfort, even in face of low air temperatures. But the method still works for the radiatively coupled case because the surface temperatures of a radiantly coupled mass differ from the air temperature only by a few degrees. The difference is so slight because the mass conducts the majority of the impinging solar energy to its interior during the day. On the other hand, a space that is convectively coupled will always feel much warmer during the day than the air temperature suggests because the sun is striking insulated surfaces, which elevate drastically in surface temperature.

Example 8-1. A 929 m^2 (10,000 ft^2) loft with 204 m^2 (2200 ft^2) of low-e south-facing glass is located in Boston (latitude = 42°N) where the average March outdoor temperature, T_{out}, is 3.4 °C (38.1°F). The average March minimum and maximum temperatures, T_{min}, T_{max}, are - 0.3°C (31.5°F) and 7 °C (44.6°F), respectively.

The warehouse is formed with 20 cm (8 in) concrete walls and a floor slab, which have a combined area of 1208 m^2 (13,000 ft^2). The solar collection takes place through double glazed, low-e monitor skylights, which can be expected to diffuse the sunlight over the entire storage area. The glass has a U-value of 1.53 W/°Km^2 (0.27 Btu/hr°F ft^2) and a shading coefficient of 0.74. The building heat loss rate, U_{ns}, exclusive of the south glass losses, has been calculated to be 1846 W/°K (3500 Btu/hr°F).

Step 1: *Calculate the average hourly solar gain.*

Q_s = Daylong clear day solar heat gain x SC/24 hours.

Q_s = 4499 x 0.74/24 hours = 138 W/m^2
Q_s = 1425 x 0.74/24 hours = 44 Btu/hr ft^2

Step 2: *Determine the equilibrium temperature.*

$$T_e = T_{out} + \frac{A_g \times Q_s}{UA_{total}}$$

but UA_{total} is equal to $U_{ns} + U_g \times A_g$, or

1846 + 1.53 x 204 = 2158 W/°K
3500 + 0.27 x 2200 = 4094 Btu/ hr°F

$$T_e = 3.4 + \frac{204 \times 138}{2158} = 16.5°C$$

$$T_e = 38.1 + \frac{2200 \times 44}{4094} = 61.7°F$$

Step 3: *Calculate the outdoor air temperature amplitude.*

$$ITI = \frac{7 - (-0.3)}{2} = 3.65°C$$

$$ITI = \frac{44.6 - 31.5}{2} = 6.55°F$$

Step 4: *Find the zero mass amplitude.*

From Figure 8-8

IZI = 24°C,
IZI = 44°F

Step 5: *Look up the storage heat capacity.*

From Table 8-2

MC_{sto} = 68.9 Wh/m^2°K of surface area
MC_{sto} = 12.14 Btu/ ft^2 °F of surface area

Step 6: *Determine the storage surface film conductance.*

Because most of the storage mass is in the floor, the surface film conductance becomes

h = 3.15 W/°K m^2
h = 1.0 Btu/hr °F ft^2

Step 7: *Find the convective temperature swing.*

MC_{sto}/h = 68.9/3.15 = 21.87
MC_{sto}/h = 12.14/1.0 = 12.14

Calculation

The graph parameter is

$$\frac{(T_e - T_{out}) \times h \times A_{sto}}{Q_s \times A_g}$$

$$\frac{(16.5 - 3.4) \times 3.15 \times 1208}{24 \times 204} = 10.2$$

$$\frac{(61.7 - 38.1) \times 1.0 \times 1308}{44 \times 2200} = 3.2$$

From Figure 8-9
> ICI / IZI = .25
> ICI = IZI x (ICI / IZI) = 24 x 0.25 = ±6°C
> ICI = IZI x (ICI / IZI) = 44 x 0.25 = ±11°F

Therefore, if the mass was convectively coupled

Max. air temperature = T_e + ICI = 16.5 + 6 = 22.5°C
Min. air temperature = T_e + ICI = 16.5 - 6 = 10.5°C

Max. air temperature = T_e + ICI = 61.7 + 11 = 72.7°F
Min. air temperature = T_e + ICI = 61.7 - 11 = 50.7°F

Step 8: *Find the radiative temperature swing.*

$(T_e - T_{out})$/ ITI = (16.5 - 3.4)/3.65 = 3.6
$(T_e - T_{out})$/ ITI = (61.7- 38.1)/6.55 = 3.6

From Figure 8-10
> IRI / ICI = 0.42
> IRI = ICI x (IRI / ICI) = 6 x 0.42 = 2.6°F
> IRI = ICI x (IRI / ICI) = 11 x 0.42 = 4.6°F

Therefore, since the mass is radiantly coupled
Max. air temperature = T_e + IRI = 16.5 + 2.6 = 19.1°C
Min. air temperature = T_e + IRI = 16.5 - 2.6 = 13.9°C

Max. air temperature = T_e + IRI = 61.7 + 4.6 = 66.3°F
Min. air temperature = T_e + IRI = 61.7 - 4.6 = 57°F

The preceding method for determining thermal comfort is particularly useful for checking indoor temperature swings in superinsulated houses with large, south-facing low-e windows, and no heavy internal thermal masses. This building type represents a radiatively coupled case, where the drywall acts as the thermal storage mass (assuming that the floor has light-colored coverings to diffusely reflect the solar energy to the gypsum board on the walls and ceiling). It is all too easy to overheat such a building during the winter when using low-e glazings.

Typical Low-E Values for Heating

Table 8-6 lists typical commercially available low-e products for solar heating applications. The table contains only products with shading coefficients above 0.55. These glazings maximize solar gain while minimizing thermal losses due to their low U-values.

Table 7-4 should be consulted for glazings with low shading coefficients. These glazings control normally excessive solar gains, such as those found in sun rooms with sloped glazing, or in most spaces with a western exposure.

Table 8-6. Typical Commercially Available Low-E Products for Solar Heating Applications

Low-e Type (emissivity)	Cooling Descriptors				Solar (%)			Summer U-value (air filled)	
	Outdoor Reflt. (%)	Daylight Trans.(%)	SC	Dx	Absorb.	Trans.	Reflection	W/°K sq m	Btuh/°F sq ft
Thin film (.10)	11	77	0.71	0.92	27	52	21	1.68	0.30
Pyrolytic (.18)	17	74	0.80	1.08	33	54	13	1.87	0.33
Pyrolytic (.18)*	NA	82	0.95	1.16	NA	NA	NA	3.52	0.62
Suspended(.07)	18	71	0.67	0.94	23	48	29	1.59	0.28
Suspended(.10)	18	68	0.61	0.90	36	40	24	1.76	0.31
Thin film (.10)	12	74	0.72	0.97	31	50	19	1.80	0.32
Thin film (.04)	16	69	0.67	0.97	33	45	22	1.68	0.30
Pyrolytic (.19)	16	73	0.79	1.08	33	54	13	1.90	0.33
Pyrolytic (.19)*	NA	82	0.95	1.16	NA	NA	NA	3.52	0.62
Suspended(.10)†	NA	63	0.58	0.92	NA	NA	NA	0.75	0.13

* Single glazing.

† 3 argon gaps.

European manufacturers.

The figures are from various European and North American glazing manufacturers. Any one row can serve as the basis for a glazing specification. Samples should always be evaluated outdoors on both sunny and overcast days for their color appearance. All listed U-values are for the center of the glass. All glass is clear unless otherwise noted.

9

Daylighting

Predicting Daylighting Levels

Illuminating spaces with large quantities of natural light offers the occupant an ever changing and gratifying link to the outdoors. Moving cloud patterns bring enjoyment, produce color changes, and note the passage of time. Indoor scenes become more inviting in the satisfying hues of daylight. Adequate, glare-free daylighting is always appreciated and usually boosts productivity.

Daylighting is becoming interesting again, particularly office daylighting, because low-e technology turns daylighting into a money-saving proposition. Low-e coatings, unlike any other product, can lower the solar gain without noticeably affecting the daylighting intensity. However, daylighting demands extra attention when using low-e glazing. Low-e coatings can solve the solar gain and window insulation problems, but it does nothing to address the classical lighting issues. If anything, one can get away with bigger than normal low-e windows in offices, which can lead to glare and lighting distribution problems unless lighting fundamentals are understood.

A good daylighting design must work on both sunny and cloudy days. Windows are best sized (as shown in the previous two chapters) to simultaneously provide a view and preserve thermal comfort on sunny days, unless sunny days are unlikely, in which case cloudy day conditions are used to size the windows for adequate lighting. The better insulating low-e windows lower the concern over losing too much energy through windows enlarged to give adequate daylighting when there is no direct solar exposure.

It usually isn't difficult to light an office during sunny hours. What is difficult is removing the glare and distributing the light evenly. The middle sections in this chapter offer several remedies for minimizing glare problems without interfering with the light intake. Once the windows are designed to work with the sunny conditions, they must be checked for lighting performance on cloudy days.

The following graphic methods are used to determine if any interior zones require supplemental artificial lighting during cloudy days. The first method applies only to vertical glazing. The second technique is used for spaces with large amounts of sloped glazing, such as atriums. It is particularly useful for determining if there is enough interior light to grow plants in cloudy climates. An excessive load on the air-conditioner is present anytime the interior lighting levels exceed the minimum levels for growing plants.

Daylighting Through Vertical Glazing on Cloudy Days

Light is controlled by controlling aperture, reflection, and diffusion. Specular reflections are produced by polished surfaces. Using specularly reflected sunlight is exceedingly difficult. The reflectors must track the moving sun to keep the reflected light on target. Furthermore, the reflections are not uniform unless the reflecting surfaces are optically flat. These difficulties have led to the demise of the specular reflector for daylighting work, especially as they do not even work on cloudy days. (The essentially randomly directed cloudy daylight also reflects randomly.) Only a matte, light-colored surface redirects light comfortably and practically.

Cloud-filtered daylight reaches a point in a side-lit room via three routes, as shown in Figure 9-1. Diffuse light from the sky vault reaches the point through any line that does not intersect an obstruction (shown as the sky component). Additional sky light is reflected to the same point from the nearby structures (shown as the external reflected component). Finally, light from the first two sources and light from the ground reflects diffusely off the room's interior surfaces to illuminate the point indirectly (shown as the internal reflected component).

Light levels fall off exponentially with increasing distance from a full width window in the absence of any light

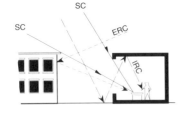

Figure 9-1. The total daylight factor (DF) is composed of the sky component (SC), the externally reflected component (ERC), and the internally reflected component (IRC).

redirecting device (Figure 9-2). Lighting levels for the maximum height window shown in the figure are shown as daylighting factors (assuming the space is wider than it is deep). The daylight factor only applies to cloudy days and is given as the horizontal illumination at an indoor point divided by the illumination received simultaneously outdoors on an unobstructed horizontal surface. It is expressed as a percentage and is always less than 100%. This ratio for a given indoor point remains unchanged as outdoor lighting levels change, as long as it remains cloudy. Thus the daylight factor provides a method for predicting the absolute interior daylight levels for any day given the measurements for one day.

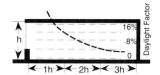

Figure 9-2. The exponential distribution of cloudy day daylight (Derived from *Daylight, International Recommendations for the calculation of Natural Daylight*, Publication CIE No. 16 [E-3.2], Commission Internationale de l'Éclairage, 1970).

Usually, the internal reflected component affects daylighting more that the sky component when the observer is positioned more than a few feet from the window. On cloudy days, the sky component is always greater than the externally reflected component.

Interior surfaces should be light in color for maximum lighting distribution. Daylighting factors in dark-colored rooms near the rear are three to four times less than in light-colored rooms. A good rule of thumb for adequate cloudy day illumination in rooms with light-colored surfaces and windows running nearly the length of one wall is the depth of the room should not exceed 1.5 to 2.5 times the height of the window. The wintertime daylight factor for residences should be at least 2%, and offices should be double that for the usual reading tasks and triple that for prolonged tasks such as drafting and machine work [17]. This assumes a minimum outdoor illumination of 5390 lux (500 footcandles).

The British Research Station (BRS) has designed a protractor, replicated in Figure 9-3, for predicting the cloudy day sky component (SC). The work is based on stimulus response and does not deal with perception response. A person may respond positively to a scene perceived as interesting and not notice any low lighting levels. Perception is also affected by contrast. High lighting levels are useless in a room with dark walls. Nevertheless, the BRS method provides a reasonable means for predicting lighting levels and distribution.

The protractor is designed for use with architectural plans and sections. Any conveniently sized drawing works because daylighting behavior is independent of scale. Figure 9-4 shows how the protractor is used in section for computing the average altitude of the visible sky and the uncorrected sky component. Figure 9-5 shows the pro-

Calculation

Daylighting

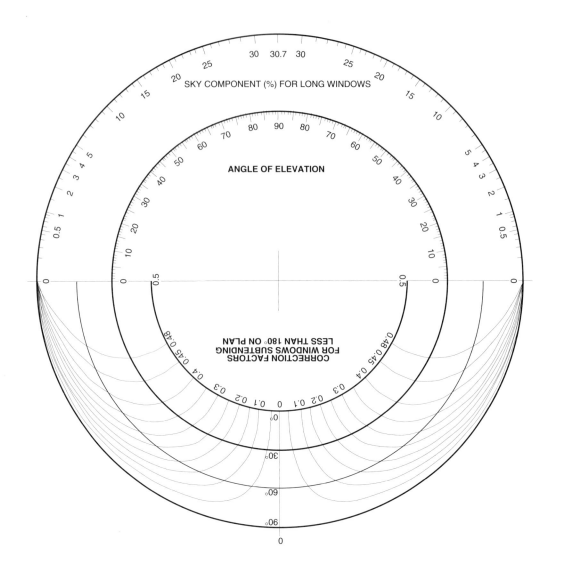

SKY COMPONENT (%) FOR LONG WINDOWS

ANGLE OF ELEVATION

CORRECTION FACTORS
FOR WINDOWS SUBTENDING
LESS THAN 180° ON PLAN

Figure 9-3. The BRS Sky Component Protractor for vertical glazing (Adapted from the British Research Station, London, England).

tractor's use in plan for determining the window length correction factor. The sequence of graphic computations is detailed next.

Select a point in the room (point P in Figure 9-4), using a section taken through the window. Draw lines from the point to the highest and lowest limits at which the sky is seen. The lower limit is determined by the sill or the surrounding buildings or vegetation. With the center of the BRS protractor superimposed on the point and the base parallel to the floor, read the values of the sky component where the upper limit line intercepts the protractor edge and at the lower limit line. Find the difference between the two values as shown in Figure 9-4. The result is the sky

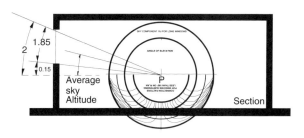

component, expressed as a daylight factor, at the selected point for a room with an infinitely long window (1.85 in this example).

Notice that the sky component is more sensitive to the header height than the sill height. The zenith is three times brighter than the horizon on a cloudy day. The higher the header, the greater the view to the zenith.

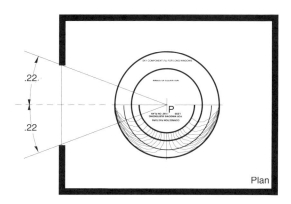

Figure 9-5. Example use of the BRS Sky Component Protractor in plan.

A correction for the actual window length is found by using the other protractor half in the plan view. Before leaving the section drawing, note on the inner semicircular scale the mean altitude of the visible sky (19° in this case). On the plan view of the room, draw lines from the point under consideration to the limits of the visible sky, which are usually coincident with the window jambs. Place the center of the correction factor side over the point in question with the protractor base parallel to the window. Using the just found mean altitude of the visible sky to select one of the concentric semicircles, estimate an appropriate correction factor for each side of the room where the limit lines intersect the mean altitude semicircle. Add these two values to obtain the total correction factor (0.22 + 0.22 = 0.44 for this example). To obtain the corrected sky component, multiply the total correction factor by the sky component found in

Calculation

the first step to get the final daylight factor (0.44 x 1.85 = 0.81). Both limit lines may end up lying in the same quadrant of the protractor if the point in question is far to the side of the window. In this case, the total correction becomes the absolute value of the difference of each correction value. The external reflected component is usually assumed to be 10% of the sky component under cloud cover.

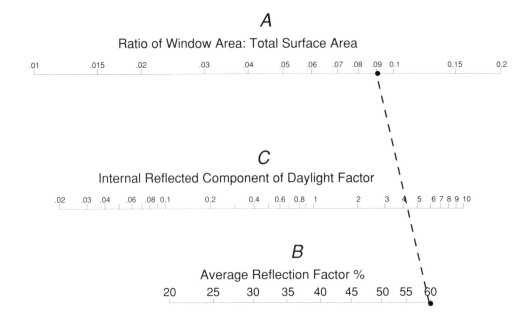

Figure 9-6. Nomograph for determining the internal reflected component.

The internal reflected component for side-lit rooms is formed with the nomograph shown in Figure 9-6. The average reflection factor referred to in Figure 9-6, point B, is found by first adding the products of the room's surface areas and their individual reflections percentages, and then dividing by the sum by the total room surface area. The windows count as part of the surface area. A typical reflection for a double-glazed window is 15%.

The ratio of the window area to the total surface area forms the second entry point, point A, in the nomograph. The internal reflected component is found by joining points A and B and reading the internal reflected component on scale C.

The internal reflected component, the external reflected component, and the sky component are then summed to give the daylight factor as a percentage at the selected point. Finally, the transparency of the windows is accounted for by multiplying the daylight factor by the window's daylight transmission. The effect of other windows is additive, so daylight factors for other exposures at the same point are merely added together.

The preceding method shows that window placement, interior reflectance, and outdoor reflectivity affect the lighting levels in a room. Opaque overhangs also detract from interior lighting since they reduce the room's sky component.

Figure 9-7 shows the effect of changing the placement of the same-sized window opening under a cloudy sky. High windows allow much better light penetration than low windows. Interior lighting uniformity increases as the window is moved into the ceiling. High, light-colored ceilings also help distribute light.

The only time a higher window header isn't better is in the presence of strong, reflected ground light, such as found at lakeside. Here, low windows provide the most illumination by distributing the reflected light to the widest possible ceiling area, insuring a luminous ceiling (Figure 9-8). Unfortunately, low windows place the light source (the ground light) near or below eye level, which increases glare at the desk top level. This is not a problem in residences where there is no specific location for a task as is the case in offices. Office workers cannot readily move work to another location to avoid glare.

Overall lighting levels are vastly increased in a mostly white room when a second high window is placed on the opposite wall, as shown in Figure 9-9. The figure shows the additive nature of light. In this example, daylighting from only one side gives adequate residential lighting levels (a daylight factor of 3) for a room depth up to 2.5 times the window height and adequate office levels (a daylight factor of 6) for a room depth of only 1.5 times the window height.

The reflectivity of outside and inside surfaces can affect the room daylighting levels as shown in Figures 9-10 and 9-11. A large decrease in outdoor reflectance does not have as great an effect at the back of the room as an equal drop in indoor reflectance. Figure 9-11 also shows the daylight factors at the rear of the room fall drastically when any surface is finished with a very dark color. For reference purposes, the interior reflectances of Figures 9-2, 9-9, 9-10, and 9-12 are the same as case A in Figure 9-11.

Figure 9-12 illustrates that an opaque overhang will greatly reduce lighting levels in a room lit from one side only. In effect, an opaque overhang moves the window away from the back wall by a distance equal to the overhang width. One way of overcoming this serious problem is to

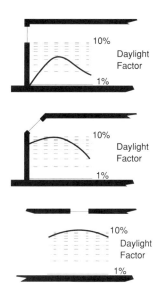

Figure 9-7: Window placement affects lighting distribution (Figures 9-7 through 9-12 are derived from *Daylight, International Recommendations for the Calculation of Natural Daylight*, Publication CIE No. 16 [E-3.2], Commission Internationale de l'Éclairage,1970).

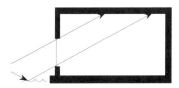

Figure 9-8. Ground reflected light penetrates farther with a low window.

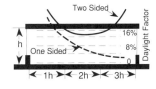

Figure 9-9. The effect of bilateral and unilateral lighting.

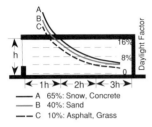

Figure 9-10. The reflectivity of outdoor surfaces can affect the internal daylighting levels.

— A 65%: Snow, Concrete
— B 40%: Sand
- - C 10%: Asphalt, Grass

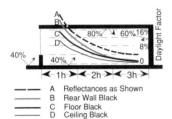

Fig 9-11. The effect of varying room reflectivity.

- - A Reflectances as Shown
— B Rear Wall Black
— C Floor Black
— D Ceiling Black

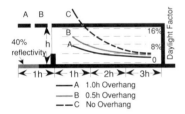

Fig 9-12. The effect of opaque overhangs.

— A 1.0h Overhang
— B 0.5h Overhang
- - C No Overhang

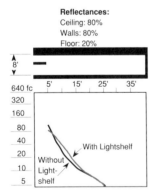

Reflectances:
Ceiling: 80%
Walls: 80%
Floor: 20%

Fig 9-13. The effect of light-shelves on cloudy days (Adapted from: Lam, W.M.C., *Sunlighting as Formgiver for Architecture*, Van Nostrand Reinhold Company, New York, 1986).

use external fixed louvers to block summer beam radiation without blocking the entire sky component. Light-colored, translucent fabrics are also used as eyebrow devices instead of opaque overhangs to admit light on cloudy days.

Lightshelves are principally used to avoid hot spots near the window and even out daylighting distribution on sunny days. They are really antiglare devices and thus are properly discussed in full detail in the section on glare reduction. Their effect on cloudy day performance is shown in Figure 9-13. Experiments [18] show the following:

- The upper window provides most of the illumination.

- The lower window provides little illumination (unlike under sunny conditions when it can be the most effective).

- Lightshelves can improve cloudy day lighting uniformity by reducing illumination substantially near the window. Illumination levels at the rear of the room remain unaffected by lightshelves.

Although office and residential lighting levels are recommended in terms of daylight factors in the preceding discussion, many times absolute lighting levels, in either footcandles or lux, are required. These figures are indirectly available from Figures 9-7 through 9-13. The daylight factor given in these figures is the ratio of the outdoor horizontal illumination to the indoor horizontal illumination, so knowing the daylight factor and the outdoor horizontal illumination determines the absolute interior lighting level.

The outdoor illuminance on average cloudy days is given for horizontal and vertical surfaces as a function of solar altitude in Figure 9-14. The readings for the vertical surface apply to all vertical surfaces because the sky brightness at a given altitude angle is the same for all compass points on a cloudy day. Data in Figures 9-14 and 9-15 are taken from United States Weather Bureau publications citing measurements at numerous weather stations throughout the country.

The exterior horizontal illuminance, E_h, on average cloudy days has also been stated in terms of empirical formulas. One formula, [19] which corresponds well with European observations is given as:

$$E_h = 300 + 21,000 \sin (\text{solar altitude}°) \quad [\text{lux}]$$
$$E_h = 28 + 1951 \sin (\text{solar altitude}°) \quad [\text{footcandles}]$$

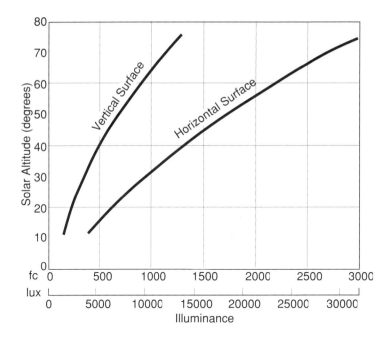

Figure 9-14. The unobstructed exterior surface illuminance on average cloudy days for horizontal and vertical surfaces as a function of solar altitude (Adapated from Stein/Reynolds/McGuinness, *Mechanical and Electrical Equipment for Buildings*, 7th ed., John Wiley & Sons, New York, 1986).

The outdoor illumination for a clear autumn or spring sky is given in Figure 9-15 for horizontal and various vertical surfaces measured with a solar azimuth angle relative to the vertical surface. The curves show the diffuse illuminance from the sky only, as is the case for a shaded window. Direct sunlight produces up to 110,000 lux (10,000 footcandles) on surfaces at right angles to the sun. The darkest part of a clear sky is approximately 90° from the

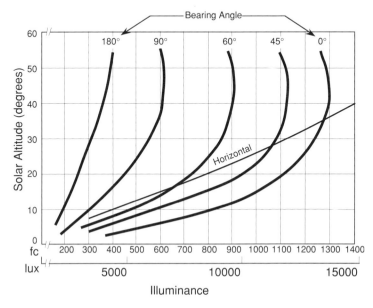

Fig 9-15. Exterior illumination for horizontal and vertical surfaces on a clear autumn or spring days with no direct sun contribution (Adapted from Stein/Reynolds/McGuinness, *Mechanical and Electrical Equipment for Buildings*, 7th ed., John Wiley & Sons, New York, 1986).

sun, which is near the horizon during most of the day. A cloudy sky is brighter than a blue sky, and the brightest part of a cloudy sky is at the zenith.

Figure 9-15 is presented for reference purposes. The daylight factor concept was originally intended for cloudy day conditions and is not directly applicable to clear day illumination figures.

The solar altitude referred to in Figures 9-14 and 9-15 depends not only on the day of the year, but also on the latitude of the site. The sun path diagrams listed for various latitudes in Chapter 6 are used to determine the solar altitude for any day of the year.

Daylighting Through Sloped Glazing on Cloudy Days

Top lighting spaces for people can occur without thermal discomfort when low-e coated skylights are used. Less skylight area is required for daylighting when compared to windows because top light is so much brighter than side light, and a skylight is naturally positioned to optimally distribute the light. Generally, a room is adequately skylit without overheating when the low-e skylight area is only 5% to 9% of the floor area—if the skylights are evenly distributed in a light-colored room and if the ceilings are high. Even this small aperture would overheat the room during sunny days if ordinary glass were used, but the clear, heat-rejecting low-e glazings easily bring the solar gains down to the level of the lights the skylights are designed to replace. Of course, the direct beam sunlight that would normally pass through the skylight must be broken up with baffles or translucent glazing to remove the glare source.

Spaces are also often daylit for the benefit of plants. Plant daylighting is most often used in atriums and other spaces with large amounts of sloped glazing. Top lighting under overcast conditions is the most demanding lighting environment for plants. It can take up to two sunny days to make up for one day of insufficient daylight, so any space that supports plant growth must provide maintenance daylighting levels on cloudy days, or 800 to 1000 lux (80 to 100 footcandles).

Figure 9-16 shows daylight factor charts for commonly encountered spaces that are mostly glazed with sloped glass (less than a 45° slope). The charts were developed from various lighting model studies conducted at the

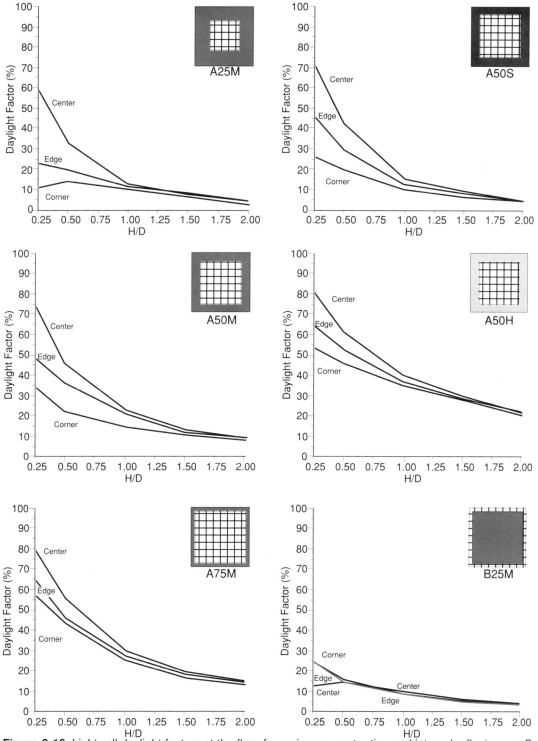

Figure 9-16. Lightwell daylight factors at the floor for various aspect ratios and internal reflectances: S = 15%, M = 40%, H = 85% (Adapted from Gardestad, K., "The Living Atrium: Design Guidelines for Quality Atriums" M.S.Arch Thesis, MIT School of Architecture, Cambridge, Massachusetts, June 1986).

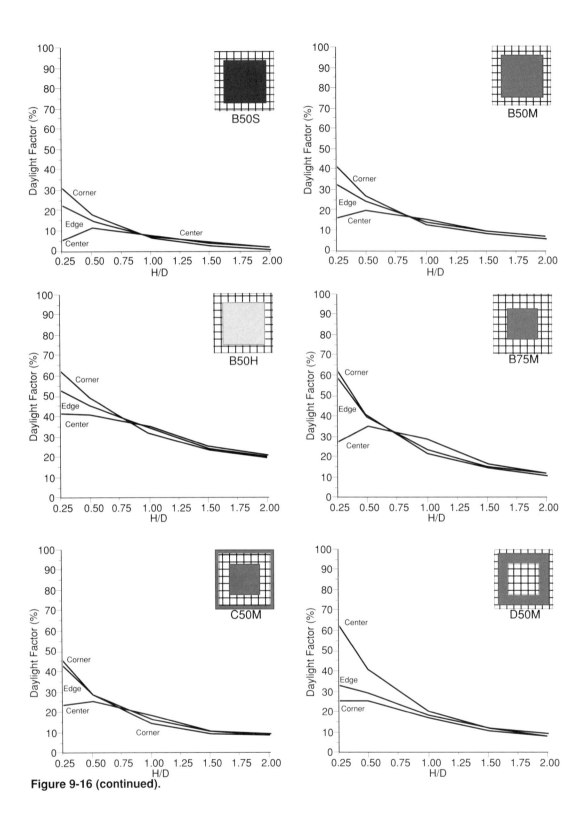

Figure 9-16 (continued).

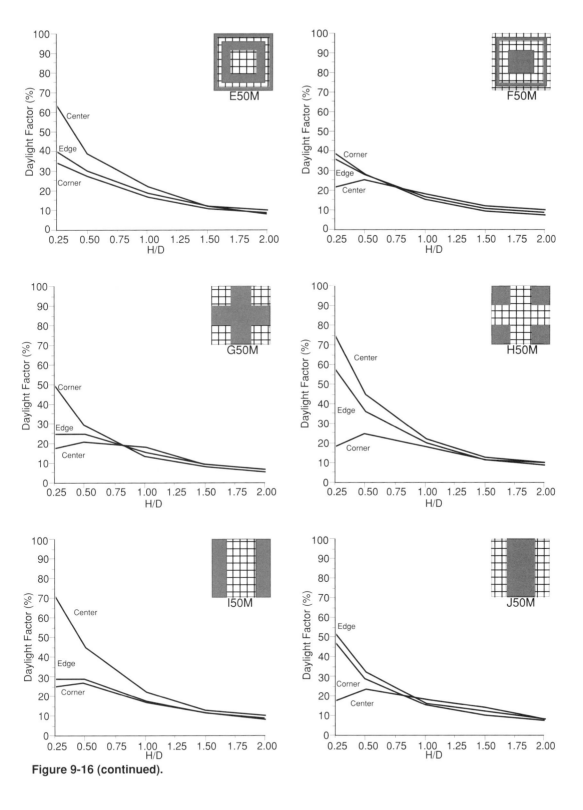

Figure 9-16 (continued).

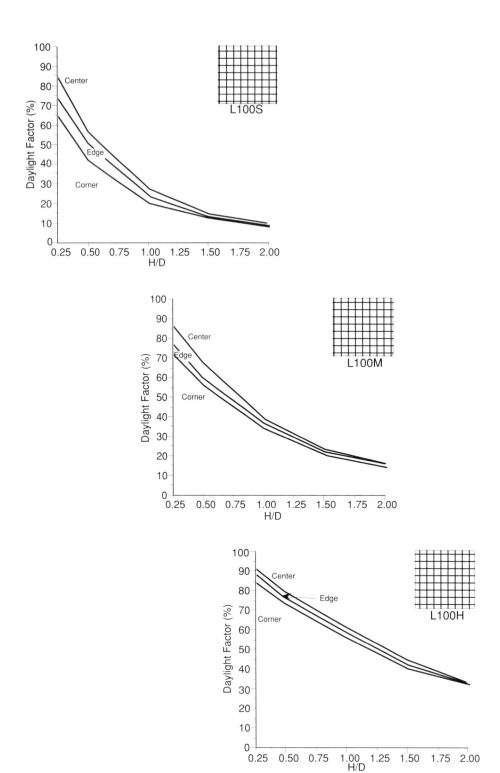

Figure 9-16 (continued).

Massachusetts Institute of Technology [10]. Nine evenly spaced photosensors were fixed to the model's square floor. The glazing opening was always configured to either 100%, 75%, 50%, or 25% of the floor area. The light well was covered with different matte papers to simulate different internal reflectances. Three shades ranging from black to white were used for the wall and ceiling reflectances (the floor was always colored dark brown):

- Near black (labeled S in the charts) = 15% reflectance simulates the reflectance of an all glass space such as an office atrium where even the spandrel panels are glass. (The window glass that rings an atrium almost behaves as a black hole to light because most of the light that enters the vertical glass never reemerges.)

- Medium (labeled M in the charts) = 40% reflectance simulates the reflectance of many earth-colored building materials.

- White (labeled H in the charts) = 85% reflectance simulates hospital white surfaces with no glass present.

Each chart is accompanied by a roof plan and a three part code describing the modeled variables. The first letter in the code labels the glazing plan shape, the middle number is the percent roof aperture, and the last letter gives the wall and ceiling reflectances. For example, the code A50H means shape A, 50% roof aperture, and H for High reflectance.

The atrium aspect ratio (given as the atrium height to depth ratio, H/D, where D is the minimum plan dimension of the light well) is used as the horizontal ordinate in the charts. Most atriums that are concerned with drawing down light to the floor have an H/D ratio between 0.5 and 2.0.

The graph's vertical axis depicts the daylight factor as a percentage. The actual daylight factor for the space is found by multiplying the daylight factor given on the graph by the daylight transmission of the sloped glazing. Multiplying this figure by the cloudy day horizontal illumination found in Figure 9-14 gives the absolute illumination levels at the listed points on the light well floor. Figure 9-17 shows where each of the labeled curves are located in plan.

For a given internal reflectance, the lighting levels are generally independent of floor position once H/D is higher than 1.0 to 1.5. High reflectances and large apertures tended

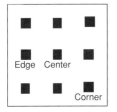

Figure 9-17. The positions of the photosensors on the modeled atrium floor.

to close the gap between different lighting levels sooner. The study shows that the total illumination level is not proportional to the relative aperture until H/D is close to 2.0, as long as the light is evenly distributed. The graphs also show that illumination levels for light wells with medium reflectances are not drastically higher than the light levels for nearly black light wells. Finally, by interpolation, one can see deep light wells (H/D greater than 2.5) absorb most of the light before it reaches the floor.

Evenly distributed skylights produce such an even light in one story spaces that simple rules of thumb are often all that is needed to accurately predict the daylight factors. The following design rules of thumb [17] give average wintertime daylight factors for light-colored spaces:

Vertical Monitors:
$$DF_{ave} = 0.20 \times (\text{skylight glazing area/floor area})$$

45° sloped sawtooth:
$$DF_{ave} = 0.33 \times (\text{skylight glazing area/floor area})$$

Horizontal skylights:
$$DF_{ave} = 0.50 \times (\text{skylight glazing area/floor area})$$

As usual, the daylight factor must be multiplied by the glazing daylight transmission to form the actual daylight factor. The same formulas can be used for north, east, or west glazing on clear, winter days [17]. Much more light and heat will be available on summer days, so the use of heat-rejecting low-e glazing becomes mandatory.

Glare Reduction

Windows often bring unwelcome glare when adequate interior daylighting levels are reached. The problem is not solved by switching to low-e glazing, but only by knowledgeably applying good architectural detailing.

Many glare issues arise on sunny days, but cloudy days can also cause some forms of glare. The various types of glare discussed in this section are associated with side-lit rooms. The type of glare that occurs when overhead daylight sources reflect off of glossy surfaces and veil the material is not normally encountered in office daylighting schemes.

An unusual form of glare is disability glare, which causes indistinct vision in an area around a large, bright light source. The bright light is scattered sideways inside the eye, casting a haze across the view. This effect is particularly pronounced in the elderly because their internal eye fluid becomes cloudier, resulting in more light scattering. Windows that look on a large sky area can produce this form of glare. Disability glare is overcome by reducing the aperture, the contrast, or raising the interior lighting levels with more windows.

Discomfort glare, the more common form of glare encountered in buildings, is caused by a bright light source in the line of vision as seen against a darker object. Discomfort glare, which does not impair vision, occurs when areas of the sky are seen against dark mullions or frames, or other dark surfaces adjacent to the window. The silhouetting of a person's face that sometimes occurs when he or she stands between the observer and a large window is an example of discomfort glare. Meaningless patches of sunlight that fall onto dark areas also cause the same problem. Generally, measured light intensity ratios should be less than 10 to 1 in the field of view to avoid discomfort glare.

Glare is also a perception effect, not just a stimulus effect. High contrast will no longer annoy if the bright areas offer visual delight. Shafts of bright sunlight falling on a planter make the room sparkle; but one person's sparkle may be another person's glare.

Generally, contrast between room surfaces and the outdoor scene should be minimized by using bright surfaces near the windows to produce a gradual transition in brightness from outside to inside. Only clear glass should be used, for translucent materials make the opening even brighter, and tinted glazing makes the interior appear gloomy on cloudy days. Corner or side windows are used to move light to the rear of the room and reduce contrast ratios.

Reveals. Windows should be located against a light colored wall, rather than just punched into the center of a weather wall. The interior wall acts like a large reveal, which becomes intermediately bright with reflected light. When this is not possible, a light colored, splayed reveal (Figure 9-18) is used at the window edges to ease the transition from the bright outdoors to the darker indoors. Mullions should be white to reduce contrast at the window itself.

Glare problems usually worsen on sunny days. Large pools of sunlight on a bland floor, or even worse, large areas of sunlight falling on a white wall make the space visually, if not thermally uncomfortable. One way to avoid this problem is to make the scene interesting. Another way to over-

Figure 9-18. The splayed reveal eases the contrast between the bright outdoors and the darker interior.

---

come the problem is to break up the sunlight, either by reflecting it to the ceiling or by diffusing it through baffles.

Venetian Blinds. Upside down venetian blinds work well as light diffusers if they are narrow enough to appear as a screen rather than a collection of broad stripes. The upper surface of the blind must reflect the light specularly rather than diffusely, so the louvers do not appear as bright light sources. The underside of the blades must have a matte finish so light isn't specularly reflected to the eye. It does not matter if the louvers have imperfect reflecting surfaces once the louvers are small enough. So many reflections add up to a uniform field of light on the ceiling rather than a splotchy collection of hot spots. Lightshelves are also used to diffuse light to the ceiling.

An ideal light diffuser should accomplish the following:

- provide an unimpaired view to the outside

- move the light without becoming a light source

- redistribute the light evenly

- not affect the solar gain and/or lighting levels

- allow ventilation

Of course, no diffuser meets all the listed requirements. In fact, a good diffuser has not been designed yet. Patterned glass can cause glare when the faceted structure breaks the sun down into a thousand tiny images. Translucent glazings suffer from one of three problems, depending on the level of transparency. Nearly transparent diffusing glazings, such as the fiberglass reinforced plastic products, enlarge the sun disk to painful proportions. If the diffusion is increased, such as in ground glass, the sun disk spreads over the whole glass area and the window becomes intolerably bright. If the translucency is lowered to reduce the brightness, the daylighting levels (and sometimes the desirable solar gain) are washed out.

The narrow, upside down venetian blinds come close to the ideal because they do not produce light at the window and they do not interfere with the view when set nearly horizontally.

Lightshelves. Overhead lightshelves, or one or two large louvers, also work well; but their massive presence is sometimes overbearing unless they are carefully designed as an integral part of the facade. Lightshelves work by optimizing the use of reflected light. A proper lightshelf design carefully coordinates the lightshelf's height, width, finishes, and glazing position into a functioning whole.

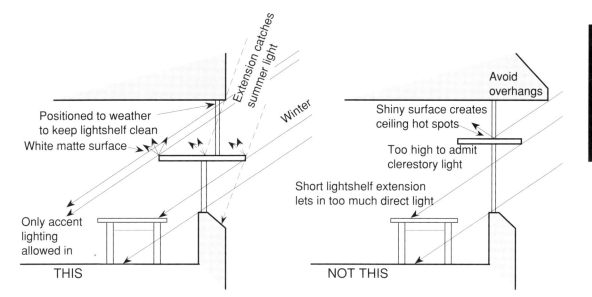

Extension catches summer light

Positioned to weather to keep lightshelf clean

White matte surface

Winter

Only accent lighting allowed in

THIS

Avoid overhangs

Shiny surface creates ceiling hot spots

Too high to admit clerestory light

Short lightshelf extension lets in too much direct light

NOT THIS

Figure 9-19 depicts the elements of good lightshelf (or reflecting glass block or large louver) design. Lightshelves are located as low to the floor as possible to reflect the most light to the ceiling. Of course the lightshelf must provide head room and clearance for doors or other structures, so ceilings tend to become high and painted white. Lightshelf design is highly dependent on the latitude of the site. The front to back depth of the shelf must be large enough to shade most of the room during sunny days and to even out the distribution of light. Some sunlight can enter the room as an accent, as long as large sunny areas do not fall on the work area. Light intake through the window's clerestory section is kept at high intensities by avoiding overhangs. Extending the lightshelf past the facade grabs more light for the clerestory window, which is doing most of the daylighting work anyway. Sloping the lightshelf down provides additional shading for the lower window, but at the expense of moving the light through the clerestory window. A backward tilt reverses the trade-off. The lower glazing can reject even more heat in temperate or hot climates if it is inset relative to the outside edge of the lightshelf. The clerestory glazing is best positioned outboard as far as possible so that the majority of the lightshelf remains inside, free of dirt.

The reflectance of both the inner and outer upper sections of the lightshelf should be as high as possible without using specularly reflecting surfaces, which create visual hot spots on the ceiling. Matte surfaces work very well, but

Figure 9-19. The elements of good lightshelf design.

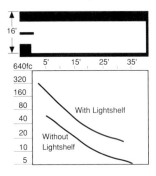

White Ceiling, Back, and Side Walls; Black Foreground

Figure 9-20. The interior lighting levels on a sunny day with and without a lightshelf at various depths (Adapted from: Lam, W.M.C., *Sunlighting as Formgiver for Architecture*, Van Nostrand Reinhold Company, New York, 1986).

semiglossy surfaces are easier to clean. The bottom surface of the shelf is finished to balance the room's lighting. Darker finishes reduce any excessive ground-reflected light, and lighter finishes reduce contrast glare.

Lightshelves are constructed from any durable, easily maintained building material; but they must be thermally broken in cold climates to avoid condensation problems. They can serve other functions, such as spandrels, catwalks, duct enclosures, or sprinkler enclosures. Whatever their sculptural form, they remain strong horizontal elements, which strongly affect the appearance of the building's facade.

Lightshelves function best on sunny days at sites with ground reflectances less than 40% (grass-covered sites have ground reflectances around 30%). They reduce glare by shading the front reaches of a room, but more important, they even out the lighting (and solar heat) distribution in sun-filled rooms by lifting the levels at the back of the room. Figure 9-20 shows the lighting levels with and without a lightshelf at various depths in a modeled [18] room finished with white walls and ceilings. The sun is 45° above the horizon at the left of the diagram, so there is no direct sun at the measured room locations. The outside ground is dark colored, so ground reflections do not play an important role. The illumination at the 20-foot mark is twice as high when using a lightshelf due to the light that is bounced off the ceiling. Light levels are lower than normal at the front of the room due to the shading by the shelf.

Lightshelves do not affect the lighting levels at the back of the room when ground reflections are high. The rising ground light produces a luminous ceiling, which negates the need for any light-redirecting device.

Atrium Louvers. Diffusing daylight becomes particularly important in atriums ringed with offices. One way or another, most of the direct sunlight must be excluded from the offices. Rather than intercepting the sunlight at each office window that faces on the atrium, the sunlight can be equally well diffused at the sloped glazing that roofs over the atrium, without interfering with most of the view to the sky. This approach has typically been taken with either fixed or operable linear louvers suspended near the sloped glazing. (Exterior installations do not work in snow climates and they must resist heavy wind loads.) The light-colored louvers are angled so that the surrounding office openings are shaded, while allowing a view to the sky from below. Fixed louvers only work well for atriums whose long axes run either north-south or east-west. For the east-west orientation, the louvers are run the length of the atrium and angled perpendicular to the floor so, a view to the sky is possible from the floor. The profile angle that the sun's rays make with the openings formed by the louvers is nearly constant throughout the day, so it becomes easy to shade the atrium walls. For the north-south oriented atrium, the louvers are run from north to south and also angled perpendicular to the floor. Although the sun does penetrate the atrium roof for a half hour either side of solar noon, only the offices on the atrium's narrow north end will see the sun's direct light during the short incursion.

Unfortunately, louvers are very expensive since a superstructure is required to carry their weight and to hold them off the glass. Figure 9-21 shows an alternative, that has been used successfully by the author in several commercial atriums that are oriented north-south. The white louvers double as shading devices by taking on a large width relative to the gap between neighboring louvers. More important, the extra width makes it possible to glue the lightweight louvers, which are more like mullions than louvers, to the sloped glazing; so the high cost of the louver superstructure is dispensed with. The mullions are hollow vinyl extrusions that have a white plastic cellular foam adhered to the broad face. The sponge is treated with a pressure-sensitive adhesive to hold the mullions against the glass. The sponge is necessary to compensate for the different thermal expansion rates of the plastic and the glass. The amount of shading is controlled by the mullion spacing. Shading is almost always called for in atriums to lower the solar load on the air-conditioner.

Usually more than enough daylight is available when the sloped glazing forms most of the atrium roof. The designer can use the atrium lighting charts given earlier in this chapter to guarantee the mullions are not spaced so close together that the space becomes dark (multiply the daylight factor found on the chart by the glazing transmission times the ratio of the mullion coverage to the glass area). The mullions must be used with clear low-e glazing, so the light reflected off the white sponge does not heat up the glass as it reflects back to the outside. The mullions have a trapezoidal (or better yet, a semicircular cross section) to act as miniature reveals so the light is eased into the space without creating glaring bright light at the mullions. The lighting effect in atriums more than two stories tall is reminiscent of the light that filters through the horizontal bamboo screens used to bridge the streets in the Middle Eastern bazaars.

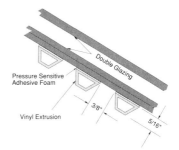

Figure 9-21. Vinyl extrusions adhered to the underside of an atrium glazing for shading and glare reduction.

One of the benefits of low-e glazings for curators and home owners who are worried about fabrics and displayed works of art succumbing to ultraviolet attack is the exceptionally low ultraviolet transmission of most low-e coatings. Most of the remaining ultraviolet light that gets through the low-e glazing is absorbed in the first object it strikes. For this reason, louvers, deep reveals, or other light baffling devices are used in good museum designs to intercept all direct sunlight that would normally reach the daylit galleries. The more durable architecture is sacrificed to the aging effects of ultraviolet light, rather than the works of art. Now, some of the low-e coatings can save the architecture as well.

Physical Models. The best way to predict interior daylighting behavior is to build a model and measure the levels with a light meter. Every aspect of lighting behavior is independent of scale, even the glare conditions.

Short of the real space, a scale physical model is the only trustworthy method for studying glare. (Computer models are not yet up to the task.) The model should be large enough to place an eye or head inside the the scale space for a qualitative inspection.

Daylight levels are affected by surface reflectance and specularity, so the model interior should be a reasonable facsimile of the real thing. This goal is difficult to achieve, so in practice, adhering to the following rules will guarantee enough of a correspondence to ensure the readings:

- Model accurately the window mullion, reveals, and sills. These surfaces produce the first light.

- Model in scale level changes and interior partitions. Furniture need not be modeled unless it reaches significantly into the light distribution volumes.

- Give the interior surfaces the correct reflectances and specular finishes. Hue and chroma do not matter, but the degree of shininess does. The interior reflected component has the biggest influence on interior lighting levels away from the window.

- Make sure the model is outdoors, in the open, and "seeing" a ground reflectance similar to that of the real site's. Nearby buildings will cut off most of the source light. The model must be able to withstand a strong wind.

- Model large exterior obstructions, such as trees or nearby buildings, as two-dimensional objects. Large neighboring objects eclipse the light.

- Model ordinary clear glass by leaving the openings uncovered. All meter readings are corrected by multiplying the readings by the actual window transmission. Translucent glazings can be modeled with vellum of equal diffusing quality.

- Never use a translucent material, such as white cladded Foamcore®, to model the space; make the joints light-tight with black tape. Admitting the light through the ceiling and floor material is the usual cause of spurious readings.

- Keep the model and the light meter strictly horizontal. The diffuse sky component is strongest at the zenith, so the zenith must be overhead for the model too. Rotate the model in plan at different times on sunny days to simulate the various sun angles.

- Measure the illumination inside the model and outdoors simultaneously on a cloudy day with two light meters in order to ratio the readings as an accurate daylight factor. The daylight factor depends on simultaneous indoor and outdoor readings.

- Consider a day cloudy if no shadows are perceived when waving an object near the ground. The daylight factor concept only holds for cloudy days. Measurements must be gathered within 4 hours either side of solar noon to avoid false readings from too low a light.

Daylight models also serve nicely as presentation models, except that the exterior appearance has no effect on the meter readings.

Verifying the Glazing's Daylight Transmission

Although manufacturers list the daylight transmission of their low-e products, many times it is necessary to confirm the published material in the field. A simple $50 analog lux or footcandle meter makes the job simple (a photographic light meter does not give usable readings).

Acquire a large glazing sample, at least 0.30 m (1 ft) on a side, or locate a comparable window bathed in sunlight. Test the glazing in the sunlight. Point the meter at the sun and anchor it so that the meter's attitude remains fixed during the measurements. (It is not necessary to precisely align the meter with the sun because the measurements are relative.) Record the meter's lighting level when there is nothing between the meter and the sun. Quickly (before the sun moves or before the ambient light level changes) place the glazing between the meter and the sun so that the glazing is parallel to the detector and just barely gapped away from the meter. (This approach assures the only light the meter "sees" is the light transmitted by the glazing.) Divide this reading by the first to get the daylight transmission. Take two more sets of measurements and average the results.

Low-E Color and Detection

As is the case with all coated glazings, low-e coatings color the fenestration in certain conditions. Each type of soft coat and thick hard coat low-e coating adds its distinctive pastel color component to reflected light. The only exception is the new pyrolytic coating, which just barely colors the transmitted or reflected light. Accordingly, the exact color of a coated glass is only noticed when the window is viewed in natural daylight against a dark background. Low-e coated glazings are not only uniform in color, but uniform through a given manufacturer's production runs. Color mismatches are only expected when mixing low-e types or runs from different manufacturers.

Chapters 7 and 8 show how important it is to coat the correct window surface. The color shift seen in reflected light from the nonpyrolytic coatings is useful for determining the location of the coated surface in glazing assemblies. Hold a light colored cylinder, such as a piece of chalk or a cigarette, perpendicularly against the glazing surface and note the various reflections. Each receding surface in a multiple glazed unit will mirror an ever weaker image of the cylinder, depending on the distance of the surface from the object. The reflection off the low-e surface will appear in its telltale color, usually as a pastel shade of blue or yellow.

Determining the presence of the new pyrolytic coatings isn't so easy. (The old, intermediate emissivity pyrolytic coatings were all too easy to detect—they looked like gasoline diluted, iridescent oil slicks.) The only large-scale visible effect produced by the pyrolytic coatings is a very slight surface haze when seen from the outside in bright light. The window looks like it had been washed with dirty water. This effect is almost impossible to detect with small coated samples.

The only sure way to determine the presence of a pyrolytic coating is to test for what it does best, either infrared heat reflection or electrical current conduction. The first test works only for single glazing, but no instrumentation is required. The second test requires an inexpensive ohmmeter, and the test also works with double-glazed units.

Detecting infrared heat reflection is easily accomplished without instrumentation with just the aid of a high intensity incandescent lamp in a draft-free room. Think of the coated sample as a heat mirror. First hold one side and then the other below the lamp so that it will reflect the maximum amount of light (and heat) to your face. Your face is also best placed below the lamp out of the way of convective updrafts. One glass side will produce noticeable reflected warmth on your face, and the other will make no discernible difference.

The investment in an inexpensive electrical resistance ohmmeter makes the testing job even easier for single glazing. Place the two current probes diametrically opposite on one side of the glass and note the measured electrical resistance. Repeat the process for the opposite side. The side with the noticeably lower resistance is the side with the pyrolytic coating. This test works on all types of exposed low-e coatings.

Pilkington markets a hand-held meter that detects the presence of pyrolytic coatings in both single- and double-glazed units. It becomes difficult to test for the whereabouts of the pyrolytic coating in a sealed double-glazed unit without this meter because the insulated glass unit must be temporarily removed from the window frame for testing. The following test only works for insulated glass units with conventional edge spacers and double organic seals—taped or welded edges must be left intact.

A double organic seal is evidenced by the sealants' different colors as seen through the band of glass over the edge spacer. The inner sealant is usually much darker than the outer sealant. Unlike the softcoats, which are stripped off the glass at the edge seal, the corrosion-proof pyrolytic coatings are left as is, so the coating comes to the very edge of the glass. The outer seal is there to provide mechanical strength; it does not act as the gas barrier to keep any sealed gas in or water vapor out. This outer seal can be safely pricked a millimeter or so with an ohmmeter current probe so that the probe rests firmly on the glass surface next to the edge spacer. The second probe is placed on the same glass surface at the opposite edge of the window to see if the coating is present. Try the other pane if a large resistance is indicated.

Specification Guidelines

Guide Specification for Low-E Glazings

The previous chapters have singled out the important parameters that differentiate the various low-e glazings. This chapter formally summarizes this information in a specification guide. The guide is intended to aid in preparing specifications for low-e projects, which are characterized by performance. It is also useful when writing prescriptive specifications for particular products or when working from manufacturer's specifications because of the guide's extensiveness.

Each article of a typical glazing specification section is named along with an outline discussion on how the article differs from a traditional glazing specification. The listed information is not meant to act as a literal specification. Adjacent remarks in the column above the page number list alternatives and point the reader to the relevant book passages.

This guide is based on North American practice; consequently, it follows the Construction Specifications Institute's format for specification sections. Some of the articles are based on the American Institute of Architects' *Masterspec* for low-e glazings.

This chapter covers only single glass glazing, low-e insulated glass units and their sealants, or, in the case of retrofit films, the glass and film combination. It does not cover any other item related to the window opening. The following paragraphs are listed for informational purposes and are not intended for verbatim insertion in a specification document.

Specs

Part 1 General

Summary

Specifiers should use the same references to related work in other sections that are used for traditional glazing because the mechanical aspects of low-e glazing are the same as for ordinary glazing.

See pages 46, 62, 85, 86, 99, 100, and 107 for a discussion on HVAC impacts.

Low-e glazings, like any other high performance glass, will influence related sections on luminaires, heating, ventilating, shading, and air-conditioning due to the product's superior daylighting and thermal performance. Mechanical equipment specifiers should be alerted when low-e glass is used.

Unit pricing in the United States does not fluctuate abnormally from the norm, so cost allowances can be designated with confidence.

References

Refer to the low-e paragraphs in *Masterspec* by the American Institute of Architects, and manufacturer's literature.

Definitions

This numerical definition of emissivity is according to the English 1990 edition of the Building Regulations. There is no comparable definition in the North American building codes. Using an emissivity of 0.23 to 0.29 instead of 0.20 will include the retrofit films (see page 57).

Low-emissivity glazing: A glazing with a coating that has an emissivity of less than 0.20.

Emissivity: A measure of a surface's ability to emit long-wave infrared radiation (room temperature radiant heat energy). Emissivity varies from 0 (no emitted infrared) to 1 (100% emitted infrared).

There are three types of low-e coatings for glazings: low temperature vacuum-deposited, high temperature vacuum-deposited, and pyrolytic vapor-deposited.

See page 52.

Low temperature vacuum-deposited glazings: Manufacturer's standard unit with at least one glazing (glass or suspended polyester film in a sealed unit, or retrofit film) coated with a thin metallic or metallic oxide layer by the manufacturer's standard deposition process.

High temperature vacuum-deposited glazings: Manufacturer's standard unit with at least one glass surface coated with a durable and stable thick metallic or metallic oxide layer by the manufacturer's standard deposition process. This coating is currently not commonly available.

See page 59.

Pyrolytic coated glazings: Manufacturer's standard unit with at least one glass surface impregnated with a durable and stable metallic oxide coating by the manufacturer's standard pyrolytic deposition process, either at the time of manufacture, or during heat treatment.

See page 58.

System Description

The performance characteristics designated for coated insulating glazings and/or films are nominal values based on manufacturer's published data:

Performance characteristics:

Visible light transmittance of:_____
Shading coefficient of: _____
Outdoor daylight reflectance: _____

COG summer U-value of: _____
COG winter U-value of: _____

Average summer U-value of: _____
    based on a unit dimension of _____
Average winter U-value of: _____
    based on a unit dimension of _____

Manufacturers have not standardized their published performance figures. Center-of-glass figures for U-values are the norm (see pages 70-71). European manufacturers sometimes characterize solar heat gains in terms of total solar transmission, rather than the shading coefficient (see page 46). Some producers omit the daylight reflectance figure. Additional information is usually furnished on request.

See Tables 7.4 and 8.6 for typical values.

See Tables 5.1-5.4, 7.4, and 8.6 for typical values. COG refers to the Center of Glass (see page 51). Choose either COG or average performance (see discussion on pages 70-71).

Submittals

Submitted product data should be consistent with specified requirements.

Specs

Some of the multigap sealed units are quite thick and require custom mounts (see page 34).

See pages 45 and 148 for a discussion on color. The designers and/or owners should inspect a full-size mock-up in the intended frame for color rendition.

Use ASTME E 774 Class A or equivalent for standard testing.

Use the West German standard DIN 52293 or equivalent (see page 32).

Shop drawings in other sections should be reviewed for mounting and sealant compatibilities.

Samples are required for field verification and for inspecting color rendition and uniformity.

The standard references on traditional glazings apply. For double glazing: The preassembled units consisting of organically sealed panes of glass enclosing a hermetically sealed dehydrated space shall comply with _____. For units filled with a gas other than air, the organic seal leakage rate is determined according to _____ .

Quality control submittals are based on the same tests used for ordinary glazings.

Quality Assurance

Because a low-e glazing's mechanical properties are the same as ordinary glazing, the same qualifications, certifications, and mock-ups used for ordinary glazings apply to low-e glazings. In addition, low-e glazings units are installed like any other glass unit.

Delivery, Storage, and Handling

Low-e double glazing units should be handled with care to avoid damage to the edge seal. They should be unpacked on receipt, and any wet units must be dried. All units must be stored on edge in dry ventilated conditions, out of direct sunlight. Avoid storage temperatures above 66°C (150°F), which can deteriorate the edge seals and any suspended or retrofit polyester films.

Project/Site Conditions

The environmental requirements are the same as those for ordinary glass glazings.

Low-e technology is moving fast enough to expect some delays on the newer production lines. Heat treated low-e glass may impose additional delays depending on the type of coating (see Materials in Part 2 of this chapter).

Sequence and Scheduling

The specifier should confirm availability with the manufacturer, especially if a new product.

Warranty

Most low-e units carry the same warranty as ordinary glass units because the same edge seals are used. Warranties do vary widely, however, for some of the multigap units and the retrofit films.

Maintenance

Maintenance is usually the same as for ordinary glass units, except for the retrofit films, which require washing with nonabrasive cleaners and tools.

Part 2 Products
Manufacturers

Most major flat glass producers and roll coaters produce low-e products.

A list of all major low-e manufacturers in Europe and North America is given in Appendix A.

Materials

The same heat treatments specified for ordinary glass units may be specified for low-e glazings. Glass coated with low temperature vacuum depositions must be tempered before the coating is applied, whereas glass coated with pyrolytic coatings may be posttempered.

Although color uniformity is maintained throughout a given company's production runs for a given low-e coating type, color matching is not practical among different manufacturers, or even over different low-e types from the same manufacturer.

The organic edge sealants used in certain double-glazed low-e products are incompatible with exterior flush glazing or butt-joint glazing applications.

Always check with the glazing manufacturer for sealant UV resistance if exterior flush glazing or butt-joint glazing applications are under consideration (see page 33).

Manufactured Units

Low-e coating type _____
(specify either low temperature vacuum-deposited on glass or polyester film, high temperature vacuum-deposited, pyrolytic, or manufacturer's standard)

Specs

Usually one gas space, unless interior films are used to produce additional gaps (see page 50).

Depends on the gas fill, see page 41 for best gap spacing. Usually each gap is identical.

Air is still the common fill for commercial applications. See page 38 for other available fills.

Surfaces are numbered from the outside in. Delete one of these clauses. Coating surface number 1 is not possible with low temperature vacuum deposited coatings, and not recommended even when using the corrosion resistant pyrolytic coatings (page 87).

Specify clear, or see Tables 5.1, 5.2, and 7.4 for the common tints.

The specifier should use either *as indicated, heat strengthened, or fully tempered.* The low temperature vacuum-deposited coating cannot be heat treated or tempered after coating, while the pyrolytic coatings can be posttempered (see pages 52 and 58).

Delete one of these clauses. Coating surface number 3 is not recommended (see pages 87 and 104). Facing two low-e surfaces opposite each other across a gap is not necessary because the thermal resistance is not noticeably improved by the second coating.

Thickness of each glass pane, from the outside in:_____x_____ (usually 6 mm x 6 mm [.25 in. x .25 in] for commercial double glazing, depending on loading conditions). There are no additional loading criteria for low-e units. The thickness of any interior suspended polyester film is not considered.

Number of gas spaces:_____

Gas space thickness, from the outside in:____x____

Gas:_____

Exterior pane: <u>Tinted float glass coated on the second surface</u>, or <u>Tinted float glass coated on the first surface</u>

Tint:_____

  Heat treatment:_____

Interior pane: <u>Uncoated, clear float glass</u>, or <u>Clear float glass—third surface coated</u>

  Heat treatment:_____
  (use the same clauses as above)

Sealing system: _____

Spacer material:_____
(usually aluminum or galvanized steel, else specify as manufacturer's standard)

Spacer finish:_____
(usually clear anodized or mill finish for aluminum; aluminum spacers are available from certain manufacturers in color anodized finishes)

Desicant:_____
(the specifier should use manufacturer's standard; either molecular sieve or silica gel, or blend of both)

Spacer corner construction _____
(specify the manufacturer's corner construction; bent corners are preferable to fabricated corners)

The low-e coating shall be free of color variation.

The film shall be adhered to the glass with a _____.

Usually a *dual seal*; using primary and secondary sealants as presented on page 32, else specify as *manufacturer's standard*. Always check with the glazing manufacturer for sealant UV resistance if exterior flush glazing or butt-joint glazing applications are under consideration (see page 33).

Equipment, Components, and Accessories

No special, equipment, components or accessories are required.

This paragraph only applies to retrofit films. Usually a water release adhesive, or a pressure sensitive adhesive with a temporary detackifying overcoat (see page 36).

Fabrication

No unusual tolerances or finishing requirements

Source Quality Control

Verifying the performance of the low-e coatings falls into two classes:

1) Inspection: determining the presence and positioning of the highly transparent low-e coating.

2) Verification: confirming the manufacturer's published performance data.

The presence and positioning of the low-e coating is determined in the field either visually or with a meter.

See pages 148 and 149.

The U-value determination method is based on comparing temperature drops across the center of a window and a material of known U-value, which is adhered to the room side of the window (see page 74).

See pages 147 and 148.

The U-value for low-e insulated glass units is roughly verified in the field by comparing the window's insulation value with a reference insulation material. The specifier must send samples to an independent testing laboratory for more accurate figures.

Daylight transmission is determined in the field with a lux or footcandle meter.

Shading coefficients must be determined by an independent testing laboratory.

Part 3 Execution
Summary

The normal paragraphs under the Construction Specifications Institute's Part 3 on Examination, Preparation, Installations, Field Quality Control, Adjusting, Cleaning, Demonstration, and Protection are the same as for traditional glazings.

Any useful specification is really a snapshot of current technology. Specifiers should always verify the state of the art with the manufacturer.

11

The Future

Which Will Win—Soft Coats or Hard Coats?

This book demonstrates that each type of low-e coating excels in some applications and falls short in others. But, as technology advances, each low-e category will tend to acquire the best features of their competitors. Will an eventual victor emerge from this race for the perfect coating and market penetration? It depends on which industry is doing the talking.

Glass producers naturally feel that the pyrolytic coatings will win out. Coating the glass on-line is inherently less expensive than maneuvering it to another line for coating as is the case for soft-coat production. This fact, and the ability to posttemper pyrolytically coated glass, means the product would probably win out if the race depended only on cost. In addition, the on-line method can theoretically produce a higher volume as demand for the low-e coatings inevitably soars, although currently yields are only moderate. But the real reason pyrolytic coatings will become a serious contender is that the primary glass manufacturers not only produce it, they also have a major marketing force in place. Today's omnipresent glass salesforce are tomorrow's hard-coat salesforce. Most of the world's major primary glass manufacturers have launched on-line coating projects.

Those in the vacuum-coating industry, of course, feel otherwise. Except for some solar heating applications, off-line coatings and roll-coated products will certainly outperform pyrolytics for some time to come, particularly since the coating parameters are easily varied. This inherent flexibility also means soft-coat products are easily tailored to different markets and climates. An on-line production facility cannot quickly switch over from one type of coating to the next. Moreover, volume production is already established and growing because of the soft-coat industry's recent entry into the electrically conducting automobile windshield market. Furthermore, the pyrolytics cannot currently match the desirable low shading coefficient/high daylight transmission coupling that is possible with soft coats, although this advantage is already under attack. (Pyrolytic coatings for single glazings that give a shading coefficient of 0.50 and a daylight transmission of 63% are under development. This development is particularly attractive for residences in hot climates, which traditionally use single glazing.)

It is simply too early to tell which approach will predominate. Perhaps the irony is that the biggest market will become the windshield market, not the architectural market.

The New Achilles' Heels—the Edge Spacer and the Frame

Low-e bulk glazing performance has improved steadily so that today, for small windows, the heat lost through the frames and edge seals is approaching the heat lost through the glazing itself. Clearly, the edge spacers and most of the current frames must improve thermally or the low-e performance advantage will suffer.

Two companies that manufacture or use multiple low-e coated polymers have already developed thermally broken edge seals, which effectively contain exotic gas fills while maintaining resiliency (see Chapter 4). Others are working on simpler and less expensive solutions. Even some of today's products will work after slight modification.

An example of such a product is Tremco's Swiggle Strip, a desiccated butyl cast about a metal corrugated strip. The corrugated strip performs the mechanical duty of spacing the glazing apart under the usual compression forces. Very little heat bridges the gap because there are no metal faces acting as heat fins, as is the case with the today's box-shaped metal edge spacers. The design is resilient enough to account for the different thermal coefficients of expansion at the glass and the spacer. The metal stops most of the gas fill migration through the butyl, but unfortunately, it does not stop all of it. Some permeates tangentially out the boundary between the glass and the strip. Thus the butyl is desiccated to soak up the water vapor, which would normally permeate into the unit and fog it. The gas permeation problem is solvable now using the same barrier wrap technique advanced by Southwall Technologies for use on their multiple low-e film unit.

The search is on for a cheaper homogenous material that performs the nearly impossible job of thermal break, gas permeation barrier, and mechanical spacer, while simultaneously exhibiting the same coefficient of expansion as glass so that the edge seal remains intact. The fiberglass spacers on the market today do not fill this bill, but a promising new material is emerging from the aerospace industry that just might do the trick—polymer-ceramics.

Polymer-ceramics are engineered materials that theoretically can take on any combination of properties that lie between the properties of the two materials, depending on the compound's ratio of polymers to ceramics. Either polymers or ceramics can individually solve some of the edge spacer problems, but taken together they can solve all of them. Perhaps the most promising feature of this new material is its predicted method of attachment—the resilient material can weld to glass. Research is just beginning on this material, so the hoped for miracle is still some years away.

The thermal losses through the windows frames are similar to the losses through the edge spacers. Today's thermally broken metal frames are really designed to stop condensation, not excessive heat loss. Wood frames insulate only as well as ordinary double glazing. Better insulating materials than wood or metal are necessary to keep pace with low-e windows and the walls in which they sit.

The Europeans have taken the lead in high-performance frames using reaction injected molding (RIM) technology. The technology makes it possible to form a graded density foam frame from urethanes (or fireproof phenolics) so the interior is porous and resistant to heat flow, while the exterior is dense and hard enough to resist wear and tear and to take on a finish. The frame is strengthened with an interior longitudinal steel rod to maintain dimensional stability, particularly when the outdoor temperatures rise. The frame was test marketed in the U.S. high-end residential window market only to find that the sampled home owners did not like the plastic look on the room side of the window.

The U.S. residential window and frame manufacturers are, for the most part, preoccupied with meeting market demand for higher quality, lower maintenance frames because demand for energy conservation has temporarily faded in North America. In the meantime, the U.S. Forest

Products Laboratory* continues to investigate wood and plastic composites frames, whereas companies that normally manufacture other building components, such as plastic trim and insulation, are beginning to break into the field with innovative products.

An example is Owens-Corning-Fiberglass's recent entry into the finished window market with their fiberglass frame. A dense fiberglass core acts as the insulator with a U-value of 1.41 W/°K m² (0.25 Btu/ hr°F ft²). The mechanical strength and the finish skin is provided by an outer sheath of gel-coated, glass-reinforced polyester, which is integrally bonded to the fiberglass core. The outer material has the same appearance and strength as an ordinary fiberglass small boat hull, but this material is formulated to have the same temperature coefficient of expansion as wood. This practice guarantees that the frame continues to mate well with the glass glazing throughout the year. Dimensional stability is reportedly quite good because of the extra fiberglass reinforcing at the core-to-skin bond.

Where Does It All End?

Low-e performance is reaching its theoretical and economical limits. Soft coat emissivity has been lowered from 10% to 3%. Further decreases would not noticeably improve the glazing's thermal resistance.

Pyrolytic coatings have lifted the solar gain by 4% to within 2% to 3% of clear double glazing. A 4% rise in the shading coefficient is important for solar heating applications, but pyrolytic technology does not lend itself to much more improvement in the shading coefficient.

The desirable low-shading coefficient, high daylight transmission combination for offices has reached new performance levels. The lowest shading coefficient available with soft coat technology is now 38% at a 60% daylight transmission. The lowest theoretical shading coefficient for this daylight transmission is 21.6%, so improvement is still needed. Further advances in this area will depend on advanced low-e coatings with sharper cut offs in the near infrared spectrum and better heat absorbing glazings that maintain a high daylight transmission.

With low-e performance near its peak, is there any glazing technology on the horizon that promises to better low-e

*Madison, Wisconsin.

technology? Two candidates have often been cited as potentially better approaches: evacuated glazings for maximum R-value and electrochromic glazings for better solar gain control. So far, the two approaches have only generated controversy.

Evacuated Glazings

Convective heat losses in double-glazed windows are completely eliminated if the air space is evacuated. Of course the glass must be internally supported or the atmospheric pressure will shatter the glass. One approach is to provide support with 3 mm (0.125 in) glass beads arrayed over the inner glass surface on a 5 cm (2 in) grid (Figure 11-1). Current research [20] indicates that this approach can achieve an R-value of 1.8 m^2°K/W (10 ft^2°F hr/Btu) in double-glazed units with a good low-e coating to arrest the radiant heat losses. The R-value is not higher because the thermal bridging through the glass beads and edge seal becomes the heat loss mechanism.

A high vacuum must be maintained over 20 years in order for the window to become practical. Only all-glass seals can currently do this job. A laser has been used experimentally to adequately seal the borosilicate glass edges. Most of the soft coat low-e coatings cannot withstand the high heat of laser welding. Although the pyrolytic coatings can withstand this onslaught, their emissivities are not low enough for vacuum windows.

Another problem arises because of the glass's limited strength—the glass deflects over the glass beads causing disturbing reflections. Closer bead spacing minimizes these optical distortions, but the denser spacing increases the thermal bridging and view interference.

Another approach to withstanding the atmospheric crush is to hold the two glass panes apart with a mostly transparent open-cell foam insulation. The vacuum also evacuates every microscopic cell in the foam, so heat transfer by convection cannot occur. The heat transfer due to infrared radiation is miniscule because each infrared exchange between two cell walls in the foam is progressively attenuated by the nearly endless cells, which chain from one side of the foam to the other.

Most foams are not transparent, of course, but an unusual foam, called aerogel, is tantalizingly clear. Aerogel is a microporous silica material with a 99% void fraction. It is specularly transparent (although it appears slightly hazy) rather than translucent because the pore diameter is much

Figure 11-1. A 56 x 71 cm (22 x 28 in.) evacuated window showing 3 mm (0.125 in) glass spacer beads arrayed on a 5 x 5 cm (2 x 2 in) grid in scale.

smaller than a wavelength of light. The extraordinarily small diameter pores cannot scatter light because the relatively large lightwaves wash right over them. The amount of silica in the material is so low that thermal bridging in not an issue when the foam is evacuated. It is possible to reach an R-value of 3.6 m^2 °K/W (20 ft^2°F hr/Btu) over 2.5 cm (1 in) of material when 90% of the air is removed.

Aerogel is difficult to prepare in large sizes. The first step mixes alkoxide, water, and a solvent to produce a very fine mix of particles in an alcohol solution, which finally links together to form the open-pore foam [21]. The second step is crucial. The foam must undergo careful drying in an autoclave above the critical point of the flammable liquid or it will collapse or fracture. This step can take many hours because of the material's fragility.

Despite the difficulty and the cost, the material is being produced commercially in Sweden* for solar collector insulation and radiation detectors. A U.S. company[†] hopes to manufacture the material as a refrigerator insulation because a refrigerator's steel cabinet can hold a vacuum.

Although thin sections of aerogel appear mostly transparent, the material does refract enough light to create color fringing. The material also has a distinct yellow tinge. These optical difficulties must be overcome before the material is architecturally acceptable as a window. In the meantime, aerogels might find uses where the view isn't important, such as in glass blocks or in certain types of skylights.

All evacuated glazings are vulnerable to fracture because of the large temperature differences, which build up across the perimeter glass weld due to the unit's high insulation value. The thermal stresses are high enough to break ordinary glass, so expensive, high-strength glass becomes necessary.

The experimental vacuum glazings based on glass bead spacers only insulate 20% more than the best low-e unit. Although there are more promising alternatives, all of them are optically disappointing. No one wants to return to the days before float glass when windows reflected and refracted light like funhouse mirrors.

---

*Airglass, Staffanstorp, Sweden.
[†]Thermalux, Richmond, California.

Electrochromic Glazings

Many see electrochromic glazings as the ultimate high-technology window, which definitively solves the office solar gain problem. Others see it as an inherently expensive laboratory curiosity. Whether or not electrochromics is a panacea, this section demonstrates that the approach only saves appreciable amounts of energy in hot, humid climates when compared to the best of today's low-e glazings.

Electrochromic windows are made from either liquid crystals or organic or inorganic materials coated over a low-e base on a glass or polyester film substrate. The low-e layer is used to carry the electrical energy for switching the coating from a transparent state to a solar heat-rejecting state.

Liquid crystals are commonly used as the display media in digital watches. They switch from the reflective to the transparent state when the normally randomly arranged crystals are aligned by an electric field. The molecular structure of liquid crystals can be realigned easily by electric and magnetic fields, mechanical stress and pressure, and temperature. The last two alteration methods create control problems when liquid crystals are used for large-scale windows. In addition, where most electrochromic materials require energy only during switching, liquid crystals require continuous power to maintain the reflective state. Currently, the material costs over $75 per square foot, which is 250 times the cost of clear single glazing. Extremely large economies of scale must materialize before this alternative becomes economically feasible.

A typical inorganic electrochromic metal stack on glass consists of vacuum-deposited indium-tin oxide, amorphous tungsten oxide (the layer that does the switching), and magnesium fluoride [22]. The organic alternatives use layers of laminated transparent dyes and emulsions.

Under the influence of a small voltage, most inorganic electrochromic materials undergo an intense color change from a clear state to a reflective state. Organic electrochromics change their near infrared absorption without greatly changing their color or transparency. These materials have been experimentally applied to windows as coatings and laminates [22].

A flick of an electric switch can change an electrochromic window from its normal high solar transmission state to a heat-rejecting glazing. The switch is normally set to change the glazing after the welcome early morning solar gain becomes unnecessary.

A computer simulation was conducted at the Massachusetts Institute of Technology to determine if the concept could save office air-conditioning and lighting energy in various U.S. climates when compared with various low-e and reflective glazings [23]. A spacious 18.6 m² (192 ft²) lightweight perimeter office with 6.2 m² (64 ft²) of glazing was modeled on an hourly basis for various exposures. The double glazings

Table 11-1. Double Glazing Parameters Simulated in the MIT Office Energy Use Study						
Glass Type	Visible Transmission Clear/Switched	Shading Coefficient Clear/Switched	U-value Winter Summer (Btu/hr sq ft °F)		U-value Winter Summer (W/sq m°K)	
Clear	0.81	0.81	0.58	0.61	3.29	3.46
Reflective	0.18	0.21	0.46	0.52	2.61	2.95
Low-E	0.51	0.39	0.28	0.32	1.59	1.82
Electro-2	0.73/0.43	0.72/0.31	0.33	0.33	1.87	1.87
Electro-4	0.70/0.16	0.64/0.16	0.31	0.31	1.76	1.76
Electro-5	0.50/0.11	0.41/0.11	0.30	0.30	1.70	1.70

shown in Table 11-1 were simulated, where the *Electro* entries represented the best known laboratory properties for both organic and inorganic electrochromic windows.

The simple switching strategy for the electrooptical group was based on the outdoor air temperature and lighting requirements. The windows remained in the clear state until the office became too warm. The glass was never switched when daylighting became necessary, such as on cloudy days and during the late afternoon hours. The auxiliary lighting was provided by three independently controlled rows of lights.

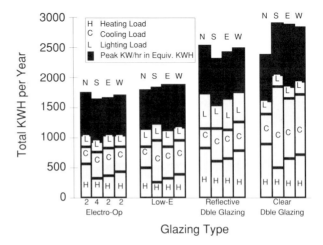

Figure 11-2. Annual office energy load comparison between base glazings and electrooptical glazings in a heating climate—Boston (Adapted from Bartovicks, W.A., "The Thermal Performance of Fixed and Variable Selective Transmitters in Commercial Architecture," S.M. Arch Thesis, Department of Architecture, MIT, February 1984).

The stacked column graphs in Figures 11-2 and 11-3 show the annual total energy consumption for four office orientations (north, south, east, and west) in two U.S. cities. The black bars represent the peak kilowatts in terms of equivalent kilowatt hours for the year. The best possible electrochromic type was used on each orientation as indicated by the numerals at the base of the columns.

In the heating climate (Figure 11-2), the electrochromic fenestration produced the same low lighting load (L) as the clear double glazing. The electrochromic cooling loads (C) were comparable to the loads produced by the low-e glazing except for the southern orientation. Both the low-e and the electrochromic windows showed essentially the same savings over reflective and clear double glazing for all orientations. The annual energy consumption for the low-e windows was nearly independent of orientation. Load reduction among all the glazing types was most affected by the U-value.

As seen in Figure 11-3, electrochromic windows in cooling climates theoretically offer a 20% savings in total load over low-e glazings facing south, east, and west, mainly due to the solar gain reduction. The electrochromic glazing was switched to the dark state most of the time because of the incessantly high lighting levels from the larger than normal amounts of diffuse light created by the high humidity. The excessive light was more than enough to daylight the office even with the windows switched off. The study suggests that a low-e window with a slightly lower shading coefficient might have fared as well as the electrochromic windows. The north glazings faired the same for both win-

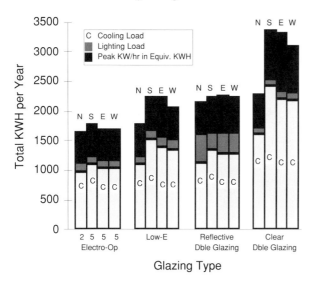

Figure 11-3. Annual office energy load comparison between base glazings and electro-optical glazings in a cooling climate—Miami (Adapted from: W.A., Bartovicks, "The Thermal Performance of Fixed and Variable Selective Transmitters in Commercial Architecture," S.M. Arch Thesis, Department of Architecture, MIT, February 1984).

dow types. The U-value was less important here than for heating climates.

One of the visually disturbing aspects of most inorganic electrochromic windows is the abrupt color change that the coating undergoes when switched to reject solar energy. Seen from the inside, the current laboratory models switch from a clear to a transparent, dark blue, or bronze color. The inorganic varieties don't exhibit such visually discontinuous behavior with their more subtle color change. Perhaps, given the expected expense of these devices, electrochromics is better applied as high-technology window overhangs. A switchable overhang can control the entire window below it using a much smaller area of electrochromic material without interrupting the view.

Conclusion

Like the Emperor's new clothes, the super-thin low-e coatings that clothe our modern windows are indeed "as light and delicate as a spider's web"; but unlike the fabled wardrobe, the low-e coating definitely works. New levels of thermal insulation for windows that were unheard of a few years ago are available now because of the advances in low-e and gas fill technology.

Low-e coatings are still quite capable of fooling our eye. Witness some of the low-e windows with their exceptionally low shading coefficients; they look as transparent as the old triple glazings. Chapter 4 indicated how this technology works, and Chapter 5 compared the benefits and drawbacks. Whereas Chapters 6 through 8 introduced several design methods for effectively using the coating architecturally, the end of Chapter 9 demonstrated how to make sure the coating was really there, just in case someone yelled "but the emperor has no clothes!"

Appendix

A

Low-E Manufacturers

Belgium
Glaverbel SA
Chee De la Hulpe 166
Bruxelles, Brabant 1170

Canada
AFG Glass Inc.
3650 Victoria Park Avenue
Willowdale, On M4V 1M9

France
Saint Gobain Vitrage
Les Miroirs
Courbevoie, Hauts-De S
92400

Germany
Flachglas
Auf der Reihe 2
Postfach 10 08 51
D-4650 Gelsenkirchen

Interpane
Postfach 20
D-3471 Lauenförde

Leybold-Heraeus A.G.
Wilhelm Rohn Str. 25
D-6450 Hanau 1

Vegla AG
Viktoriaallee 3-5
D-5100 Aachen

Holland
Glasfabriek Sas Van Gent

Italy
Societa Vetri Speciali
29 Viale Restell
Milano 20124

Japan
Asahi Glass Co. Ltd.
1-2 Marunouchi 2-Chome
Chiyoda-KU
Tokyo 100

Nippon Sheet Glass Co. Ltd.
8 Doshomachi 4-Chome
Osaka 541

Mexico
Vidrio Plano De Mexico SA
Ex Hacienda De La Santa
Cruz S N San Juan Ixhuatep
Tiainepantia 54180

Spain
Cristaleria Espanola SA
Paseo De La Castellana 77
Madrid 28046

Switzerland
Geilinger AG
Postfach
CH-8401 Winterthur

United Kingdom
Pilkington Glass LTD
Prescot Road
St Helens WA10 3TT
England

United States
3M
220 8E 3M Center
St. Paul, MN 55144

Alpen Inc.
5400 Spine Road
Boulder, CO 80301

Cardinal IG
12301 Whitewater Drive
Minnetonka, MN 55343

Gila Energy Products
6615 W. Boston St.
Chandler, AZ 85226

Guardian Industries
14600 Romine Rd.
Carleton, MI 48117

Interpane Coatings, Inc
Deerfield, MI 49238

LOF Co.
811 Madison Ave.
Toledo, OH 43695

PPG Industries Inc.
One PPG Place
Pittsburgh, PA 15272

Southwall
3961 East Bayshore Rd.
Palo Alto, CA 94303

Viracon, Inc.
Owatonna, MN 55060

WINDOW 3.1

WINDOW 3.1 is a public domain computer program developed by the Windows and Daylighting Group at Lawrence Berkeley Laboratory for analyzing heat flow through windows. The program has been used to design and develop new products, to assess and compare performance characteristics of all types of window products, to assist educators in teaching heat transfer through windows, and to help public officials in developing building energy codes. WINDOW 3.1 was also used by ASHRAE's Technical Committee on Fenestration to calculate data on standard window products for the *1989 Handbook of Fundamentals*. The program uses an iterative technique to calculate the following:

- one-dimensional temperature profile across a user-defined window system while accounting for edge effects

- center-of-glass U-value

- insulated glass unit U-value

- window's average U-value

- shading coefficient

- relative humidity point where condensation will occur

- shading coefficient

- relative heat gain

- total solar transmittance

- visible transmittance

- inside visible and solar reflectance

- outside visible and solar reflectance

The user can vary the following:

- environmental conditions

- window size

- window tilt

- number of glazing layers

- layer properties (emissivity, solar, and visible optical properties, and thermal conductance)

- gap widths

- composition of gap gas mixture

- spacer and frame composition

Over 300 compositions for the glass, gas, frame, and spacer materials are stored in libraries for direct use. All stored data is laboratory-measured data.

The user can choose among air, argon, krypton, and sulphur hexaflouride, or any combination of these, for a gas fill.

The frame and spacer library includes choices for aluminum, aluminum with thermal break, wood, cladded wood, and vinyl frames. The spacer options are metal, glass edge, butyl, wood, and fiberglass.

Nonglass shading systems, such as venetian blinds, are not modeled, but these capabilities are planned for future versions.

The program provides an extensive series of help screens. A library on environmental conditions is also available. Presentations are either in SI or metric units.

WINDOW 3.1 runs on IBM PC compatibles with at least 256 Kbytes of RAM and DOS 2.1 or higher. A math coprocessor is recommended.

The program is available for free on a 5.25-inch IBM formatted diskette by requesting it in writing from:

Bostik Construction Products
P.O. Box 8
Huntingdon Valley, PA 19006
USA
Telephone (800) 523-6530

WINDOW 3.1 Window Configuration

ID No: 1   Name: Sample   Layer:2   Tilt: 90   Units: 2 IP
Frame: 3 Al. w/o break   Frame width: 2.250 in   Spacer: 1 Aluminum
Size: Residential   Window Width: 36.00 in   Height: 40.00 in   Mul:1 Horiz

	No.	Name	D(in)	Tsol	1 Rsol 2		Tvis	1 Rvis 2		Tir	1 Emis 2	
Lay1	1	CLEAR	0.000	.856	.077	.077	.902	.002	.002	.000	.040	.040
Gap1	1	Air	0.500									
Lay2	1	CLEAR	0.000	.856	.077	.077	.902	.002	.002	.000	.040	.040

• Unit System (1-SI or 2- Inch Pound) [+,-]

Results

Condition	U-Val (Btu/h-ft2-F)			Inside T °F	% Rel Humid	SC	Rel Ht Gain	Optical Properites		
	Center	IG	Window						Solar	Visible
Winter	0.49	0.53	0.07	45.3	41			Trans	0.74	0.82
Summer	0.55	0.50	0.91	78.3		0.909	109	Rout	0.13	0.15
User								Rin	0.13	0.15

Sample Main Screen from WINDOW 3.1. The window configuration appears on the top half of the main screen and the results are displayed on the bottom half.

Appendix # C

Solar Geometry

Date	Declination (deg)
Jan 21	-20.0
Feb 21	-10.8
Mar 21	0
Apr 21	+11.6
May 21	+20.0
June 21	+23.45
July 21	+20.6
Aug 21	+12.3
Sept 21	0
Oct 21	-10.5
Nov 21	-19.8
Dec 21	-23.45

Figure C-1. The solar declination at the 21st of each month.

The sun's position is expressed absolutely as two measures, the solar altitude, α, above the horizontal and the solar azimuth, ø, measured from the south (Figure 6-9). The solar azimuth is positive for afternoon hours and negative for morning hours. These angles in turn depend on the local latitude, L, the solar declination, ∂, which depends on the date (Figure C-1), and the apparent solar time, which is sometimes expressed in degrees as the hour angle, H, where

H = 0.25°/min. x (no. of minutes from local solar noon).

Table C-1   Solar Geometry Nomenclature

Term	Definition	Units
H	Hour angle	degrees
SM	Standard meridian (longitude) (Table 6-4)	degrees
LST	Local standard time	degrees
ET	Equation of time (Figure 6-10)	minutes
LON	Observer's longitude	degrees
α	Solar altitude	degrees
ø	Solar azimuth; south = 0, negative for morning hours	degrees
∂	Declination (Figure C-1)	degrees
L	Observer's latitude	degrees

f	The azimuth angle relative to the window	degrees
Ω	The local window azimuth relative to south (east is negative)	degrees
Σ	Surface tilt angle	degrees
Δ	Angle of incidence	degrees

Trigonometric Solar Positions. The following trigonometric equations relate α and ϕ to the three angles H, ∂, and L.

$$\sin \alpha = \cos L \cos \partial \cos H + \sin L \sin \partial \qquad (a)$$
$$\cos \phi = (\sin \alpha \sin L - \sin \partial) / (\cos \alpha \cos L) \qquad (b)$$

These angles are related to the position of the window by the angles Ω, the local window azimuth relative to south, and the surface tilt angle Σ as shown in Figure 6-9. The angle Ω is negative when it swings to the east. The azimuth angle relative to the sun, f, is given by:

$$f = \text{Absolute Value of } (\phi - \Omega). \qquad (c)$$

The window is in the shade if f is greater than 90° or less than 270°.

The angle of incidence, Δ, for any surface is the angle the sun's rays make with a perpendicular to the surface (Figure 6-9) and is given by:

$$\cos \Delta = \cos \alpha \cos f \sin \Sigma + \sin \alpha \cos \Sigma, \qquad (d)$$

When the window is horizontal, $\Sigma = 0$, so the angle of incidence is only related to the solar altitude, and equation (d) simplifies to:

$$\cos \Delta = \sin \alpha$$

When the window is vertical, $\Sigma = 90°$, so the angle of incidence is related to just the solar altitude and f, and equation (d) simplifies to:

$$\cos \Delta = \cos \alpha \cos f$$

Example 1. Find the solar azimuth and altitude at 08:30 United States Central Standard Time on October 21 at 32°N latitude and 95°W latitude. Also determine the angle of incidence the sun makes with a vertical southeast facing window at this site.

Solution:
From Figure 6-10 and Table 6-4, the apparent solar time = LST + ET + 4 minutes/°(SM - LON), or 08:30 + 15 + 4(90-95) = 08:25, or 3 hours and 35 minutes (215 minutes) before solar noon. The hour angle, H, becomes 0.25 x 215 = 53.8°. Figure C-1 gives the solar declination ∂ on October 21 as -10.5°.

Thus by equation (a):

$$\sin \alpha = \cos 32 \cos (-10.5) \cos (53.8) + \sin 32 \sin (-10.5)$$
$$= 0.396$$
$$\alpha = 23.3°$$

By equation (b):

$$\cos \varnothing = (\sin 23.3 \sin 32 - \sin [-10.5]) / (\cos 23.3 \cos 32)$$
$$= 0.503$$
$$\varnothing = 59.8°$$

Ω, the local window azimuth, is -45°. Both $\varnothing$ and Ω are negative, so equation (c) becomes:

$$f = \text{Absolute Value of } (- 59.8° - [- 45°]) = 14.8°$$

The angle of incidence for a vertical window is given by :

$$\cos \Delta = \cos \alpha \cos f, \text{ or}$$
$$\cos \Delta = \cos 23.3 \cos 14.8 = 0.888$$
$$\Delta = 27.4°$$

The shadow line cast by the top of a window, or an overhang, is most easily determined by the profile angle, or vertical shadow angle. The profile angle is the angle between the horizon and the projection of the sun's rays in a plane perpendicular to the window (Figure 6-13), or:

$$\tan (\text{Profile Angle}) = \tan (\alpha) / \cos (f)$$

The distance from the window wall to the shadow line on the floor in Figure 6-15 is:

$$\text{Shadow Penentration} = \frac{\text{Window Header Height off floor}}{\tan (\text{Profile Angle})}$$

Example 2. Find the distance from the window wall to the shadow line on the floor for the window given in Example 1 above. Assume the window header is 2.5 meters above the floor.

$$\text{Distance} = 2.5 / (\tan (\alpha) / \cos (f))$$
$$= 2.5 / (\tan 23.3) / \cos (14.8))$$
$$= 2.5 / (0.43 / 0.97) = 5.6 \text{ meters}$$

Unit Conversions

LENGTH

1 m	= 1.09361 yd	(0.9144)
	= 3.28084 ft	(0.3048)
1 cm	= 0.3937 in	(2.54)
1 mile	= 1.6093 km	(0.6214)

AREA

1 m^2	= 1.19591 yd^2	(0.8362)
	= 10.7636 ft^2	(0.0929)
1 cm^2	= 0.155 in^2	(6.4516)
1 hectare	= 2.47 acres	(0.4049)
1 acre	= 43,560 ft^2	(2.2957 x 10^{-5})

VOLUME

1 m^3	= 1.30795 yd^3	(0.7646)
	= 35.3147 ft^3	(0.0283)
1 cm^3	= 0.061 in^3	(16.3934)
1 liter	= 0.0354 ft^3	(28.3170)
	= 0.2642 gal	(3.7854)
1 barrel (bbl)	= 42 gal	(0.0238)

MASS

1 kg	= 2.2046	(0.4536)

TEMPERATURE

t °C	= 0.556 (t °F -32)
t °F	= 1.8 t°C + 32
T °K	= t °C + 273
T °R	= t °F +460

DENSITY

1 kg/m^3	= 0.0624 lb/ft^3	(16.0256)

ENERGY, HEAT

1 MJ	= 0.2778 kWh	(3.600)

1 kJ	= 0.9478 Btu	(1.0551)
1 J	= 0.7376 ft-lbf	(1.3557)
1 kWh	= 3412.4 Btu	(2.93 x 10^{-4})

FLOW

1 liter/s	= 2.1189 ft^3/min (CFM)	(0.4719)

HEAT STORAGE

1 KJ/°C	= 0.5269 Btu/°F	(1.8979)
1 Wh/°C	= 1.8969 Btu/°F	(0.5272)
1 kJ/m^2 °C	= 0.04895 x 10^{-3} Btu/ft^2 °F	(20.4290)
1 kJ/kg °C	= 0.2390 Btu/lb °F	(4.1841)

HEAT TRANSFER

1 W/m °C	= 0.5782 Btu ft/hr ft^2 °F	(1.7295)
	= 6.9380 Btu in/hr ft^2 °F	(0.1441)
1 W/m^2 °C	= 0.1762 Btu/hr ft^2 °F	(5.6745)
1 W/°C	= 1.8956 Btu/hr °F	(0.5275)
1 W/m^2	= 0.3172 Btu/hr ft^2	(3.1526)

POWER

1 W	= 3.4144 Btu/hr	(0.2929)

VELOCITY

1 m/s	= 196.85 ft/min	(0.0051)
	= 2.2369 mph	(0.4470)

BUILDING HEAT LOSS

1 Wh/DD(°C)	= 3.600 kJ/DD (°C)	(0.2778)
	= 1.896 Btu/DD (°F)	(0.5274)
1 Wh/m^{2}DD (°C)	= 3.600 kJ/m^{2}DD (°C)	(0.2778)
	= 20.4 Btu/hrft^{2}DD(°F)	(0.0490)

ILLUMINANCE

1 lux	= 0.0929 lm/ft^2 (footcandle)	

U-Value Calculation

The following method for calculating a window's U-value from its material properties is a simple manual alternative to the WINDOW 3.1 computer program listed in Appendix B. This method is based on Pilkington's 7th edition of *Glass and Transmission Properties of Windows*, as prepared by the Environmental Advisory Service.

The heat conductance, or center-of-glass U-value for any glazing assembly is given by the equation:

(1) Basic U-value Equation

$$U = \frac{1}{1 \, / \, h_e + 1 \, / \, h_t + 1 \, / \, h_i}$$

where
h_e and h_i are the external skin and internal skin heat-transfer coefficients,
and h_t is the heat conductance of the multiple glazing.

(2) Glazing Conductance

$$\frac{1}{h_t} = \frac{1}{h_{s1}} + \frac{1}{h_{s2}} + \ldots + \frac{1}{h_{sn}} + D_{glass} \times R_{glass} + D_{other} \times R_{other}$$

where
h_{s1} through h_{sn} are the gas space conductance for the gaps,
D_{glass} is the total thickness (in meters, or feet) of all the glass lights,
R_{glass} is thermal resistance of glass (1.0 m°K/W (5.67 hr°F ft/ Btu)),
D_{other} is the total thickness (in meters, or feet) of all other nonglass lights,

Table E-1. U-values from Material Properties Nomenclature

Term	Definition	Units (SI)	Units (Imperial)
U	Thermal conductance	$W/m^2{}^\circ K$	$Btu/hr{}^\circ F\ ft^2$
h_e	External skin conductance	$W/m^2{}^\circ K$	$Btu/hr{}^\circ F\ ft^2$
h_i	Internal skin conductance	$W/m^2{}^\circ K$	$Btu/hr{}^\circ F\ ft^2$
h_t	Multiple glazing conductance	$W/m^2{}^\circ K$	$Btu/hr{}^\circ F\ ft^2$
$h_{s1} \dots h_{sn}$	Gas space conductance for n gaps	$W/m^2{}^\circ K$	$Btu/hr{}^\circ F\ ft^2$
D_{glass}	Total thickness of all the glass panes	meters	feet
R_{glass}	Thermal resistance of glass	$m\ {}^\circ K/W$	$hr{}^\circ F\ ft^2/\ Btu$
D_{other}	Total thickness of all other nonglass lights	meters	feet
R_{other}	Thermal resistance of all other nonglass lights (0 for plastics)	$m\ {}^\circ K/W$	$hr{}^\circ F\ ft^2/\ Btu$
h_g	Conductance by convection/conduction	$W/m^2{}^\circ K$	$Btu/hr{}^\circ F\ ft^2$
h_r	Conductance by radiation	$W/m^2{}^\circ K$	$Btu/hr{}^\circ F\ ft^2$
β	Radiation linearization constant	$W/m^2{}^\circ K$	$Btu/hr{}^\circ F\ ft^2$
e_1	Emissivity	none	none
e_2	Emissivity	none	none
h_{ri}	Interior skin radiation coefficient	$W/m^2{}^\circ K$	$Btu/hr{}^\circ F\ ft^2$
h_c	Interior skin convection coefficient	$W/m^2{}^\circ K$	$Btu/hr{}^\circ F\ ft^2$

R_{other} is thermal resistance of the other nonglass lights, in m°K/W (hr°F ft/ Btu). R_{other} is taken as zero for plastic films since they are so thin.

There are no h_s terms in single-glass glazing, so equation (2) simplifies to:

(2a) Single Glazing Conductance $1/h_t = D_{glass} \times 1.0 \text{ m }^\circ K/W = D_{glass} \times 5.67 \text{ ft hr } ^\circ F/Btu$

For multiple glazing, any h_s is the sum of the heat conductance by radiation, h_r, and the conductance by convection/conduction, h_g, across the gap, or:

(3) Gap Conductance $h_s = h_r + h_g$.

The expression h_g depends not only on the gas fill's properties, but also on the gap dimension and the average temperature over the gap. The complex relationships for these dependencies are given at the end of this appendix. Figure E-1 lists h_s values for the common air and argon-filled gaps

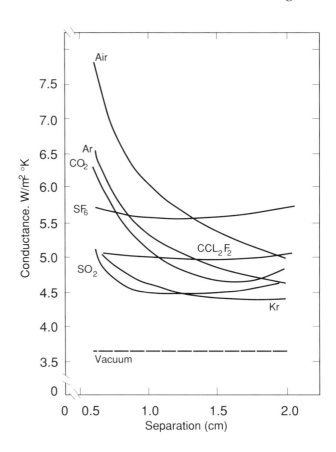

Figure E-1. Total glass space coefficient (h_s) for horizontal heat transfer vs. glass separation for double glazing ($\Delta T = 10^\circ C$ and emissivity = 0.84). (Reprinted by permission from the 1989 ASHRAE *Handbook—Fundamentals* published by the American Society of Heating, Refrigeration and Air-Conditioning Engineers, Inc.)

over a $10^\circ C$ ($18^\circ F$) temperature difference using ordinary glass with an emissivity of 0.84. Note the figure for a vacuum—3.76 $W/m^2 {}^\circ K$ (0.66 $Btu/hr.fts^\circ F$)—is equivalent to h_r for ordinary glass, so h_g is equal to $h_s - h_r$.

Low-E Glazing Design Guide

The radiation conductance, h_r, for each gas space faced with surfaces of given emissivities ε_1 and ε_2 is given for windows by the equation:

$$h_r = \beta / (\frac{1}{\varepsilon_1} + \frac{1}{\varepsilon_2} - 1)$$

(4) Radiation Conductance

The term β is essentially constant for temperatures around room temperature [24]. For normal winter and summer operating temperature, β is taken as 5.14 $W/m^{2\circ}K$ (0.906 $Btu/hr\ ft^{2\circ}F$).

ε_1 and ε_2 are the emissivities of the surrounding glazings. Emissivity is 0.84 for uncoated glass and 0.72 for uncoated polyester and vinyl film.

The exterior heat transfer coefficient, h_e, depends mostly on the wind speed. The emissivity of the outside glass light is always taken as 0.84 because wind driven convective heat transfer overrides any radiation reduction due to the low-e coating.

h_e is standardized as:

(5) Exterior Coefficient

16.7 $W/m^{2\circ}K$ in the U.K. for vertical glazing,
25.0 $W/m^{2\circ}K$ in the U.K. for sloped glazing,
and for vertical glazing in the United States as*:

6.0 $Btu/hr\ ft^{2\circ}F$ during the winter,
4.0 $Btu/hr\ ft^{2\circ}F$ during the summer.

The interior heat transfer coefficient, h_i, is given by the expression:

$$h_i = h_{ri} + h_c,$$

(6) Interior Coefficient

where
h_{ri} is the radiation coefficient, and
h_c is the convection coefficient.

The radiation coefficient depends only on the emissivity of the room side of the window:

h_{ri} = 5.3 $W/m^{2\circ}K$ x ε / 0.84, or
h_{ri} = 0.93 $Btu/hr\ ft^{2\circ}F$ x ε / 0.84.

---

*The English value is given in Table A3.5 of the CIBSE Guide A3, 1980. The U.S. value in ASHRAE 1989 Fundamentals.

In still air, h_c is standardized as*:

h_c= 8.3 W/m$^{2\circ}$K for vertical glazing, and
h_c= 10.0 W/m$^{2\circ}$K for sloped glazing in winter conditions,

and in the United States,

h_c= 1.39 Btu/hr ft$^{2\circ}$F for vertical glazing.

Equations 1 through 6 are sufficient to predict the behavior of any sealed window assembly operating within ±39 °C (70 °F) of room temperature.

Example. Find the center-of-glass U-value for a triple-glazed window fabricated from the following three plates of glass spaced 12.5 mm (0.50 in) apart:

    6.0 mm glass,
    1.5 mm glass with an emissivity = 0.02 on each side,
    6.0 mm glass.

The window is filled with argon.

Solution:

The gas conductance, h_g, of each 12.5 mm argon-filled gap is calculated from Figure E-1 by subtracting out the effect of an h_r of 3.76 W/m$^{2\circ}$K for ordinary glass, giving 5.1 - 3.76 = 1.34 W/m$^{2\circ}$K (0.24 Btu/hr ft$^{2\circ}$F) for h_g.

The corresponding radiation conductance, h_r, for each gap with emissivities 0.02 and 0.84 is given by Equation (4):

h_r = 5.14 / [1/.02 + 1/.84 - 1] = 0.102 W/m$^{2\circ}$K,
h_r = 0.906 / [1/.02 + 1/.84 - 1] = 0.018 Btu/hr ft$^{2\circ}$F.

From Equation (3):
h_s = h_r + h_g,
h_s = 0.102 + 1.34 = 1.44 W/m$^{2\circ}$K,
h_s = 0.018 + 0.24 = 0.26 Btu/hr ft$^{2\circ}$F.

All the glass lights total up to a thickness of 0.0135 m (0.0443 ft).

From Equation (2):
1/h_t = 1/ 1.44 + 1/ 1.44 + 0.0135 x 1.0 = 1.40 (metric)
1/h_t = 1/ 0.26 + 1/ 0.26 + 5.67 x 0.0443 = 7.94 (imperial)

The exterior heat transfer coefficient, h_e, is taken as the standard value 16.7 W/m$^{2\circ}$K (4.0 Btu/hr ft$^{2\circ}$F), so 1/ h_e = 0.599 m$^{2\circ}$K/W (0.25hr ft$^{2\circ}$F/Btu).

---

*Table A3.5 of the CIBSE Guide A3, 1980. The U.S. value in ASHRAE 1989 Fundamentals.

The interior heat transfer coefficient has two components. The radiation component is

h_{ri} = 5.3 W/m²°K x ε / 0.84 = 5.3 W/m²°K (0.93 Btu/hr ft²°F).

In still air, h_c, the convective component is standardized as h_c= 8.3 W/m²°K (1.39 Btu/hr ft²°F).

From Equation (6), h_i, the interior heat transfer coefficient is
h_i = 5.3 + 8.3 = 13.6 W/m²°K
h_i = 0.93 + 1.39 = 2.32 Btu/hr ft²°F,
so 1/ h_i = 0.074 m²°K/W   (0.43 hr ft²°F/Btu).

The U-value as given by Equation (1) is
U-value =1 / (0.599 + 1.40 + 0.074) = 0.482 W/m²°C
U-value =1 / (0.250 + 7.94 + 0.43) = 0.116 Btu/hr ft²°F.
(The metric and imperial U-values do not equal each other because different standards are used for the interior and exterior film coefficients.)

The gas conductance, h_g, is given by the equation:
  $h_g = C (Gr\ Pr)^n \lambda / s$
where
  s   is the mean width of the space (m)
  λ   is the thermal conductivity (W/mK)
  $Gr = (G\ s^3\ \Delta T\ \rho^2) / (T_m\ \mu^2)$
  $Pr = (\mu\ Cp) / \lambda$
  ΔT = temperature difference over gap (K)
  ρ = gas density (kg/m³)
  μ = dynamic viscosity (kg/m s)
  Cp = gas specific heat (J/kg K)
  G = gravitational acceleration (9.81 m/s²)
  C and n are given in the following table:

Direction of Heat Flow	Space	C	n	For GrPr Less Than:
Horizontal	Vertical	0.035	0.38	6780
Upwards	45°	0.10	0.31	1680
Upwards	Horizontal	0.16	0.28	696

Solar Heat Gain Factors

The following tables present clear day data. The solar intensity and solar heat gain factors are listed for five latitudes in both SI and imperial units. The solar heat gain factors are the solar gains through one layer of clear double-strength (DSA) glass measuring 3 mm (0.125 in) thick, based on a ground reflectance of 0.20 (Note a in the tables). The half day totals are computed by Simpson's rule, time interval = 10 minutes (Note b in the tables).

The solar intensity is given as direct normal data. The data are based on an "average cloudless" day at each latitude.

SI Units—Solar Intensity and Solar Heat Gain Factors for 24° North Latitude

Date	Solar Time	Direct Solar W/m²	Solar Heat Gain Factors, W/m² Normal																HOR	Time
			N	NNE	NE	ENE	E	ESE	SE	SSE	S	SSW	SW	WSW	W	WNW	NW	NNW		
Jan 21	7	223	7	8	65	143	194	212	200	154	80	9	7	7	7	7	7	7	15	5
	8	754	37	39	131	404	600	698	689	571	360	89	37	37	37	37	37	37	173	4
	9	908	58	58	72	335	598	757	798	716	522	229	61	58	58	58	58	58	381	3
	10	972	73	73	75	166	454	667	772	759	631	395	119	74	73	73	73	73	543	2
	11	1001	82	82	82	86	229	491	667	737	695	546	299	91	82	82	82	82	642	1
	12	1010	85	85	85	85	90	257	504	662	716	662	504	257	90	85	85	85	676	12
	Half Day Totals		301	303	466	1172	2117	2971	3392	3276	2648	1592	759	379	303	301	301	301	2094	
Feb 21	7	482	19	38	212	359	444	458	405	283	105	20	19	19	19	19	19	19	53	5
	8	825	47	51	252	521	694	758	705	541	281	52	47	47	47	47	47	47	263	4
	9	938	68	70	144	434	655	770	767	646	419	132	69	68	68	68	68	68	482	3
	10	989	83	83	87	241	494	659	720	673	521	276	89	83	83	83	83	83	646	2
	11	1012	92	92	92	99	252	465	601	641	583	431	213	97	92	92	92	92	750	1
	12	1019	95	95	95	95	100	221	421	558	604	558	421	221	100	95	95	95	785	12
	Half Day Totals		355	375	809	1663	2540	3189	3381	3042	2203	1180	630	401	357	355	355	355	2585	
Mar 21	7	613	33	141	364	517	585	566	457	272	54	31	31	31	31	31	31	31	115	5
	8	842	58	111	390	613	737	748	642	436	152	60	58	58	58	58	58	58	352	4
	9	931	78	84	269	520	678	731	674	513	260	84	78	78	78	78	78	78	567	3
	10	973	94	96	130	325	510	610	616	528	352	148	97	94	94	94	94	94	730	2
	11	993	103	103	106	132	267	407	486	487	411	272	135	106	103	103	103	103	833	1
	12	999	106	106	106	108	112	177	301	397	432	397	301	177	112	108	106	106	868	12
	Half Day Totals		420	597	1328	2185	2856	3187	3057	2451	1445	784	534	439	420	418	418	418	3031	
Apr 21	6	126	19	67	104	123	124	105	70	21	7	6	6	6	6	6	6	6	12	6
	7	639	62	278	476	595	621	554	400	172	47	44	44	44	44	44	44	44	183	5
	8	808	76	251	500	659	719	669	519	277	77	70	70	70	70	70	70	70	416	4
	9	882	94	169	397	572	655	641	531	332	122	92	90	90	90	90	90	90	615	3
	10	920	107	116	236	394	496	520	466	338	177	110	104	104	104	104	104	104	769	2
	11	938	113	118	125	185	267	325	336	296	220	143	119	116	113	113	113	113	863	1
	12	944	116	118	119	121	123	143	184	221	235	221	184	143	123	121	119	118	892	12
	Half Day Totals		530	1069	1914	2605	2963	2913	2436	1558	770	569	515	495	489	488	487	486	3306	
May 21	6	270	80	181	248	276	264	209	120	25	18	18	18	18	18	18	18	20	40	6
	7	641	136	370	539	626	618	515	332	101	54	54	54	54	54	54	54	56	229	5
	8	781	121	358	561	675	688	598	417	169	82	78	78	78	78	78	78	80	448	4
	9	848	111	277	474	594	625	565	417	208	104	97	97	97	97	97	97	97	634	3
	10	883	119	186	323	431	474	446	349	212	121	114	111	111	111	111	111	114	777	2
	11	901	126	134	175	227	262	265	235	184	139	127	124	120	120	120	120	124	863	1
	12	906	129	129	130	131	132	134	139	144	146	144	139	134	132	131	130	129	889	12
	Half Day Totals		749	1551	2359	2865	2970	2648	1934	972	591	556	547	544	542	542	542	551	3433	
Jun 21	6	307	112	222	294	318	298	229	122	26	22	22	22	22	22	22	22	26	54	6
	7	633	175	401	557	628	605	490	297	82	57	57	57	57	57	57	57	62	244	5
	8	764	157	397	580	674	668	563	370	135	85	82	82	82	82	82	82	86	456	4
	9	829	136	322	500	597	607	529	367	168	106	101	101	101	101	101	101	104	635	3
	10	864	129	227	357	442	462	412	301	172	122	114	114	114	114	114	114	118	773	2
	11	881	132	157	204	244	259	242	200	154	132	128	126	122	122	122	126	129	855	1
	12	886	135	135	135	135	135	135	135	135	136	135	135	135	135	135	135	135	880	12
	Half Day Totals		897	1771	2530	2941	2938	2512	1717	803	590	572	567	565	565	565	567	589	3455	
Jul 21	6	255	81	176	241	266	253	200	114	25	19	19	19	19	19	19	19	21	42	6
	7	615	142	367	529	610	600	498	319	98	56	56	56	56	56	56	56	59	229	5
	8	755	128	361	556	664	673	583	404	163	85	81	81	81	81	81	81	83	444	4
	9	823	117	284	474	588	615	553	406	202	107	100	100	100	100	100	100	100	626	3
	10	858	123	194	328	431	469	437	340	206	124	117	114	114	114	114	114	117	767	2
	11	876	130	140	182	232	263	262	230	180	139	130	127	122	122	122	122	127	851	1
	12	882	133	133	133	134	135	137	141	145	146	145	141	137	135	134	133	133	876	12
	Half Day Totals		779	1572	2352	2830	2916	2585	1877	947	602	570	562	559	557	557	558	570	3394	
Aug 21	6	109	19	62	93	110	110	93	61	19	7	7	7	7	7	7	7	7	13	6
	7	588	69	273	455	564	586	521	374	161	51	47	47	47	47	47	47	47	183	5
	8	759	82	257	491	640	693	642	496	264	82	74	74	74	74	74	74	74	409	4
	9	837	100	181	398	563	638	621	512	319	123	97	95	95	95	95	95	95	603	3
	10	876	113	125	245	394	488	507	451	325	174	116	109	109	109	109	109	109	752	2
	11	896	121	124	134	193	269	320	327	287	214	145	125	121	118	118	118	118	844	1
	12	902	121	124	125	127	130	148	184	216	229	216	184	148	130	127	125	124	872	12
	Half Day Totals		565	1094	1896	2543	2869	2803	2335	1493	766	588	539	521	516	514	513	512	3242	
Sep 21	7	544	35	133	333	471	533	516	417	250	55	33	33	33	33	33	33	33	111	5
	8	781	61	112	374	584	701	711	611	418	151	64	61	61	61	61	61	61	340	4
	9	875	82	89	265	504	654	705	650	497	256	88	82	82	82	82	82	82	548	3
	10	920	97	100	134	320	498	593	599	514	346	151	101	97	97	97	97	97	706	2
	11	942	106	106	111	136	265	400	476	477	404	270	139	111	106	106	106	106	806	1
	12	948	110	110	110	112	117	180	298	391	424	391	298	180	117	112	110	110	840	12
	Half Day Totals		438	600	1280	2084	2721	3040	2925	2363	1424	793	550	457	438	435	435	435	2921	
Oct 21	7	434	20	39	197	329	406	418	369	258	96	21	20	20	20	20	20	20	53	5
	8	778	49	54	248	502	666	725	674	517	268	54	49	49	49	49	49	49	258	4
	9	896	70	72	148	426	637	746	742	624	405	130	72	70	70	70	70	70	473	3
	10	950	85	85	91	242	484	643	701	654	506	269	92	85	85	85	85	85	634	2
	11	974	95	95	95	103	251	456	586	624	568	420	210	100	95	95	95	95	735	1
	12	982	98	98	98	98	104	220	411	544	589	544	411	220	104	98	98	98	770	12
	Half Day Totals		366	388	803	1616	2453	3071	3254	2930	2129	1156	631	412	369	366	366	366	2535	
Nov 21	7	210	7	8	63	137	185	201	190	146	76	9	7	7	7	7	7	7	15	5
	8	732	38	40	131	397	587	682	672	557	351	87	38	38	38	38	38	38	173	4
	9	889	59	59	74	333	590	745	785	703	513	235	62	59	59	59	59	59	378	3
	10	954	59	59	77	167	450	658	761	748	621	389	118	75	59	59	59	59	539	2
	11	984	83	83	83	87	229	486	658	726	685	538	295	92	83	83	83	83	638	1
	12	992	86	86	86	86	91	255	498	653	706	653	498	255	91	86	86	86	671	12
	Half Day Totals		305	307	469	1160	2085	2919	3330	3215	2600	1567	753	382	307	305	305	305	2079	
Dec 21	7	93	3	3	22	56	79	89	85	68	38	5	3	3	3	3	3	3	5	5
	8	710	33	33	92	352	548	655	659	561	372	111	34	33	33	33	33	33	139	4
	9	887	54	54	59	293	566	738	794	727	547	266	58	54	54	54	54	54	336	3
	10	959	68	68	70	139	432	659	779	779	659	432	139	70	68	68	68	68	496	2
	11	990	77	77	77	81	217	493	681	761	725	579	328	92	77	77	77	77	594	1
	12	999	80	80	80	80	85	266	526	691	747	691	526	266	85	80	80	80	627	12
	Half Day Totals		277	278	371	987	1927	2834	3322	3286	2737	1734	810	369	280	277	277	277	1886	
			N	NNW	NW	WNW	W	WSW	SW	SSW	S	SSE	SE	ESE	E	ENE	NE	NNE	HOR	PM

Reprinted by permission from the 1989 ASHRAE *Handbook—Fundamentals* published by the American Society of Heating, Refrigerating and Air-Conditioning Engineers, Inc.

SI Units—Solar Intensity and Solar Heat Gain Factors for 32° North Latitude

Date	Solar Time	Direct Solar W/m²	Solar Heat Gain Factors, W/m² Normal																HOR	Time
			N	NNE	NE	ENE	E	ESE	SE	SSE	S	SSW	SW	WSW	W	WNW	NW	NNW		
Jan 21	7	4	0	0	1	3	4	4	4	3	2	0	0	0	0	0	0	0	0	5
	8	640	28	29	93	330	505	597	596	502	326	88	29	28	28	28	28	28	102	4
	9	848	48	48	53	286	553	721	775	710	534	248	52	48	48	48	48	48	278	3
	10	931	63	63	64	129	427	659	784	788	669	444	144	64	63	63	63	63	430	2
	11	966	71	71	71	75	213	502	697	784	750	602	347	90	71	71	71	71	524	1
	12	977	74	74	74	74	79	276	548	718	777	718	548	276	79	74	74	74	556	12
	Half Day Totals		249	250	338	897	1796	2700	3201	3197	2692	1745	831	353	251	249	249	249	1614	
Feb 21	7	352	13	23	148	258	323	335	299	212	83	14	13	13	13	13	13	13	30	5
	8	771	41	43	203	469	646	719	683	537	300	53	41	41	41	41	41	41	200	4
	9	905	60	60	100	386	627	764	782	680	471	174	63	60	60	60	60	60	401	3
	10	963	75	75	78	195	475	670	759	733	595	352	99	75	75	75	75	75	556	2
	11	990	83	83	83	88	240	491	656	717	670	519	275	89	83	83	83	83	651	1
	12	998	86	86	86	86	91	250	489	643	696	643	489	250	91	86	86	86	684	12
	Half Day Totals		314	324	635	1405	2317	3085	3406	3186	2460	1425	718	384	316	314	314	314	2180	
Mar 21	7	582	30	116	331	483	555	544	447	276	63	29	29	29	29	29	29	29	100	5
	8	820	54	77	338	575	716	746	660	472	195	57	54	54	54	54	54	54	314	4
	9	914	74	77	203	475	662	745	716	577	339	95	74	74	74	74	74	74	515	3
	10	958	88	88	96	273	498	637	676	615	455	221	93	88	88	88	88	88	666	2
	11	980	96	96	98	108	258	446	563	591	529	380	185	101	96	96	96	96	762	1
	12	986	99	99	99	99	105	209	385	511	553	511	385	209	105	99	99	99	795	12
	Half Day Totals		392	511	1130	1983	2758	3255	3281	2799	1856	1029	608	429	393	391	391	391	2754	
Apr 21	6	210	29	110	172	205	207	177	119	38	11	11	11	11	11	11	11	11	23	6
	7	648	53	253	462	593	631	574	427	204	49	45	45	45	45	45	45	45	191	5
	8	804	73	192	452	632	715	689	559	337	95	69	69	69	69	69	69	69	408	4
	9	876	89	113	324	531	648	669	590	418	183	92	87	87	87	87	87	87	593	3
	10	913	101	106	165	342	489	558	543	444	275	123	104	101	101	101	101	101	735	2
	11	931	109	109	115	149	262	371	426	415	340	221	126	113	109	109	109	109	824	1
	12	937	112	112	112	116	119	167	259	335	362	335	259	167	119	116	112	112	854	12
	Half Day Totals		507	932	1733	2498	3002	3127	2804	2032	1135	720	559	496	482	479	478	478	3201	
May 21	6	374	103	244	340	381	367	295	175	39	26	26	26	26	26	26	26	26	67	6
	7	665	112	350	535	637	642	550	373	134	59	57	57	57	57	57	57	59	256	5
	8	787	92	295	519	654	693	628	470	229	86	80	80	80	80	80	80	80	460	4
	9	848	103	194	403	557	624	600	487	293	117	99	97	97	97	97	97	97	632	3
	10	881	114	127	240	382	472	490	434	313	170	117	110	110	110	110	110	110	766	2
	11	898	121	124	132	186	260	312	321	285	215	147	125	122	118	118	118	118	846	1
	12	903	121	123	124	127	130	148	186	219	232	219	186	148	130	127	124	123	872	12
	Half Day Totals		699	1380	2212	2837	3107	2940	2353	1407	787	627	576	557	551	549	548	550	3461	
Jun 21	6	412	140	289	388	425	401	314	174	39	32	32	32	32	32	32	32	35	89	6
	7	662	148	384	556	644	634	529	342	109	62	62	62	62	62	62	62	65	279	5
	8	773	115	335	539	656	676	596	427	188	89	84	84	84	84	84	84	84	476	4
	9	831	110	234	431	563	609	567	440	244	111	101	101	101	101	101	101	101	642	3
	10	863	120	150	272	395	461	458	387	261	143	119	114	114	114	114	114	114	770	2
	11	879	126	130	148	202	258	287	279	237	177	135	128	125	122	122	122	122	847	1
	12	884	128	129	130	132	134	144	164	183	191	183	164	144	134	132	130	129	871	12
	Half Day Totals		824	1588	2402	2949	3107	2828	2137	1174	710	621	595	585	581	579	579	586	3537	
Jul 21	6	357	106	240	332	370	355	285	168	39	27	27	27	27	27	27	27	30	70	6
	7	640	118	349	526	623	626	533	361	129	62	59	59	59	59	59	59	61	257	5
	8	761	98	300	515	645	679	613	456	221	89	82	82	82	82	82	82	82	457	4
	9	823	107	202	405	553	615	588	474	284	117	100	100	100	100	100	100	100	626	3
	10	856	118	133	247	383	467	481	424	303	167	120	113	113	113	113	113	113	757	2
	11	873	124	128	137	191	261	308	314	276	210	147	129	125	121	121	121	121	836	1
	12	878	126	126	128	130	133	150	184	214	226	214	184	150	133	130	128	126	861	12
	Half Day Totals		728	1402	2210	2808	3051	2876	2289	1365	783	637	591	574	568	566	565	568	3431	
Aug 21	6	187	30	103	158	188	189	161	108	35	12	12	12	12	12	12	12	12	25	6
	7	599	59	250	444	565	598	542	402	192	53	49	49	49	49	49	49	49	192	5
	8	756	79	200	446	614	690	662	535	321	96	74	74	74	74	74	74	74	403	4
	9	830	95	124	328	523	632	648	570	402	179	98	93	93	93	93	93	93	583	3
	10	869	106	113	175	344	482	544	526	429	266	126	110	106	106	106	106	106	721	2
	11	888	114	117	122	157	264	365	414	401	328	217	131	119	114	114	114	114	808	1
	12	894	117	117	117	122	126	170	255	324	350	324	255	170	126	122	117	117	837	12
	Half Day Totals		539	957	1721	2442	2909	3013	2693	1950	1109	729	581	523	510	507	506	506	3151	
Sep 21	7	514	32	109	301	437	502	492	405	252	62	30	30	30	30	30	30	30	97	5
	8	758	57	81	324	546	678	706	626	449	190	61	57	57	57	57	57	57	303	4
	9	857	77	81	201	459	637	717	688	557	330	99	77	77	77	77	77	77	498	3
	10	905	91	91	101	270	485	617	655	596	444	220	97	91	91	91	91	91	644	2
	11	927	100	100	102	113	257	437	549	575	516	373	187	106	100	100	100	100	737	1
	12	934	103	103	103	103	110	210	379	499	540	499	379	210	110	103	103	103	769	12
	Half Day Totals		409	518	1088	1887	2620	3096	3131	2688	1811	1025	620	446	411	407	407	407	2663	
Oct 21	7	312	13	24	136	233	291	301	268	190	75	14	13	13	13	13	13	13	30	5
	8	723	42	46	200	450	616	684	649	510	285	54	42	42	42	42	42	42	198	4
	9	862	63	63	104	378	608	730	755	655	454	170	65	63	63	63	63	63	394	3
	10	923	77	77	81	197	465	652	737	710	576	342	101	77	77	77	77	77	546	2
	11	951	86	86	86	91	239	480	639	697	651	505	269	93	86	86	86	86	639	1
	12	959	89	89	89	89	95	247	477	626	676	626	477	247	95	89	89	89	671	12
	Half Day Totals		325	335	632	1324	2233	2967	3274	3066	2375	1390	714	393	327	325	325	325	2142	
Nov 21	7	5	0	0	1	3	4	5	4	3	2	0	0	0	0	0	0	0	0	5
	8	619	28	29	93	323	492	580	579	488	316	86	29	28	28	28	28	28	102	4
	9	828	49	49	55	283	544	708	761	696	523	253	53	49	49	49	49	49	277	3
	10	912	64	64	65	130	423	650	772	775	658	436	142	65	64	64	64	64	427	2
	11	948	72	72	72	76	213	496	688	772	739	593	342	91	72	72	72	72	521	1
	12	959	75	75	75	75	80	274	540	707	766	707	540	274	80	75	75	75	552	12
	Half Day Totals		253	254	342	889	1768	2651	3141	3136	2641	1716	823	355	256	253	253	253	1606	
Dec 21	8	556	22	22	59	265	425	515	523	451	305	98	23	22	22	22	22	22	69	4
	9	811	43	43	46	243	512	686	750	701	539	281	48	43	43	43	43	43	228	3
	10	907	57	57	57	106	401	642	777	791	683	466	163	59	57	57	57	57	375	2
	11	948	66	66	66	69	200	496	700	795	766	620	367	92	66	66	66	66	468	1
	12	960	69	69	69	69	73	281	559	733	794	733	559	281	73	69	69	69	499	12
	Half Day Totals		223	233	265	717	1576	2498	3042	3109	2687	1822	868	339	225	233	233	233	1389	
			N	NNW	NW	WNW	W	WSW	SW	SSW	S	SSE	SE	ESE	E	ENE	NE	NNE	HOR	PM

Reprinted by permission from the 1989 ASHRAE *Handbook—Fundamentals* published by the American Society of Heating, Refrigerating and Air-Conditioning Engineers, Inc.

Low-E Glazing Design Guide

SI Units—Solar Intensity and Solar Heat Gain Factors for 40° North Latitude

Solar Heat Gain Factors, W/m² (Normal)

Date	Solar Time	Direct Solar W/m²	N	NNE	NE	ENE	E	ESE	SE	SSE	S	SSW	SW	WSW	W	WNW	NW	NNW	HOR	Time
Jan 21	8	446	17	17	55	223	350	417	420	358	236	68	17	17	17	17	17	17	44	4
	9	753	37	37	41	233	485	648	706	658	504	260	42	37	37	37	37	37	172	3
	10	865	51	51	51	97	390	627	761	776	671	460	161	53	51	51	51	51	303	2
	11	912	59	59	59	62	193	493	699	796	769	623	372	89	59	59	59	59	390	1
	12	926	62	62	62	62	66	283	563	739	802	739	563	283	66	62	62	62	419	12
	Half Day Totals		194	194	231	627	1425	2315	2851	2941	2565	1770	860	318	196	194	194	194	1117	
Feb 21	7	175	6	10	71	127	160	167	150	107	43	6	6	6	6	6	6	6	11	5
	8	691	33	35	158	407	576	651	704	504	296	56	33	33	33	33	33	33	136	4
	9	856	52	52	70	337	587	738	773	688	496	209	55	52	52	52	52	52	304	3
	10	926	65	65	67	155	449	666	777	768	640	408	120	66	65	65	65	65	450	2
	11	957	73	73	73	77	224	503	690	768	729	579	325	86	73	73	73	73	538	1
	12	967	76	76	76	76	80	271	536	702	759	702	536	271	80	76	76	76	567	12
	Half Day Totals		266	266	478	1139	2042	2887	3307	3201	2590	1601	789	360	276	266	266	266	1729	
Mar 21	7	540	27	92	295	440	514	509	425	271	69	26	26	26	26	26	26	26	83	5
	8	789	50	57	288	533	686	731	664	494	232	54	50	50	50	50	50	50	267	4
	9	888	67	70	147	428	639	749	743	624	404	127	69	67	67	67	67	67	450	3
	10	937	80	80	85	225	482	653	722	682	538	299	91	80	80	80	80	80	587	2
	11	960	88	88	88	94	247	475	623	672	622	473	244	94	88	88	88	88	672	1
	12	967	91	91	91	91	97	238	457	601	650	601	457	238	97	91	91	91	702	12
	Half Day Totals		358	439	953	1775	2624	3261	3425	3052	2189	1269	693	416	359	357	357	357	2409	
Apr 21	6	282	36	144	228	275	279	241	164	56	16	15	15	15	15	15	15	15	34	6
	7	651	50	223	442	583	633	588	451	235	51	45	45	45	45	45	45	45	193	5
	8	794	69	140	402	600	705	703	593	391	130	69	67	67	67	67	67	67	389	4
	9	864	84	91	253	488	637	690	640	493	260	91	84	84	84	84	84	84	557	3
	10	901	96	99	117	291	480	589	608	538	380	177	101	96	96	96	96	96	684	2
	11	919	104	104	107	122	255	411	506	522	459	323	163	109	104	104	104	104	766	1
	12	925	106	106	106	109	114	196	341	448	486	448	341	196	114	109	106	106	793	12
	Half Day Totals		486	835	1579	2389	3018	3312	3133	2464	1538	935	628	495	467	464	463	463	3018	
May 21	5	3	1	2	3	3	3	2	1	0	0	0	0	0	0	0	0	0	0	7
	6	452	113	284	403	458	445	363	223	56	33	33	33	33	33	33	33	35	96	6
	7	681	89	320	520	638	658	579	442	172	63	59	59	59	59	59	59	59	275	5
	8	787	86	230	470	629	693	654	518	294	92	80	80	80	80	80	80	80	460	4
	9	843	99	131	330	517	620	631	550	382	168	100	96	96	96	96	96	96	616	3
	10	874	107	114	171	332	467	529	512	418	262	127	111	107	107	107	107	107	736	2
	11	890	114	114	121	152	255	357	409	400	330	221	133	120	114	114	114	114	811	1
	12	895	117	117	117	121	126	171	321	355	329	355	329	171	126	121	117	117	835	12
	Half Day Totals		679	1274	2100	2816	3228	3229	2775	1895	1128	779	629	568	553	550	549	552	3414	
Jun 21	5	68	32	54	68	70	63	46	20	5	4	4	4	4	4	4	4	7	8	7
	6	488	150	329	450	501	478	380	222	53	39	39	39	39	39	39	39	43	126	6
	7	681	118	355	543	647	654	562	385	145	68	65	65	65	65	65	65	67	306	5
	8	776	94	268	492	632	680	626	480	252	93	85	85	85	85	85	85	85	483	4
	9	829	105	160	358	524	606	601	507	332	142	104	100	100	100	100	100	100	633	3
	10	858	112	121	197	345	457	499	466	366	218	122	115	112	112	112	112	112	749	2
	11	874	119	123	128	166	254	332	367	347	279	188	130	124	119	119	119	119	821	1
	12	879	121	121	121	127	131	163	227	281	301	281	227	163	131	127	121	121	844	12
	Half Day Totals		799	1482	2314	2967	3274	3150	2579	1649	995	743	642	602	592	588	587	594	3550	
Jul 21	5	7	3	5	7	7	6	5	2	0	0	0	0	0	0	0	0	1	1	7
	6	434	116	281	395	447	433	352	216	55	34	34	34	34	34	34	34	37	100	6
	7	656	95	321	513	625	643	564	400	166	66	62	62	62	62	62	62	62	278	5
	8	762	90	236	468	620	680	639	505	285	94	83	83	83	83	83	83	83	459	4
	9	818	102	138	333	513	610	618	537	371	165	104	99	99	99	99	99	99	611	3
	10	850	110	118	177	333	462	519	501	407	254	128	114	110	110	110	110	110	729	2
	11	866	117	120	125	157	256	352	400	389	321	217	135	123	117	117	117	117	802	1
	12	871	120	120	120	125	130	172	253	320	344	320	253	172	130	125	120	120	826	12
	Half Day Totals		705	1296	2102	2791	3180	3164	2706	1842	1110	783	643	586	572	568	567	570	3395	
Aug 21	6	255	38	137	214	256	259	223	151	52	18	17	17	17	17	17	17	17	38	6
	7	603	55	223	426	557	602	557	426	222	55	49	49	49	49	49	49	49	196	5
	8	747	75	149	397	584	681	675	569	373	128	74	72	72	72	72	72	72	386	4
	9	819	89	97	259	481	621	669	618	475	251	97	89	89	89	89	89	89	549	3
	10	857	102	105	126	294	472	573	589	519	367	175	107	102	102	102	102	102	674	2
	11	876	109	109	113	130	257	403	492	505	443	313	165	116	109	109	109	109	753	1
	12	882	112	112	112	115	120	197	333	434	469	434	333	197	120	115	112	112	779	12
	Half Day Totals		518	860	1571	2338	2928	3014	2851	2370	1495	932	647	523	496	492	492	492	2982	
Sep 21	7	471	28	87	265	395	460	456	381	244	66	27	27	27	27	27	27	27	80	5
	8	725	52	61	275	504	646	689	626	467	224	57	52	52	52	52	52	52	258	4
	9	830	71	73	148	413	613	717	712	599	390	129	73	71	71	71	71	71	434	3
	10	881	84	84	89	224	468	630	696	658	521	293	95	84	84	84	84	84	567	2
	11	906	92	92	92	99	245	463	604	652	603	461	242	99	92	92	92	92	650	1
	12	914	95	95	95	95	101	237	446	584	631	584	446	237	101	95	95	95	679	12
	Half Day Totals		374	447	917	1683	2483	3091	3256	2917	2119	1250	699	432	376	373	373	373	2329	
Oct 21	7	152	6	10	64	113	142	148	132	94	38	7	6	6	6	6	6	6	12	5
	8	643	35	37	155	387	545	615	592	475	279	56	35	35	35	35	35	35	136	4
	9	811	54	54	73	329	567	710	742	661	476	202	57	54	54	54	54	54	305	3
	10	884	67	67	70	157	439	646	752	742	619	395	119	69	67	67	67	67	443	2
	11	917	76	76	76	80	223	491	690	745	707	562	317	89	76	76	76	76	529	1
	12	927	78	78	78	78	84	267	521	681	737	681	521	267	84	78	78	78	557	12
	Half Day Totals		277	282	479	1105	1964	2770	3073	3053	2493	1555	780	369	279	277	277	277	1704	
Nov 21	8	429	17	17	55	217	339	404	406	346	228	66	18	17	17	17	17	17	44	4
	9	732	38	38	42	230	476	634	690	643	492	254	42	38	38	38	38	38	173	3
	10	846	52	52	52	99	385	616	748	762	658	451	159	54	52	52	52	52	303	2
	11	894	60	60	60	63	192	486	688	783	756	613	367	89	60	60	60	60	388	1
	12	907	63	63	63	63	67	280	555	728	789	728	555	281	67	63	63	63	417	12
	Half Day Totals		197	197	235	623	1402	2271	2795	2882	2515	1737	849	319	199	197	197	197	1115	
Dec 21	8	279	9	9	25	129	212	259	264	230	157	52	10	9	9	9	9	9	20	4
	9	684	31	31	33	188	427	584	645	611	477	260	40	31	31	31	31	31	124	3
	10	824	45	45	45	78	357	594	732	755	661	462	173	47	45	45	45	45	243	2
	11	881	53	53	53	55	177	477	685	786	764	623	379	90	53	53	53	53	327	1
	12	897	56	56	56	56	60	281	560	736	798	736	560	281	60	56	56	56	356	12
	Half Day Totals		165	165	178	461	1180	2045	2593	2735	2445	1757	869	298	167	165	165	165	891	
			N	NNW	NW	WNW	W	WSW	SW	SSW	S	SSE	SE	ESE	E	ENE	NE	NNE	HOR	PM

Reprinted by permission from the 1989 ASHRAE *Handbook—Fundamentals* published by the American Society of Heating, Refrigerating and Air-Conditioning Engineers, Inc.

SI Units—Solar Intensity and Solar Heat Gain Factors for 48° North Latitude

Solar Heat Gain Factors, W/m² Normal

Date	Solar Time	Direct Solar W/m²	N	NNE	NE	ENE	E	ESE	SE	SSE	S	SSW	SW	WSW	W	WNW	NW	NNW	HOR	Time
Jan 21	8	116	4	4	13	57	90	109	110	94	63	18	4	4	4	4	4	4	7	4
	9	584	24	24	26	168	371	505	554	523	405	217	30	24	24	24	24	24	79	3
	10	754	37	37	37	69	333	553	682	702	615	429	159	39	37	37	37	37	174	2
	11	823	45	45	45	47	166	455	656	753	733	598	365	83	45	45	45	45	244	1
	12	842	48	48	48	48	51	271	541	712	772	712	541	271	51	48	48	48	269	12
	Half Day Totals		134	134	144	368	995	1787	2298	2447	2212	1616	817	267	136	134	134	134	639	
Feb 21	7	11	0	1	5	8	10	11	10	7	3	0	0	0	0	0	0	0	1	5
	8	568	24	25	114	324	469	537	524	428	259	52	24	24	24	24	24	24	78	4
	9	780	42	42	49	284	530	683	726	660	488	225	45	42	42	42	42	42	210	3
	10	869	54	54	55	120	414	640	764	768	653	434	137	55	54	54	54	54	330	2
	11	908	61	61	61	64	205	497	696	786	755	607	355	84	61	61	61	61	408	1
	12	919	63	63	63	63	68	280	555	728	789	728	555	280	68	63	63	63	435	12
	Half Day Totals		214	215	336	864	1707	2574	3053	3050	2564	1676	824	328	216	214	214	214	1246	
Mar 21	7	481	23	71	253	387	457	457	387	253	71	23	22	22	22	22	22	22	64	5
	8	743	44	48	239	485	644	700	651	498	257	49	44	44	44	44	44	44	214	4
	9	852	60	60	104	381	608	737	752	651	448	164	62	60	60	60	60	60	371	3
	10	905	71	71	75	182	459	655	748	727	596	363	104	71	71	71	71	71	493	2
	11	931	79	79	79	83	232	491	662	730	688	541	297	88	79	79	79	79	568	1
	12	939	81	81	81	81	86	261	509	665	720	665	509	261	86	81	81	81	593	12
	Half Day Totals		317	372	789	1556	2444	3190	3467	3196	2418	1464	768	398	318	316	316	316	2004	
Apr 21	6	340	39	167	271	330	337	294	203	74	20	19	19	19	19	19	19	19	46	6
	7	646	49	191	417	567	628	595	468	263	56	45	45	45	45	45	45	45	189	5
	8	778	64	99	350	565	689	708	619	435	173	67	64	64	64	64	64	64	359	4
	9	846	79	83	191	443	621	703	679	554	335	105	79	79	79	79	79	79	506	3
	10	883	90	90	97	243	466	609	659	612	472	251	97	90	90	90	90	90	618	2
	11	902	97	97	97	105	245	442	569	608	557	419	217	103	97	97	97	97	688	1
	12	908	97	97	97	97	106	224	414	543	586	543	414	113	106	97	97	97	712	12
	Half Day Totals		463	764	1453	2284	3018	3463	3409	2823	1907	1168	713	492	445	441	441	441	2760	
May 21	5	129	52	97	125	133	122	91	44	9	8	8	8	8	8	8	8	10	16	7
	6	510	112	305	443	511	503	410	266	75	38	38	38	38	38	38	38	40	125	6
	7	689	73	283	498	630	667	603	448	214	66	61	61	61	61	61	61	61	287	5
	8	781	82	170	417	598	688	675	561	358	120	78	78	78	78	78	78	78	448	4
	9	833	92	101	259	474	611	655	604	462	243	100	92	92	92	92	92	92	584	3
	10	863	103	106	124	282	457	560	579	512	365	179	109	103	103	103	103	103	689	2
	11	879	109	109	113	127	248	396	487	504	446	319	170	116	109	109	109	109	755	1
	12	883	111	111	111	114	120	198	336	438	474	438	336	198	120	111	111	111	778	12
	Half Day Totals		678	1223	2033	2814	3356	3511	3173	2361	1523	996	738	578	549	545	545	545	3294	
Jun 21	5	243	111	192	241	252	228	166	75	19	17	17	17	17	17	17	17	24	38	7
	6	544	146	348	487	552	534	434	266	70	46	46	46	46	46	46	46	49	162	6
	7	693	93	317	521	642	667	591	427	188	72	67	67	67	67	67	67	67	324	5
	8	774	90	202	440	604	678	651	529	320	107	84	84	84	84	84	84	84	479	4
	9	822	98	114	285	482	600	629	567	418	208	105	98	98	98	98	98	98	610	3
	10	849	108	113	142	296	450	534	540	465	319	157	114	108	108	108	108	108	711	2
	11	864	114	114	120	138	248	373	448	456	396	279	156	121	114	114	114	114	774	1
	12	868	116	116	116	120	126	189	303	391	423	391	303	189	126	120	116	116	796	12
	Half Day Totals		811	1446	2278	3012	3453	3476	3012	2139	1376	941	718	620	597	593	592	602	3494	
Jul 21	5	135	57	104	133	141	129	96	46	11	9	9	9	9	9	9	9	12	18	7
	6	492	116	302	436	501	492	407	259	74	40	40	40	40	40	40	40	43	130	6
	7	666	78	285	491	619	653	588	436	207	69	63	63	63	63	63	63	63	290	5
	8	757	86	176	416	590	675	660	547	348	119	81	81	81	81	81	81	81	448	4
	9	809	96	106	263	471	601	642	591	450	237	104	96	96	96	96	96	96	581	3
	10	839	106	109	130	284	453	550	566	500	355	177	112	106	106	106	106	106	684	2
	11	854	112	112	117	132	249	390	477	492	435	312	169	119	112	112	112	112	749	1
	12	859	114	114	114	117	124	198	329	428	462	428	329	198	124	117	114	114	771	12
	Half Day Totals		705	1246	2038	2794	3311	3445	3101	2303	1496	993	721	598	570	565	565	569	3287	
Aug 21	6	311	42	161	256	310	316	275	190	70	22	21	21	21	21	21	21	21	51	6
	7	599	53	193	403	543	598	565	444	250	59	49	49	49	49	49	49	49	193	5
	8	732	69	108	347	549	665	681	593	417	168	73	69	69	69	69	69	69	358	4
	9	801	84	90	198	437	605	680	655	534	323	108	84	84	84	84	84	84	501	3
	10	839	95	95	104	247	458	593	639	592	456	245	103	95	95	95	95	95	610	2
	11	858	102	102	102	112	247	433	553	589	539	406	215	110	102	102	102	102	678	1
	12	864	104	104	104	104	113	224	404	526	568	526	404	224	113	104	104	104	702	12
	Half Day Totals		495	790	1449	2237	2928	3342	3282	2719	1851	1156	728	521	475	471	471	471	2740	
Sep 21	7	414	24	66	224	342	403	403	342	224	66	24	23	23	23	23	23	23	62	5
	8	678	46	51	228	455	602	654	608	467	244	52	46	46	46	46	46	46	206	4
	9	792	63	63	107	366	580	702	716	621	430	162	66	63	63	63	63	63	358	3
	10	848	75	75	79	182	444	630	718	698	573	353	107	75	75	75	75	75	476	2
	11	875	82	82	82	88	230	476	639	704	664	524	292	93	82	82	82	82	549	1
	12	883	84	84	84	84	91	257	493	643	695	643	493	257	91	84	84	84	573	12
	Half Day Totals		332	380	757	1467	2299	3006	3278	3038	2323	1428	766	412	334	331	331	331	1937	
Oct 21	7	12	0	1	5	9	11	12	11	8	3	0	0	0	0	0	0	0	1	5
	8	521	25	27	111	304	439	501	488	398	242	51	25	25	25	25	25	25	79	4
	9	734	44	44	52	276	508	652	693	629	465	216	47	44	44	44	44	44	208	3
	10	825	56	56	58	122	402	618	735	739	628	418	136	58	56	56	56	56	326	2
	11	866	63	63	63	67	203	483	673	759	729	586	345	86	63	63	63	63	403	1
	12	878	66	66	66	66	71	274	538	704	763	704	538	274	71	66	66	66	428	12
	Half Day Totals		223	225	340	838	1636	2460	2917	2917	2458	1618	808	334	226	223	223	223	1233	
Nov 21	8	115	4	4	13	57	90	108	109	93	62	18	4	4	4	4	4	4	7	4
	9	565	25	25	27	165	362	492	540	509	394	211	31	25	25	25	25	25	80	3
	10	734	38	38	38	70	327	542	668	687	602	420	156	40	38	38	38	38	175	2
	11	803	46	46	46	48	165	448	644	739	719	587	358	83	46	46	46	46	244	1
	12	822	48	48	48	48	53	267	531	699	757	699	531	267	53	48	48	48	269	12
	Half Day Totals		138	138	147	367	979	1751	2249	2394	2164	1582	804	268	139	138	138	138	642	
Dec 21	9	442	16	16	18	113	272	378	420	401	316	176	25	16	16	16	16	16	42	3
	10	675	30	30	30	51	286	491	612	635	563	398	155	32	30	30	30	30	119	2
	11	765	38	38	38	40	146	421	614	708	693	569	351	80	38	38	38	38	181	1
	12	789	41	41	41	41	44	256	514	679	734	679	514	256	44	41	41	41	204	12
	Half Day Totals		105	105	107	231	735	1444	1924	2097	1943	1476	778	239	107	185	105	105	444	
			N	NNW	NW	WNW	W	WSW	SW	SSW	S	SSE	SE	ESE	E	ENE	NE	NNE	HOR	PM

Reprinted by permission from the 1989 ASHRAE *Handbook—Fundamentals* published by the American Society of Heating, Refrigerating and Air-Conditioning Engineers, Inc.

SI Units—Solar Intensity and Solar Heat Gain Factors for 56° North Latitude

Date	Solar Time	Direct Solar W/m²	N	NNE	NE	ENE	E	ESE	SE	SSE	S	SSW	SW	WSW	W	WNW	NW	NNW	HOR	Time
Jan 21	9	245	8	8	9	66	154	212	234	222	173	94	12	8	8	8	8	8	17	3
	10	537	21	21	21	40	232	396	492	509	451	317	121	23	21	21	21	21	65	2
	11	653	29	29	29	30	125	365	533	613	600	492	302	65	29	29	29	29	108	1
	12	684	31	31	31	31	34	225	453	599	646	599	453	225	34	31	31	31	125	12
	Half Day Totals		73	73	74	145	514	1081	1476	1632	1535	1192	651	193	75	73	73	73	251	
Feb 21	8	363	13	14	65	202	298	344	338	279	172	36	13	13	13	13	13	13	31	4
	9	654	30	30	33	223	440	578	621	573	430	210	33	30	30	30	30	30	115	3
	10	774	41	41	41	88	363	580	703	715	617	420	142	43	41	41	41	41	204	2
	11	827	47	47	47	50	178	465	662	755	731	592	354	78	47	47	47	47	266	1
	12	842	50	50	50	50	54	270	539	709	768	709	539	270	54	50	50	50	288	12
	Half Day Totals		156	156	209	574	1289	2102	2588	2668	2325	1604	797	281	158	156	156	156	759	
Mar 21	7	403	18	51	204	320	382	385	330	219	67	18	18	18	18	18	18	18	45	5
	8	678	37	40	192	428	584	646	611	479	264	47	37	37	37	37	37	37	156	4
	9	799	51	51	73	331	565	705	735	651	466	193	54	51	51	51	51	51	281	3
	10	859	61	61	63	144	429	640	750	744	623	403	122	63	61	61	61	61	384	2
	11	888	67	67	67	71	214	491	677	759	724	579	333	85	67	67	67	67	448	1
	12	897	69	69	69	69	74	273	535	700	758	700	535	273	74	69	69	69	470	12
	Half Day Totals		268	304	632	1320	2204	3014	3376	3204	2521	1583	814	371	270	268	268	268	1548	
Apr 21	5	1	0	1	1	1	1	1	1	0	0	0	0	0	0	0	0	0	0	7
	6	386	39	181	301	371	382	337	237	92	24	22	22	22	22	22	22	22	57	6
	7	633	46	160	388	544	615	594	479	287	67	43	43	43	43	43	43	43	178	5
	8	754	60	73	299	526	666	703	633	467	216	64	60	60	60	60	60	60	318	4
	9	820	73	75	139	398	598	704	704	597	396	138	75	73	73	73	73	73	443	3
	10	857	82	82	87	200	447	619	695	667	540	321	103	82	82	82	82	82	536	2
	11	876	88	88	88	94	232	462	614	672	630	493	271	96	88	88	88	88	595	1
	12	882	90	90	90	90	97	248	470	612	661	612	470	248	97	90	90	90	615	12
	Half Day Totals		437	714	1355	2188	2999	3569	3615	3095	2204	1379	796	485	416	412	412	413	2436	
May 21	5	292	114	215	280	299	276	208	104	22	19	19	19	19	19	19	19	19	23	7
	6	553	103	310	465	548	547	463	306	99	44	43	43	43	43	43	43	44	152	6
	7	691	68	241	469	616	669	622	480	256	68	61	61	61	61	61	61	61	290	5
	8	770	78	121	362	564	677	688	597	414	164	80	76	76	76	76	76	76	425	4
	9	818	88	93	195	430	596	671	648	529	321	112	88	88	88	88	88	88	539	3
	10	846	97	97	105	236	444	582	631	589	457	251	105	97	97	97	97	97	626	2
	11	861	102	102	102	111	238	426	550	589	543	412	223	110	102	102	102	102	681	1
	12	866	104	104	104	104	112	225	406	530	572	530	406	225	112	104	104	104	700	12
	Half Day Totals		700	1231	2030	2856	3503	3787	3531	2768	1903	1237	806	589	541	537	537	544	3107	
Jun 21	4	67	42	60	69	67	55	35	9	4	4	4	4	4	4	4	5	16	8	8
	5	385	167	296	377	398	362	268	127	33	29	29	29	29	29	29	29	37	78	7
	6	584	133	350	506	585	575	478	307	93	51	51	51	51	51	51	51	53	195	6
	7	699	78	272	492	629	672	614	465	235	75	68	68	68	68	68	68	68	332	5
	8	767	86	146	384	571	670	670	571	383	146	86	83	83	83	83	83	83	462	4
	9	809	94	101	218	438	588	650	617	493	287	109	94	94	94	94	94	94	571	3
	10	835	103	103	113	249	438	560	598	549	417	224	111	103	103	103	103	103	655	2
	11	849	108	108	110	119	239	407	517	549	500	375	204	110	108	108	108	108	709	1
	12	853	110	110	110	110	119	216	376	490	529	490	376	216	119	110	110	110	727	12
	Half Day Totals		866	1493	2327	3118	3665	3808	3414	2591	1773	1184	819	640	600	595	595	617	3375	
Jul 21	4	1	1	1	1	1	1	1	0	0	0	0	0	0	0	0	0	0	0	8
	5	288	117	217	281	300	276	208	104	24	21	21	21	21	21	21	21	25	50	7
	6	534	107	309	458	537	535	452	299	97	47	45	45	45	45	45	45	47	158	6
	7	668	71	244	464	605	655	607	468	250	71	64	64	64	64	64	64	64	294	5
	8	746	81	127	362	557	665	674	583	404	162	83	79	79	79	79	79	79	426	4
	9	794	91	97	200	427	587	659	634	516	314	114	91	91	91	91	91	91	538	3
	10	822	100	100	109	238	440	572	618	575	446	247	109	100	100	100	100	100	623	2
	11	837	105	105	105	115	239	420	539	576	530	403	220	114	105	105	105	105	677	1
	12	842	107	107	107	107	116	224	399	518	559	518	399	224	116	107	107	107	696	12
	Half Day Totals		729	1257	2039	2841	3461	3722	3457	2709	1871	1229	817	610	563	559	559	567	3113	
Aug 21	5	4	1	2	3	4	4	3	2	0	0	0	0	0	0	0	0	0	0	7
	6	355	43	176	287	351	361	318	223	88	26	24	24	24	24	24	24	24	63	6
	7	588	51	162	375	521	587	565	455	273	69	47	47	47	47	47	47	47	183	5
	8	708	65	80	296	511	642	676	607	448	209	70	65	65	65	65	65	65	320	4
	9	775	78	81	146	392	581	681	679	575	382	138	80	78	78	78	78	78	441	3
	10	812	87	87	93	204	438	601	672	645	522	312	107	87	87	87	87	87	532	2
	11	832	93	93	93	101	233	452	596	650	610	478	266	103	93	93	93	93	589	1
	12	838	95	95	95	95	103	246	457	593	640	593	457	246	103	95	95	95	599	12
	Half Day Totals		470	740	1352	2144	2911	3444	3482	2983	2139	1358	807	514	447	443	443	443	2433	
Sep 21	7	339	18	47	177	276	329	332	284	190	60	19	18	18	18	18	18	18	44	5
	8	611	39	43	182	397	540	596	564	443	247	49	39	39	39	39	39	39	151	4
	9	736	54	54	76	316	535	665	693	615	442	188	58	54	54	54	54	54	272	3
	10	799	64	64	67	145	412	611	714	709	595	387	123	66	64	64	64	64	371	2
	11	829	71	71	71	75	211	472	649	726	693	556	324	89	71	71	71	71	433	1
	12	839	73	73	73	73	79	267	515	672	727	672	515	267	79	73	73	73	454	12
	Half Day Totals		282	313	604	1233	2055	2817	3166	3020	2400	1528	803	382	284	282	282	282	1495	
Oct 21	8	327	14	15	63	186	274	315	310	255	158	35	14	14	14	14	14	14	33	4
	9	608	32	32	36	214	416	545	585	539	406	199	35	32	32	32	32	32	116	3
	10	729	43	43	43	90	349	555	671	682	588	401	138	45	43	43	43	43	203	2
	11	782	50	50	50	52	176	448	636	724	700	568	342	80	50	50	50	50	264	1
	12	798	52	52	52	52	57	263	519	681	738	681	519	263	57	52	52	52	285	12
	Half Day Totals		164	164	215	557	1229	1996	2457	2535	2214	1536	774	284	166	164	164	164	757	
Nov 21	9	238	8	8	9	6	151	207	228	217	169	92	12	8	8	8	8	8	17	3
	10	520	22	22	22	41	227	386	480	496	439	308	118	24	22	22	22	22	66	2
	11	634	30	30	30	31	123	357	520	598	586	481	296	65	30	30	30	30	109	1
	12	665	32	32	32	32	35	221	443	585	632	585	443	221	35	32	32	32	126	12
	Half Day Totals		76	76	76	147	506	1058	1593	1593	1498	1163	637	192	77	76	76	76	255	
Dec 21	9	16	0	0	1	4	10	14	15	15	12	7	1	0	0	0	0	0	1	3
	10	356	12	12	12	22	148	259	325	338	302	215	85	13	12	12	12	12	29	2
	11	523	20	20	20	21	94	289	427	493	485	399	247	53	20	20	20	20	60	1
	12	568	23	23	23	23	26	187	378	500	539	500	378	187	26	23	23	23	73	12
	Half Day Totals		45	45	45	64	276	683	982	1117	1081	874	514	149	47	45	45	45	127	
			N	NNW	NW	WNW	W	WSW	SW	SSW	S	SSE	SE	ESE	E	ENE	NE	NNE	HOR	PM

Reprinted by permission from the 1989 ASHRAE *Handbook—Fundamentals* published by the American Society of Heating, Refrigerating and Air-Conditioning Engineers, Inc.

Solar Intensity and Solar Heat Gain Factors for 24° North Latitude

Date	Solar Time	Direct Normal Btu/h·ft²	N	NNE	NE	ENE	E	ESE	SE	SSE	S	SSW	SW	WSW	W	WNW	NW	NNW	HOR	Solar Time
Jan 21	0700	71	2	3	21	45	62	67	63	49	25	3	2	2	2	2	2	2	5	1700
	0800	239	12	12	41	128	190	221	218	181	114	28	12	12	12	12	12	12	55	1600
	0900	288	18	18	23	106	190	240	253	227	166	73	19	18	18	18	18	18	121	1500
	1000	308	23	23	24	53	144	211	245	241	200	125	38	24	23	23	23	23	172	1400
	1100	317	26	26	26	27	73	156	211	234	220	173	95	29	26	26	26	26	204	1300
	1200	320	27	27	27	27	29	82	160	210	227	210	160	81	29	27	27	27	214	1200
	HALF DAY TOTALS		95	96	148	372	671	942	1076	1039	840	505	241	120	96	95	95	95	664	
Feb 21	0700	153	6	12	67	114	141	145	128	90	33	6	6	6	6	6	6	6	17	1700
	0800	262	15	16	80	165	220	240	224	172	89	17	15	15	15	15	15	15	83	1600
	0900	297	21	22	46	138	208	244	243	205	133	42	22	21	21	21	21	21	153	1500
	1000	314	26	26	28	76	157	209	228	213	165	87	28	26	26	26	26	26	205	1400
	1100	321	29	29	29	31	80	148	191	203	185	137	68	31	29	29	29	29	238	1300
	1200	323	30	30	30	30	32	70	134	177	192	177	133	70	32	30	30	30	249	1200
	HALF DAY TOTALS		113	119	257	527	806	1011	1072	965	699	374	200	127	113	113	113	113	820	
Mar 21	0700	194	11	45	115	164	186	180	145	86	17	10	10	10	10	10	10	10	36	1700
	0800	267	18	35	124	195	234	237	204	138	48	19	18	18	18	18	18	18	112	1600
	0900	295	25	27	85	165	215	232	214	163	82	27	25	25	25	25	25	25	180	1500
	1000	309	30	31	41	103	162	194	195	168	112	47	31	30	30	30	30	30	232	1400
	1100	315	33	33	34	42	85	129	154	155	139	86	43	34	33	33	33	33	264	1300
	1200	317	34	34	34	34	35	56	96	126	137	126	95	56	35	34	34	34	275	1200
	HALF DAY TOTALS		133	189	422	693	906	1011	970	778	458	249	169	139	133	133	133	133	962	
Apr 21	0600	40	6	21	33	39	39	33	22	7	2	2	2	2	2	2	2	2	4	1800
	0700	203	20	88	151	189	197	176	127	55	15	14	14	14	14	14	14	14	58	1700
	0800	256	24	80	159	209	228	212	164	88	24	22	22	22	22	22	22	22	132	1600
	0900	280	30	54	126	181	208	203	169	105	39	29	28	28	28	28	28	28	195	1500
	1000	292	34	37	75	125	157	165	148	107	56	35	33	33	33	33	33	33	244	1400
	1100	298	36	37	40	59	85	103	106	94	70	45	38	37	36	36	36	36	274	1300
	1200	299	37	37	38	38	39	46	59	70	75	70	58	45	39	38	38	37	283	1200
	HALF DAY TOTALS		168	339	607	826	940	924	773	494	244	180	163	157	155	155	154	154	1048	
May 21	0600	86	25	57	79	87	84	66	38	8	6	6	6	6	6	6	6	6	13	1800
	0700	203	43	117	171	199	196	163	105	32	17	17	17	17	17	17	17	18	73	1700
	0800	248	38	114	178	214	218	190	132	54	26	25	25	25	25	25	25	26	142	1600
	0900	269	35	88	150	188	198	179	132	66	33	31	31	31	31	31	31	31	201	1500
	1000	280	38	59	103	137	150	141	111	67	39	36	35	35	35	35	35	36	247	1400
	1100	286	40	43	55	72	83	84	75	58	44	40	39	38	38	38	38	39	274	1300
	1200	288	41	41	41	41	42	43	44	46	46	46	44	43	42	41	41	41	282	1200
	HALF DAY TOTALS		238	492	749	909	943	840	614	308	187	176	174	173	172	172	172	175	1089	
Jun 21	0600	97	36	70	93	101	94	73	39	8	7	7	7	7	7	7	7	8	17	1800
	0700	201	55	127	177	199	192	155	94	26	18	18	18	18	18	18	18	20	77	1700
	0800	242	50	126	184	214	212	179	117	43	27	26	26	26	26	26	26	27	145	1600
	0900	263	43	102	158	189	192	168	116	53	34	32	32	32	32	32	32	33	201	1500
	1000	274	41	72	113	140	146	131	96	55	39	36	36	36	36	36	36	38	245	1400
	1100	279	42	50	65	77	82	77	64	49	42	41	40	39	39	39	40	41	271	1300
	1200	281	43	43	43	43	43	43	43	43	43	43	43	43	43	43	43	43	279	1200
	HALF DAY TOTALS		284	562	802	933	932	797	544	255	187	181	180	179	179	179	180	187	1096	
Jul 21	0600	81	26	56	76	84	80	63	36	8	6	6	6	6	6	6	6	7	13	1800
	0700	195	45	116	168	194	190	158	101	31	18	18	18	18	18	18	18	19	73	1700
	0800	239	41	115	176	210	213	185	128	52	27	26	26	26	26	26	26	26	141	1600
	0900	261	37	90	150	186	195	175	129	64	34	32	32	32	32	32	32	32	198	1500
	1000	272	39	62	104	137	149	139	108	65	39	37	36	36	36	36	36	37	243	1400
	1100	278	41	44	58	73	83	83	73	57	44	41	40	39	39	39	39	40	270	1300
	1200	280	42	42	42	43	43	44	45	46	46	46	45	43	43	42	42	42	278	1200
	HALF DAY TOTALS		247	498	746	897	925	820	595	300	191	181	178	177	177	177	177	181	1076	
Aug 21	0600	35	6	20	30	35	35	30	19	6	2	2	2	2	2	2	2	2	4	1800
	0700	186	22	87	144	179	186	165	119	51	16	15	15	15	15	15	15	15	58	1700
	0800	241	26	82	156	203	220	204	157	84	26	24	24	24	24	24	24	24	130	1600
	0900	265	32	57	126	178	202	197	162	101	39	31	30	30	30	30	30	30	191	1500
	1000	278	36	40	78	125	155	161	143	103	55	37	35	35	35	35	35	35	239	1400
	1100	284	38	39	42	61	85	101	104	91	68	46	40	38	37	37	37	37	268	1300
	1200	286	38	39	40	40	41	47	58	69	72	68	58	47	41	40	40	39	277	1200
	HALF DAY TOTALS		179	347	601	806	910	889	740	473	243	186	171	165	164	163	163	162	1028	
Sep 21	0800	248	19	36	119	185	222	225	194	132	48	20	19	19	19	19	19	19	108	1600
	0900	278	26	28	84	160	207	223	206	158	81	28	26	26	26	26	26	26	174	1500
	1000	292	31	32	42	101	158	188	190	163	110	48	32	31	31	31	31	31	224	1400
	1100	299	34	34	35	43	84	127	151	151	128	86	44	35	34	34	34	34	256	1300
	1200	301	35	35	35	36	37	57	95	124	134	124	94	57	37	36	35	35	266	1200
	HALF DAY TOTALS		139	190	406	661	863	964	927	749	451	251	174	145	139	138	138	138	930	
Oct 21	0700	138	6	12	62	104	129	133	117	82	31	7	6	6	6	6	6	6	17	1700
	0800	247	16	17	79	159	211	230	214	164	85	17	16	16	16	16	16	16	82	1600
	0900	284	22	23	47	135	202	237	235	198	128	41	23	22	22	22	22	22	150	1500
	1000	301	27	27	29	77	154	204	222	207	160	85	29	27	27	27	27	27	201	1400
	1100	309	30	30	30	33	80	145	186	198	180	133	67	32	30	30	30	30	233	1300
	1200	311	31	31	31	31	33	70	131	173	187	172	130	69	33	31	31	31	244	1200
	HALF DAY TOTALS		116	123	255	512	778	974	1032	929	675	367	200	131	117	116	116	116	804	
Nov 21	0700	67	2	3	20	43	59	64	60	46	24	3	2	2	2	2	2	2	5	1700
	0800	232	12	13	42	126	186	216	213	177	111	28	12	12	12	12	12	12	55	1600
	0900	282	19	19	23	106	187	236	249	223	163	71	20	19	19	19	19	19	120	1500
	1000	303	23	23	24	53	143	209	241	237	197	123	37	24	23	23	23	23	171	1400
	1100	312	26	26	26	28	73	154	209	230	217	171	93	29	26	26	26	26	202	1300
	1200	315	27	27	27	27	29	81	158	207	224	207	158	80	29	27	27	27	213	1200
	HALF DAY TOTALS		97	97	149	368	661	926	1056	1020	825	497	239	121	98	97	97	97	659	
Dec 21	0700	30	1	1	7	18	25	28	27	21	12	2	1	1	1	1	1	1	2	1700
	0800	225	10	10	29	112	174	208	209	178	118	35	11	10	10	10	10	10	44	1600
	0900	281	17	17	19	93	180	234	252	231	174	84	18	17	17	17	17	17	107	1500
	1000	304	22	22	22	44	137	209	247	247	209	137	44	22	22	22	22	22	157	1400
	1100	314	25	25	25	26	69	156	216	241	230	183	104	29	25	25	25	25	188	1300
	1200	317	26	26	26	26	27	85	167	219	237	219	167	84	27	26	26	26	199	1200
	HALF DAY TOTALS		88	88	118	313	611	899	1054	1042	868	550	257	117	89	88	88	88	598	

Reprinted by permission from the 1989 ASHRAE *Handbook—Fundamentals* published by the American Society of Heating, Refrigerating and Air-Conditioning Engineers, Inc.

Low-E Glazing Design Guide

Date	Solar Time	Direct Normal Btu/h·ft²	N	NNE	NE	ENE	E	ESE	SE	SSE	S	SSW	SW	WSW	W	WNW	NW	NNW	HOR	Solar Time
Jan 21	0700	1	0	0	0	1	1	1	1	1	1	0	0	0	0	0	0	0	0	1700
	0800	203	9	9	29	105	160	189	189	159	103	28	9	9	9	9	9	9	32	1600
	0900	269	15	15	17	91	175	229	246	225	169	82	17	15	15	15	15	15	88	1500
	1000	295	20	20	20	41	135	209	249	250	212	141	46	20	20	20	20	20	136	1400
	1100	306	23	23	23	24	68	159	221	249	238	191	110	29	23	23	23	23	166	1300
	1200	310	24	24	24	24	25	88	174	228	246	228	174	88	25	24	24	24	176	1200
	HALF DAY TOTALS		79	79	107	284	570	856	1015	1014	853	553	264	112	80	79	79	79	512	
Feb 21	0700	112	4	7	47	82	102	106	95	67	26	4	4	4	4	4	4	4	9	1700
	0800	245	13	14	65	149	205	228	216	170	95	17	13	13	13	13	13	13	64	1600
	0900	287	19	19	32	122	199	242	248	216	149	55	20	19	19	19	19	19	127	1500
	1000	305	24	24	25	62	151	213	241	232	189	112	31	24	24	24	24	24	176	1400
	1100	314	26	26	26	28	76	156	208	227	212	165	87	28	26	26	26	26	207	1300
	1200	316	27	27	27	27	29	79	155	204	221	204	155	79	29	27	27	27	217	1200
	HALF DAY TOTALS		100	103	201	445	735	978	1080	1010	780	452	228	122	100	100	100	100	691	
Mar 21	0700	185	10	37	105	153	176	173	142	88	20	9	9	9	9	9	9	9	32	1700
	0800	260	17	25	107	183	227	237	209	150	62	18	17	17	17	17	17	17	100	1600
	0900	290	23	25	64	151	210	237	227	183	107	30	23	23	23	23	23	23	164	1500
	1000	304	28	28	30	87	158	202	215	195	144	70	29	28	28	28	28	28	211	1400
	1100	311	31	31	31	34	82	142	179	188	168	120	59	32	31	31	31	31	242	1300
	1200	313	32	32	32	32	33	66	122	162	176	162	122	66	33	32	32	32	252	1200
	HALF DAY TOTALS		124	162	359	629	875	1033	1041	888	589	326	193	136	125	124	124	124	874	
Apr 21	0600	66	9	35	54	65	66	56	38	12	4	3	3	3	3	3	3	3	7	1800
	0700	206	17	80	146	188	200	182	136	65	16	14	14	14	14	14	14	14	61	1700
	0800	255	23	61	144	200	227	219	177	107	30	22	22	22	22	22	22	22	129	1600
	0900	278	28	36	103	168	206	212	187	133	58	29	28	28	28	28	28	28	188	1500
	1000	290	32	34	52	108	155	177	172	141	87	39	33	32	32	32	32	32	233	1400
	1100	295	35	35	36	47	83	118	135	132	108	70	40	36	35	35	35	35	262	1300
	1200	297	36	36	36	37	38	53	82	106	115	106	82	53	38	37	36	36	271	1200
	HALF DAY TOTALS		161	296	550	792	952	992	889	645	360	228	177	157	153	152	152	152	1015	
May 21	0600	119	33	77	108	121	116	94	56	13	8	8	8	8	8	8	8	9	21	1800
	0700	211	36	111	170	202	204	174	118	42	19	18	18	18	18	18	18	19	81	1700
	0800	250	29	94	165	208	220	199	149	73	27	25	25	25	25	25	25	25	146	1600
	0900	269	33	61	128	177	198	190	155	93	37	32	31	31	31	31	31	31	201	1500
	1000	280	36	40	76	121	150	156	138	99	54	37	35	35	35	35	35	35	243	1400
	1100	285	38	39	42	59	83	99	102	90	68	47	40	39	37	37	37	37	269	1300
	1200	286	38	39	40	40	41	47	59	70	74	70	59	47	41	40	40	39	277	1200
	HALF DAY TOTALS		222	438	702	900	985	933	747	447	250	199	183	177	175	174	174	175	1098	
Jun 21	0600	131	44	92	123	135	127	99	55	12	10	10	10	10	10	10	10	11	28	1800
	0700	210	47	122	176	204	201	168	108	35	20	20	20	20	20	20	20	21	88	1700
	0800	245	36	106	171	208	214	189	135	60	28	27	27	27	27	27	27	27	151	1600
	0900	264	35	74	137	178	193	180	139	77	35	32	32	32	32	32	32	32	204	1500
	1000	274	38	47	86	125	146	145	123	83	45	38	36	36	36	36	36	36	244	1400
	1100	279	40	41	47	64	82	91	89	75	56	43	41	40	39	39	39	39	269	1300
	1200	280	41	41	41	42	42	46	52	58	60	58	52	46	42	42	41	41	276	1200
	HALF DAY TOTALS		261	504	762	935	985	897	678	372	225	197	189	185	184	184	183	186	1122	
Jul 21	0600	113	34	76	105	117	113	90	53	12	9	9	9	9	9	9	9	9	22	1800
	0700	203	38	111	167	198	198	169	114	41	20	19	19	19	19	19	19	19	81	1700
	0800	241	31	95	163	204	215	194	145	70	28	26	26	26	26	26	26	26	145	1600
	0900	261	34	64	129	175	195	186	150	90	37	32	32	32	32	32	32	32	198	1500
	1000	271	37	42	78	121	148	153	134	96	53	38	36	36	36	36	36	36	240	1400
	1100	277	39	40	43	60	83	98	99	88	66	47	41	40	38	38	38	38	265	1300
	1200	279	40	40	41	41	42	48	58	68	72	68	58	48	42	41	41	40	273	1200
	HALF DAY TOTALS		231	444	701	890	967	912	726	433	248	202	187	182	180	179	179	180	1088	
Aug 21	0600	59	10	33	50	60	60	51	34	11	4	4	4	4	4	4	4	4	8	1800
	0700	190	19	79	141	179	190	172	128	61	17	15	15	15	15	15	15	15	61	1700
	0800	240	25	63	141	195	219	210	170	102	31	23	23	23	23	23	23	23	128	1600
	0900	263	30	39	104	166	200	206	181	127	57	31	29	29	29	29	29	29	185	1500
	1000	276	34	36	55	109	153	173	167	136	84	40	35	34	34	34	34	34	229	1400
	1100	282	36	37	39	50	84	116	131	127	104	69	41	38	36	36	36	36	256	1300
	1200	284	37	37	37	39	40	54	81	103	111	103	81	54	40	39	37	37	265	1200
	HALF DAY TOTALS		171	303	546	774	922	955	854	618	352	231	184	166	162	161	160	160	999	
Sep 21	0700	163	10	35	96	139	159	156	128	80	20	10	10	10	10	10	10	10	31	1700
	0800	240	18	26	103	173	215	224	198	143	60	19	18	18	18	18	18	18	96	1600
	0900	272	24	26	64	146	202	227	218	177	105	31	24	24	24	24	24	24	158	1500
	1000	287	29	29	32	86	154	196	208	189	141	70	31	29	29	29	29	29	204	1400
	1100	294	32	32	32	36	81	139	174	182	163	118	59	34	32	32	32	32	234	1300
	1200	296	33	33	33	33	35	66	120	158	171	158	120	66	35	33	33	33	244	1200
	HALF DAY TOTALS		130	164	345	598	831	982	993	852	574	325	197	142	130	129	129	129	845	
Oct 21	0700	99	4	7	43	74	92	96	85	60	24	5	4	4	4	4	4	4	10	1700
	0800	229	13	15	63	143	195	217	206	162	90	17	13	13	13	13	13	13	63	1600
	0900	273	20	20	33	120	193	234	239	208	144	54	21	20	20	20	20	20	125	1500
	1000	293	24	24	26	62	147	207	234	225	183	109	32	24	24	24	24	24	173	1400
	1100	302	27	27	27	29	76	152	203	221	207	160	85	29	27	27	27	27	203	1300
	1200	304	28	28	28	28	30	78	151	199	215	199	151	78	30	28	28	28	213	1200
	HALF DAY TOTALS		103	106	200	433	708	941	1038	972	753	441	226	125	104	103	103	103	679	
Nov 21	0700	2	0	0	0	1	1	1	1	1	1	0	0	0	0	0	0	0	0	1700
	0800	196	9	9	29	103	156	184	184	155	100	27	9	9	9	9	9	9	32	1600
	0900	263	16	16	17	90	173	225	241	221	166	80	17	16	16	16	16	16	88	1500
	1000	289	20	20	21	41	134	206	245	246	209	138	45	21	20	20	20	20	136	1400
	1100	301	23	23	23	24	67	157	218	245	234	188	109	29	23	23	23	23	165	1300
	1200	304	24	24	24	24	25	87	171	224	243	224	171	87	25	24	24	24	175	1200
	HALF DAY TOTALS		80	81	108	282	561	841	996	995	838	544	261	113	81	80	80	80	509	
Dec 21	0800	176	7	7	19	84	135	163	166	143	97	31	7	7	7	7	7	7	22	1600
	0900	257	14	14	15	77	162	218	238	222	171	89	15	14	14	14	14	14	72	1500
	1000	288	18	18	18	34	127	204	246	251	216	148	52	19	18	18	18	18	119	1400
	1100	301	21	21	21	22	63	157	222	252	243	197	116	29	21	21	21	21	148	1300
	1200	304	22	22	22	22	23	89	177	232	252	232	177	89	23	22	22	22	158	1200
	HALF DAY TOTALS		71	71	84	227	500	792	965	986	852	578	275	107	71	71	71	71	440	

Reprinted by permission from the 1989 ASHRAE *Handbook—Fundamentals* published by the American Society of Heating, Refrigerating and Air-Conditioning Engineers, Inc.

Appendix F

Solar Intensity and Solar Heat Gain Factors for 40° North Latitude

Date	Solar Time	Direct Normal Btu/h·ft²	N	NNE	NE	ENE	E	ESE	SE	SSE	S	SSW	SW	WSW	W	WNW	NW	NNW	HOR	Solar Time
Jan 21	0800	142	5	5	17	71	111	132	133	114	75	22	6	5	5	5	5	5	14	1600
	0900	239	12	12	13	74	154	205	224	209	160	82	13	12	12	12	12	12	55	1500
	1000	274	16	16	16	31	124	199	241	246	213	146	51	17	16	16	16	16	96	1400
	1100	289	19	19	19	20	61	156	222	252	244	198	118	28	19	19	19	19	124	1300
	1200	294	20	20	20	20	21	90	179	234	254	234	179	90	21	20	20	20	133	1200
HALF DAY TOTALS			61	61	73	199	452	734	904	932	813	561	273	101	62	61	61	61	354	
Feb 21	0700	55	2	3	23	40	51	53	47	34	14	2	2	2	2	2	2	2	4	1700
	0800	219	10	11	50	129	183	206	199	160	94	18	10	10	10	10	10	10	43	1600
	0900	271	16	16	22	107	186	234	245	218	157	66	17	16	16	16	16	16	98	1500
	1000	294	21	21	21	49	143	211	246	243	203	129	38	21	21	21	21	21	143	1400
	1100	304	23	23	23	24	71	160	219	244	231	184	103	27	23	23	23	23	171	1300
	1200	307	24	24	24	24	25	86	170	222	241	222	170	86	25	24	24	24	180	1200
HALF DAY TOTALS			84	86	152	361	648	916	1049	1015	821	508	250	114	85	84	84	84	548	
Mar 21	0700	171	9	29	93	140	163	161	135	86	22	8	8	8	8	8	8	8	26	1700
	0800	250	16	18	91	169	218	232	211	157	74	17	16	16	16	16	16	16	85	1600
	0900	282	21	22	47	136	203	238	236	198	128	40	22	21	21	21	21	21	143	1500
	1000	297	25	25	27	72	153	207	229	216	171	95	29	25	25	25	25	25	186	1400
	1100	305	28	28	28	30	78	151	198	213	197	150	77	30	28	28	28	28	213	1300
	1200	307	29	29	29	29	31	75	145	191	206	191	145	75	31	29	29	29	223	1200
HALF DAY TOTALS			114	139	302	563	832	1035	1087	968	694	403	220	132	114	113	113	113	764	
Apr 21	0600	89	11	46	72	87	88	76	52	18	5	5	5	5	5	5	5	5	11	1800
	0700	206	16	71	140	185	201	186	143	75	16	14	14	14	14	14	14	14	61	1700
	0800	252	22	44	128	190	224	223	188	124	41	22	21	21	21	21	21	21	123	1600
	0900	274	27	29	80	155	202	219	203	156	83	29	27	27	27	27	27	27	177	1500
	1000	286	31	31	37	92	152	187	193	170	121	56	32	31	31	31	31	41	217	1400
	1100	292	33	33	34	39	81	130	160	166	146	102	52	35	33	33	33	33	243	1300
	1200	293	34	34	34	34	36	62	108	142	154	142	108	62	36	34	34	34	252	1200
HALF DAY TOTALS			154	265	501	758	957	1051	994	782	488	296	199	157	148	147	147	147	957	
May 21	0500	1	0	1	1	1	1	1	0	0	0	0	0	0	0	0	0	0	0	1900
	0600	144	36	90	128	145	141	115	71	18	10	10	10	10	10	10	10	11	31	1800
	0700	216	28	102	165	202	209	184	131	54	20	19	19	19	19	19	19	19	87	1700
	0800	250	27	73	149	199	220	208	164	93	29	25	25	25	25	25	25	25	146	1600
	0900	267	31	42	105	164	197	200	175	121	53	32	30	30	30	30	30	30	195	1500
	1000	277	34	36	54	105	148	168	163	133	83	40	35	34	34	34	34	34	234	1400
	1100	283	36	36	38	48	81	113	130	127	105	70	42	38	36	36	36	36	257	1300
	1200	284	37	37	37	38	40	54	82	104	113	104	82	54	40	38	37	37	265	1200
HALF DAY TOTALS			215	404	666	893	1024	1025	881	601	358	247	200	180	176	175	174	175	1083	
Jun 21	0500	22	10	17	21	22	20	14	6	2	1	1	1	1	1	1	1	2	3	1900
	0600	155	48	104	143	159	151	121	70	17	13	13	13	13	13	13	13	14	40	1800
	0700	216	37	113	172	205	207	178	122	46	22	21	21	21	21	21	21	21	97	1700
	0800	246	30	85	156	201	216	199	152	80	29	27	27	27	27	27	27	27	153	1600
	0900	263	33	51	114	166	192	190	161	105	45	33	32	32	32	32	32	32	201	1500
	1000	272	35	38	63	109	145	158	148	116	69	39	36	35	35	35	35	35	238	1400
	1100	277	38	39	40	52	81	105	116	110	88	60	41	39	38	38	38	38	260	1300
	1200	279	38	38	40	41	52	72	89	95	89	72	52	41	40	38	38	38	267	1200
HALF DAY TOTALS			253	470	734	941	1038	999	818	523	315	236	204	191	188	187	186	188	1126	
Jul 21	0500	2	1	2	2	2	2	1	1	0	0	0	0	0	0	0	0	0	0	1900
	0600	138	37	89	125	142	137	112	68	18	11	11	11	11	11	11	11	12	32	1800
	0700	208	30	102	163	198	204	179	127	53	21	20	20	20	20	20	20	20	88	1700
	0800	241	28	75	148	196	216	203	160	90	30	26	26	26	26	26	26	26	145	1600
	0900	259	32	44	106	163	193	196	170	118	52	33	31	31	31	31	31	31	194	1500
	1000	269	35	37	56	106	146	165	159	129	81	41	36	35	35	35	35	35	231	1400
	1100	275	37	38	40	50	81	111	127	123	102	69	43	39	37	37	37	37	254	1300
	1200	276	38	38	38	40	41	55	80	101	109	101	80	55	41	40	38	38	262	1200
HALF DAY TOTALS			223	411	666	885	1008	1003	858	584	352	248	204	186	181	180	180	181	1076	
Aug 21	0600	81	12	44	68	81	82	71	48	17	6	5	5	5	5	5	5	5	12	1800
	0700	191	17	71	135	177	191	177	135	70	17	16	16	16	16	16	16	16	62	1700
	0800	237	24	47	126	185	216	214	180	118	41	23	23	23	23	23	23	23	122	1600
	0900	260	28	31	82	153	197	212	196	151	80	31	28	28	28	28	28	28	174	1500
	1000	272	32	33	40	93	150	182	187	165	116	56	34	32	32	32	32	32	214	1400
	1100	278	35	35	36	41	81	128	156	160	141	99	52	37	35	35	35	35	239	1300
	1200	280	35	35	35	36	38	63	106	138	149	138	106	63	38	36	35	35	247	1200
HALF DAY TOTALS			164	273	498	741	928	1013	956	751	474	296	205	166	157	156	156	156	946	
Sep 21	0700	149	9	27	84	125	146	144	121	77	21	9	9	9	9	9	9	9	25	1700
	0800	230	17	19	87	160	205	218	199	148	71	18	17	17	17	17	17	17	82	1600
	0900	263	22	23	47	131	194	227	226	190	124	41	23	22	22	22	22	22	138	1500
	1000	280	27	27	28	71	148	200	221	209	165	93	30	27	27	27	27	27	180	1400
	1100	287	29	29	29	31	78	147	192	207	191	146	77	31	29	29	29	29	206	1300
	1200	290	30	30	30	30	32	75	142	185	200	185	142	75	32	30	30	30	215	1200
HALF DAY TOTALS			119	142	291	534	787	980	1033	925	672	396	222	137	119	118	118	118	738	
Oct 21	0700	48	2	3	20	36	45	47	42	30	12	2	2	2	2	2	2	2	4	1700
	0800	204	11	12	49	123	173	195	188	151	89	18	11	11	11	11	11	11	43	1600
	0900	257	17	17	23	104	180	225	235	209	151	64	18	17	17	17	17	17	97	1500
	1000	280	21	21	22	50	139	205	238	235	196	125	38	22	21	21	21	21	140	1400
	1100	291	24	24	24	25	71	156	212	236	224	178	101	28	24	24	24	24	168	1300
	1200	294	25	25	25	25	27	85	165	216	234	216	165	85	27	25	25	25	177	1200
HALF DAY TOTALS			88	89	152	361	623	878	1006	974	791	493	247	117	89	88	88	88	540	
Nov 21	0800	136	5	5	18	69	108	128	129	110	72	21	6	5	5	5	5	5	14	1600
	0900	232	12	12	13	73	151	201	219	204	156	80	13	12	12	12	12	12	55	1500
	1000	268	16	16	16	31	122	196	237	242	209	143	50	17	16	16	16	16	96	1400
	1100	283	19	19	19	20	61	154	218	248	240	194	116	28	19	19	19	19	123	1300
	1200	288	20	20	20	20	21	89	176	231	250	231	176	89	21	20	20	20	132	1200
HALF DAY TOTALS			63	63	75	198	445	721	887	914	798	551	269	101	63	63	63	63	354	
Dec 21	0800	89	3	3	8	41	67	82	84	73	50	17	3	3	3	3	3	3	6	1600
	0900	217	10	10	11	60	135	185	205	194	151	83	13	10	10	10	10	10	39	1500
	1000	261	14	14	14	25	113	188	232	239	210	146	55	15	14	14	14	14	77	1400
	1100	280	17	17	17	17	56	151	217	249	242	198	120	28	17	17	17	17	104	1300
	1200	285	18	18	18	18	19	89	178	233	253	233	178	89	19	18	18	18	113	1200
HALF DAY TOTALS			52	52	56	146	374	649	822	867	775	557	276	94	53	52	52	52	282	

Reprinted by permission from the 1989 ASHRAE *Handbook—Fundamentals* published by the American Society of Heating, Refrigerating and Air-Conditioning Engineers, Inc.

Low-E Glazing Design Guide

Solar Intensity and Solar Heat Gain Factors for 48° North Latitude

Date	Solar Time	Direct Normal Btu/h·ft²	Solar Heat Gain Factors, Btu/h·ft²																HOR	Solar Time
			N	NNE	NE	ENE	E	ESE	SE	SSE	S	SSW	SW	WSW	W	WNW	NW	NNW		
Jan 21	0800	37	1	1	4	18	29	34	35	30	20	6	1	1	1	1	1	1	2	1600
	0900	185	8	8	8	53	118	160	176	166	129	69	10	8	8	8	8	8	25	1500
	1000	239	12	12	12	22	106	175	216	223	195	136	50	12	12	12	12	12	55	1400
	1100	261	14	14	14	15	53	144	208	239	233	190	116	26	14	14	14	14	77	1300
	1200	267	15	15	15	15	16	86	171	226	245	226	171	86	16	15	15	15	85	1200
	HALF DAY TOTALS		43	43	46	117	316	567	729	776	701	512	259	85	43	43	43	43	203	
Feb 21	0700	4	0	0	1	3	3	3	3	2	1	0	0	0	0	0	0	0	0	1700
	0800	180	8	8	36	103	149	170	166	136	82	17	8	8	8	8	8	8	25	1600
	0900	247	13	13	16	90	168	216	230	209	155	71	14	13	13	13	13	13	66	1500
	1000	275	17	17	17	38	131	203	242	244	207	138	44	18	17	17	17	17	105	1400
	1100	288	19	19	19	20	65	158	221	249	238	192	113	27	19	19	19	19	130	1300
	1200	292	20	20	20	20	22	89	176	231	250	231	176	89	22	20	20	20	138	1200
	HALF DAY TOTALS		68	68	107	274	541	816	968	967	813	531	261	104	68	68	68	68	395	
Mar 21	0700	153	7	22	80	123	145	145	123	80	23	7	7	7	7	7	7	7	20	1700
	0800	236	14	15	76	154	204	222	206	158	82	15	14	14	14	14	14	14	68	1600
	0900	270	19	19	3	121	193	234	239	207	142	52	20	19	19	19	19	19	118	1500
	1000	287	23	23	24	58	146	208	237	231	189	115	33	23	23	23	23	23	156	1400
	1100	295	25	25	25	26	74	156	210	232	218	172	94	28	25	25	25	25	180	1300
	1200	298	26	26	26	26	27	83	161	211	228	211	161	83	27	26	26	26	188	1200
	HALF DAY TOTALS		100	118	250	494	775	1012	1100	1014	767	465	244	126	101	100	100	100	636	
Apr 21	0600	108	12	53	86	105	107	93	64	23	6	6	6	6	6	6	6	6	15	1800
	0700	205	15	61	132	180	199	189	148	84	18	14	14	14	14	14	14	14	60	1700
	0800	247	20	32	111	179	219	225	196	138	55	21	20	20	20	20	20	20	114	1600
	0900	268	25	26	60	141	197	223	215	176	106	33	25	25	25	25	25	25	161	1500
	1000	280	28	28	31	77	148	193	209	194	150	80	31	28	28	28	28	28	196	1400
	1100	286	31	31	31	33	78	140	181	193	177	133	69	33	31	31	31	31	218	1300
	1200	288	31	31	31	31	34	71	131	172	186	172	131	71	34	31	31	31	226	1200
	HALF DAY TOTALS		147	242	461	724	957	1098	1081	895	605	370	226	156	141	140	140	140	875	
May 21	0500	41	17	31	40	42	39	29	14	3	3	3	3	3	3	3	3	3	5	1900
	0600	162	35	97	141	162	160	133	85	24	12	12	12	12	12	12	12	13	40	1800
	0700	219	23	90	158	200	212	191	142	68	21	19	19	19	19	19	19	19	91	1700
	0800	248	26	54	132	190	218	214	178	113	38	25	25	25	25	25	25	25	142	1600
	0900	264	29	32	82	151	194	208	192	147	77	32	29	29	29	29	29	29	185	1500
	1000	274	33	34	39	90	145	178	184	163	116	57	35	33	33	33	33	33	219	1400
	1100	279	35	35	36	40	79	126	155	160	142	101	54	37	35	35	35	35	240	1300
	1200	280	35	35	35	36	38	63	107	139	150	139	107	63	38	36	35	35	247	1200
	HALF DAY TOTALS		215	388	645	893	1065	1114	1007	749	483	316	225	184	174	173	173	174	1045	
Jun 21	0500	77	35	61	76	80	72	53	24	6	5	5	5	5	5	5	5	8	12	1900
	0600	172	46	110	155	175	169	138	84	22	14	14	14	14	14	14	14	16	51	1800
	0700	220	29	101	165	204	211	187	135	60	23	21	21	21	21	21	21	21	103	1700
	0800	246	29	64	139	191	215	206	168	101	34	27	27	27	27	27	27	27	152	1600
	0900	261	31	36	91	153	190	199	180	133	66	33	31	31	31	31	31	31	193	1500
	1000	269	34	36	45	94	143	169	171	148	101	50	36	34	34	34	34	34	225	1400
	1100	274	36	36	38	44	79	118	142	145	126	88	49	38	36	36	36	36	246	1300
	1200	275	37	37	37	38	40	60	96	124	134	124	96	60	40	38	37	37	252	1200
	HALF DAY TOTALS		257	459	722	955	1095	1102	955	678	436	299	228	197	189	188	188	191	1108	
Jul 21	0500	43	18	33	42	45	41	30	15	3	3	3	3	3	3	3	4	6	6	1900
	0600	156	37	96	138	159	156	129	82	24	13	13	13	13	13	13	13	16	41	1800
	0700	211	25	90	156	196	207	186	138	66	22	20	20	20	20	20	20	20	92	1700
	0800	240	27	56	132	187	214	209	174	110	38	26	26	26	26	26	26	26	142	1600
	0900	256	30	34	83	149	191	204	187	143	75	33	30	30	30	30	30	30	184	1500
	1000	266	34	35	41	90	143	174	180	158	113	56	36	34	34	34	34	34	217	1400
	1100	271	36	36	37	42	79	124	151	156	138	99	54	38	36	36	36	36	237	1300
	1200	272	36	36	36	37	39	63	104	136	146	136	104	63	39	37	36	36	244	1200
	HALF DAY TOTALS		223	395	646	886	1050	1092	983	730	474	315	229	190	181	179	179	180	1042	
Aug 21	0600	99	13	51	81	98	100	87	60	22	7	7	7	7	7	7	7	7	16	1800
	0700	190	17	61	128	172	190	179	141	79	19	15	15	15	15	15	15	15	61	1700
	0800	232	22	34	110	174	211	216	188	132	53	23	22	22	22	22	22	22	114	1600
	0900	154	27	28	63	139	192	216	108	169	102	34	27	27	27	27	27	27	159	1500
	1000	266	30	30	33	78	145	188	203	188	144	78	33	30	30	30	30	30	193	1400
	1100	272	32	32	32	36	78	137	175	187	171	129	68	35	32	32	32	32	215	1300
	1200	274	33	33	33	33	36	71	128	167	189	167	128	71	36	33	33	33	223	1200
	HALF DAY TOTALS		157	251	459	709	929	1060	1040	862	587	366	231	165	151	149	149	149	869	
Sep 21	0700	131	8	21	71	108	128	128	108	71	21	8	7	7	7	7	7	7	20	1700
	0800	215	15	16	72	144	191	207	193	148	77	16	15	15	15	15	15	15	65	1600
	0900	251	20	20	34	116	184	223	227	197	136	52	21	20	20	20	20	20	114	1500
	1000	269	24	24	25	58	141	200	228	221	182	112	34	24	24	24	24	24	151	1400
	1100	278	26	26	26	28	73	151	203	223	210	166	92	29	26	26	26	26	174	1300
	1200	280	27	27	27	27	29	82	156	204	220	204	156	82	29	27	27	27	182	1200
	HALF DAY TOTALS		105	121	240	465	729	953	1040	963	737	453	243	131	106	105	105	105	614	
Oct 21	0700	4	0	0	2	3	4	4	3	2	1	0	0	0	0	0	0	0	0	1700
	0800	165	8	9	35	96	139	159	155	126	77	16	8	8	8	8	8	8	25	1600
	0900	233	14	14	16	88	161	207	220	199	148	68	15	14	14	14	14	14	66	1500
	1000	262	18	18	18	39	128	196	233	234	199	133	43	18	18	18	18	18	104	1400
	1100	274	20	20	20	21	64	153	213	241	231	186	109	27	20	20	20	20	128	1300
	1200	278	21	21	21	21	23	87	171	223	242	223	171	87	23	21	21	21	136	1200
	HALF DAY TOTALS		71	71	108	266	519	780	925	925	779	513	256	106	72	71	71	71	391	
Nov 21	0800	36	1	1	4	18	29	34	35	30	20	6	1	1	1	1	1	1	2	1600
	0900	179	8	8	9	52	115	156	171	161	125	67	10	8	8	8	8	8	26	1500
	1000	233	12	12	12	22	104	172	212	218	191	133	49	13	12	12	12	12	55	1400
	1100	255	15	15	15	15	52	142	204	234	228	186	114	26	15	15	15	15	77	1300
	1200	261	15	15	15	15	17	85	168	222	240	222	168	85	17	15	15	15	85	1200
	HALF DAY TOTALS		44	44	47	117	310	555	713	760	686	502	255	85	44	44	44	44	204	
Dec 21	0900	140	5	5	6	36	86	120	133	127	100	56	8	5	5	5	5	5	13	1500
	1000	214	10	10	10	16	91	156	194	201	179	126	49	10	10	10	10	10	38	1400
	1100	242	12	12	12	13	46	134	195	225	220	180	111	25	12	12	12	12	57	1300
	1200	250	13	13	13	13	14	81	163	215	233	215	168	81	14	13	13	13	65	1200
	HALF DAY TOTALS		33	33	34	73	233	458	610	665	616	468	247	76	34	33	33	33	141	
			N	NNW	NW	WNW	W	WSW	SW	SSW	S	SSE	SE	ESE	E	ENE	NE	NNE	HOR	PM

Reprinted by permission from the 1989 ASHRAE *Handbook—Fundamentals* published by the American Society of Heating, Refrigerating and Air-Conditioning Engineers, Inc.

Appendix F

Solar Intensity and Solar Heat Gain Factors for 56° North Latitude

Date	Solar Time	Direct Normal Btu/h·ft²	N	NNE	NE	ENE	E	ESE	SE	SSE	S	SSW	SW	WSW	W	WNW	NW	NNW	HOR	Solar Time
Jan 21	0900	78	3	3	3	21	49	67	74	70	55	30	4	3	3	3	3	3	5	1500
	1000	170	7	7	7	13	74	126	156	162	143	100	38	7	7	7	7	7	21	1400
	1100	207	9	9	9	10	40	116	169	194	190	156	96	21	9	9	9	9	34	1300
	1200	217	10	10	10	10	11	71	144	190	205	190	144	71	11	10	10	10	40	1200
	HALF DAY TOTALS		23	23	24	46	163	343	468	517	487	378	206	61	24	23	23	23	80	
Feb 21	0800	115	4	4	21	64	95	109	107	88	55	12	4	4	4	4	4	4	10	1600
	0900	203	10	10	11	71	139	183	197	182	136	66	10	10	10	10	10	10	36	1500
	1000	246	13	13	13	28	115	184	223	227	196	133	45	14	13	13	13	13	65	1400
	1100	262	15	15	15	16	57	148	210	239	232	188	112	25	15	15	15	15	84	1300
	1200	267	16	16	16	16	17	86	171	225	244	225	171	86	17	16	16	16	91	1200
	HALF DAY TOTALS		49	50	66	182	409	666	821	846	737	509	253	89	50	49	49	49	241	
Mar 21	0700	128	6	16	65	101	121	122	105	70	21	6	6	6	6	6	6	6	14	1700
	0800	215	12	13	61	136	185	205	194	152	84	15	12	12	12	12	12	12	49	1600
	0900	253	16	16	61	105	179	224	233	207	148	61	17	16	16	16	16	16	89	1500
	1000	272	19	19	20	46	136	203	238	236	198	128	39	20	19	19	19	19	122	1400
	1100	282	21	21	21	22	68	156	215	241	230	184	106	27	21	21	21	21	142	1300
	1200	284	22	22	22	22	24	86	170	222	241	222	170	86	24	22	22	22	149	1200
	HALF DAY TOTALS		85	97	200	419	699	956	1071	1016	800	502	258	118	86	85	85	85	491	
Apr 21	0600	122	13	58	95	118	121	107	75	29	7	7	7	7	7	7	7	7	18	1800
	0700	201	15	51	123	173	195	188	152	91	21	14	14	14	14	14	14	14	56	1700
	0800	239	19	23	95	167	211	223	201	148	68	20	19	19	19	19	19	19	101	1600
	0900	260	23	24	44	126	190	223	223	189	126	44	24	23	23	23	23	23	140	1500
	1000	272	26	26	27	63	142	196	220	212	171	102	33	26	26	26	26	26	170	1400
	1100	278	28	28	28	30	74	147	195	213	200	156	86	31	28	28	28	28	189	1300
	1200	280	28	28	28	28	31	79	149	194	210	194	149	79	31	28	28	28	195	1200
	HALF DAY TOTALS		139	226	430	694	951	1132	1147	982	699	437	252	154	132	131	131	131	772	
May 21	0500	93	36	68	89	95	88	66	33	7	6	6	6	6	6	6	6	7	14	1900
	0600	175	33	99	148	174	173	147	97	31	14	14	14	14	14	14	14	14	48	1800
	0700	219	21	77	149	195	212	197	152	81	22	19	19	19	19	19	19	19	92	1700
	0800	244	25	38	115	179	215	218	189	131	52	25	24	24	24	24	24	24	135	1600
	0900	259	28	30	62	136	189	213	206	168	102	36	28	28	28	28	28	28	171	1500
	1000	268	31	31	33	75	141	185	200	187	145	80	33	31	31	31	31	31	199	1400
	1100	273	32	32	32	35	76	135	174	187	172	131	71	35	32	32	32	32	216	1300
	1200	275	33	33	33	33	36	71	129	168	181	168	129	71	36	33	33	33	222	1200
	HALF DAY TOTALS		222	391	644	906	1112	1202	1120	878	604	392	256	187	172	170	170	173	986	
Jun 21	0400	21	13	19	22	21	18	11	3	1	1	1	1	1	1	2	5	3	3	2000
	0500	122	53	94	119	126	115	85	40	10	9	9	9	9	9	9	12	25	25	1900
	0600	185	42	111	160	185	182	152	97	30	16	16	16	16	16	16	17	62	62	1800
	0700	222	25	86	156	199	213	195	147	74	24	22	22	22	22	22	22	105	105	1700
	0800	243	27	46	122	181	213	213	181	122	46	27	26	26	26	26	26	26	146	1600
	0900	257	30	32	69	139	187	206	196	156	91	34	30	30	30	30	30	30	181	1500
	1000	265	33	33	36	79	139	178	190	174	132	71	35	33	33	33	33	33	208	1400
	1100	269	34	34	35	38	76	129	164	174	159	119	65	37	34	34	34	34	225	1300
	1200	271	35	35	35	35	38	68	119	155	168	155	119	68	38	35	35	35	231	1200
	HALF DAY TOTALS		275	473	738	989	1162	1207	1082	822	562	376	260	203	190	189	189	196	1070	
Jul 21	0500	91	37	69	89	95	88	66	33	8	7	7	7	7	7	7	8	16	16	1900
	0600	169	34	98	145	170	170	143	95	31	15	14	14	14	14	14	14	15	50	1800
	0700	212	23	77	147	192	208	193	148	79	23	20	20	20	20	20	20	20	93	1700
	0800	237	26	40	115	177	211	214	185	128	51	26	25	25	25	25	25	25	135	1600
	0900	252	29	31	63	135	186	209	201	164	99	36	29	29	29	29	29	29	171	1500
	1000	261	32	32	34	76	139	181	196	182	142	78	35	32	32	32	32	32	198	1400
	1100	265	33	33	33	37	76	133	171	183	168	128	70	36	33	33	33	33	215	1300
	1200	267	34	34	34	34	37	71	126	164	177	164	126	71	37	34	34	34	221	1200
	HALF DAY TOTALS		231	398	646	901	1097	1180	1096	859	593	390	259	193	179	177	177	180	987	
Aug 21	0500	1	0	1	1	1	1	1	1	0	0	0	0	0	0	0	0	0	0	1900
	0600	112	14	56	91	111	114	101	71	28	8	8	8	8	8	8	8	8	20	1800
	0700	187	16	51	119	165	186	179	144	86	22	15	15	15	15	15	15	15	58	1700
	0800	225	20	25	94	162	203	214	192	142	66	22	20	20	20	20	20	20	101	1600
	0900	246	25	26	46	124	184	216	215	182	121	44	26	25	25	25	25	25	140	1500
	1000	258	28	28	30	65	139	191	213	204	165	99	34	28	28	28	28	28	169	1400
	1100	264	30	30	30	32	74	143	189	206	193	152	84	33	30	30	30	30	187	1300
	1200	266	30	30	30	30	30	78	145	188	203	188	145	78	33	30	30	30	198	1200
	HALF DAY TOTALS		149	235	429	680	923	1092	1104	946	678	431	256	163	142	140	140	141	771	
Sep 21	0700	107	6	15	56	87	104	105	90	60	19	6	6	6	6	6	6	6	14	1700
	0800	194	12	14	58	126	171	189	179	140	78	16	12	12	12	12	12	12	48	1600
	0900	233	17	17	24	100	170	211	220	195	140	59	18	17	17	17	17	17	86	1500
	1000	253	20	20	21	46	131	194	227	225	189	123	39	21	20	20	20	20	118	1400
	1100	263	22	22	22	24	67	150	206	230	220	176	103	28	22	22	22	22	137	1300
	1200	266	23	23	23	23	25	85	163	213	231	213	163	85	25	23	23	23	144	1200
	HALF DAY TOTALS		89	99	191	391	652	893	1004	958	761	484	255	121	90	89	89	89	474	
Oct 21	0800	104	4	5	20	59	87	100	98	81	50	11	4	4	4	4	4	4	10	1600
	0900	193	10	10	11	68	132	173	186	171	129	63	11	10	10	10	10	10	37	1500
	1000	231	14	14	14	28	111	176	213	216	186	127	44	14	14	14	14	14	64	1400
	1100	248	16	16	16	17	56	142	202	229	222	180	108	25	16	16	16	16	84	1300
	1200	253	16	16	16	16	18	83	164	216	234	216	164	83	18	16	16	16	91	1200
	HALF DAY TOTALS		52	52	68	177	390	633	779	804	702	487	246	90	53	52	52	52	240	
Nov 21	0900	76	3	3	3	21	48	66	72	69	54	29	4	3	3	3	3	3	6	1500
	1000	165	7	7	7	13	72	122	152	157	139	98	37	7	7	7	7	7	21	1400
	1100	201	9	9	9	10	39	113	165	190	186	152	94	21	9	9	9	9	35	1300
	1200	211	10	10	10	10	11	70	140	186	200	186	140	70	11	10	10	10	40	1200
	HALF DAY TOTALS		24	24	24	47	161	336	457	505	475	369	202	61	24	24	24	24	81	
Dec 21	0900	5	0	0	0	1	3	4	5	5	4	2	0	0	0	0	0	0	0	1500
	1000	113	4	4	4	7	47	82	103	107	96	68	27	4	4	4	4	4	9	1400
	1100	166	6	6	6	7	30	92	135	156	154	127	78	17	6	6	6	6	19	1300
	1200	180	7	7	7	7	8	59	120	159	171	159	120	59	8	7	7	7	23	1200
	HALF DAY TOTALS		14	14	14	20	88	217	311	354	343	277	163	47	15	14	14	14	40	
			N	NNW	NW	WNW	W	WSW	SW	SSW	S	SSE	SE	ESE	E	ENE	NE	NNE	HOR	PM

Reprinted by permission from the 1989 ASHRAE *Handbook—Fundamentals* published by the American Society of Heating, Refrigerating and Air-Conditioning Engineers, Inc.

Low-E Glazing Design Guide

References

1. __, *Glass Industry*, May 1988.

2. Gläser, H.J., "Coated Heat-Insulating Glasses," *International Journal of Glass Technology*, 1989, vol. 62, p. 93-99.

3. Amstock, J., "New Technology and Testing to Improve Performance in Heat and Sound Insulation", *Glass Magazine*, April 1986.

4. Owens, R., Adhesives Applications, Bostik Construction Products, September 1987.

5. Sorrenson, C.B., "Gas—How to Retain It—Gas filling for Insulating Glassed Units", PRC Corporation, Glendale, California.

6. Johnson, T.E., *Solar Architecture: The Direct Gain Approach*, McGraw Hill, New York, 1981.

7. Fan, C.C., Reed, T.B., Goodenough, J.B., "Heat Mirrors for Solar-Energy Collection and Radiation Insulation," Proceedings of the 9th Intersociety Energy Conversion Engineering Conference, San Francisco, California, August 26-30, 1974.

8. Gillery, F.H., "The Significant Advantage of Using Zinc-Tin Oxide to Anti-Reflect Silver in Low Emissivity Coatings," PPG Industries Glass Research & Development Center, Pittsburgh, Pennsylvania, 1989.

9. Arasteh, D., Selkowitz, S., Wolfe, J.R., "The Design and Testing of a Highly Insulating Glazing System for Use With Conventional Window Systems," *Journal of Solar Engineering*, Transactions of the ASME, 1989, vol. 111.

10. Gardestad, K., "The Living Atrium: Design Guidelines for Quality Atriums," M.S.Arch. Thesis, MIT School of Architecture, Cambridge, Massachusetts, June 1986.

11. Sweitzer, G., Arateh, D., Selkowitz, S., "Effects of Low-Emissivity Glazings on Energy Use Patterns in Nonresidential Daylighted Buildings," Lawrence Berkeley Laboratory Report, Berkeley, California, LBL-21577, December 1986.

12. Elmahdy, A.H., "Joint Canadian/U.S. Research Project on Window Performance: Project Outlines and Preliminary Results," *ASHRAE Transactions*, 1990, vol. 96, Pt 1.

13. Harrison, S.J., Barakat, S.A., "A method for Comparing the Thermal Performance of Windows," *ASHRAE Transactions*, 1983, vol. 89 Part 1A.

14. Burkhart, J., Jones, R., "The Effective Absorptance of Direct Gain Rooms," Proceedings 4th National Passive Solar Conference, Kansas City, Missouri, International Solar Energy Society, October 1979.

15. Holzberlein, T., "Don't Let the Trees Make a Monkey of You," Proceedings 4th National Passive Solar Conference, Kansas City, Missouri, International Solar Energy Society, October 1979.

16. Niles, P.W., "A simple Direct Gain Passive House Performance Prediction Model," Proceedings Second National Passive Solar Conference, International Solar Energy Society, 1978.

17. Millet, M., Bedrick, J., "Manual Graphic Daylight Design Method," Department of Architecture, University of Washington, Seattle, 1980.

18. Lam, W.M.C., *Sunlighting as Formgiver for Architecture*, Van Nostrand Reinhold Company, New York, 1986.

19. Krockman, J. "Uber die horizontal Beleuchtungsstarke der Tagesbeleuchtung" *Lichtechnik*, 1963, vol. 15.

20. Benson, D.K., Tracey, C.E., "Evacuated Window Glazings for Energy Efficient Buildings," SERI/C-255-0122, Solar Energy Research Institute, Golden, Colorado.

21. Rubin, M., Lampert, C., "Transparent Silica Aerogels for Window Insulation," *Solar Energy Materials*, 1983, vol. 7, p. 393.

22. Benson, D.K., Tracey, C.E., "Solid-State Electrochromic Switchable Window Glazings", Proceedings of SPIE 502, 1984, p. 46.

23. Bartovicks, W.A., "The Thermal Performance of Fixed and Variable Selective Transmitters in Commercial Architecture," S.M. Arch Thesis, Department of Architecture, M.I.T. Cambridge, Massachusetts, February 1984.

24. Kreith, F., *Principles of Heat Transfer*, International Textbook Co., Scranton, Pennsylvania, 1958.

25. Button, D. A., Dunning, R., Fenestration 2000, Pilkington Glass Ltd., July 1989.

26. _____, Thikol Gesellschaft mbH, "Gas Permeability of IG-Sealants," Morton Thikol, Woodstock, Illinois, 1988.

Glossary

Conduction. Occurs when heat is transferred through solids or still air (or fluids) by neighboring molecular collisions.

Convection. Occurs when buoyant, moving molecules of air (or any other fluid) carry heat to or from a surface.

Emissivity. A measure of a surface's ability to emit long-wave infrared radiation or room temperature radiant heat energy. Emissivity varies from 0 (no emitted infrared) to 1 (100% emitted infrared) and is the complement of reflection for infrared opaque coatings and materials.

Light Reflectance. The fraction of visible light at normal incidence that is reflected by the glazing.

Light Transmittance. The fraction of visible light at normal incidence that is transmitted through the glazing.

Shading Coefficient. The ratio of the solar heat gain through the window to the solar heat gain through a single light of 3 mm clear glass under the same set of conditions.

Solar Absorptance. The fraction of solar radiant heat at normal incidence that is absorbed by all surfaces of the glazing.

Solar Direct Transmittance. The fraction of solar radiant heat at normal incidence that is transmitted directly through the glazing.

Solar Radiant Heat. Radiation having the same spectral distribution as the total radiation (ultraviolet, visible, and infrared) that is received at sea level directly from the sun at an altitude of 30°.

Solar Reflectance. The fraction of solar radiant heat at normal incidence that is reflected from all surfaces of the glazing.

Solar Total Transmittance. The fraction of solar radiant heat at normal incidence that is transferred through the glazing directly by transmittance and indirectly by absorbed energy that flows inward by reradiating and convecting to the interior, assuming an outside wind speed of 2 m/s.

U-value. The heat flow rate through a given glazing: the reciprocal of the thermal resistance R (U = 1 / R). The U-value is calculated for standard conditions. In England it is assumed the temperature difference across the glazing is 15°C at a mean temperature of 10°C. In the United States, values given for the summer are calculated for an outside air temperature of 89°F, an inside air temperature of 75°F, an outside air speed of 7.5 mph, and a solar intensity of 248 Btu/hr ft^2. Values given for the winter are calculated for an outside nighttime air temperature of 0°F, an inside air temperature of 70°F, and an outside air speed of 15 mph.

Index

Abrasion, 31-32, 37-38, 58-59
Absorber, 42
Adhesive tape, 34
Aerogel, 163-164
Aerospace, 161
Aetna Commercial Insurance Division Headquarters, 21
Agricultural, 36
Airco, 9, 12-13
Air-conditioner, 2, 69, 70, 88, 89,126, 145
Aircraft, 5
Alkoxide in an alcohol solution, 164
Alternative Component Package, 65, 68
Aluminized, 16, 30
Aluminum, 7-8, 71, 157
Ambient light level, 148
American Council for an Energy Efficient Economy, 3
American Institute of Architects, 151-152
Amorphous, 165
Annealed glass, 63
Annual net solar intake, 101
Anodized aluminum, 157
Antiglare, 132
Antireflection, 1, 7, 12, 25, 31-32
Aperture, 43, 48, 126, 134, 139-141
Arches, 21
Architect, 3, 15, 20, 21, 86, 151-152
Area-weighted, 63-64, 71
Argon, 11, 13, 18, 32, 38-41, 50-52, 71, 96
Art, 52, 54, 114, 146, 158
Artificial light, 67-68, 89, 95, 126
Artwork, 56
Ash, 106
ASHRAE, 65-66, 93-94
Atmosphere, 6, 9, 11, 37, 39, 48
Atmospheric pressure, 51, 163
Atoms, 6
Atriums, 4, 15, 86, 90, 96,126, 134, 139, 144-145
August, 23, 89
Autoclave, 164
Automobile, 160
Auxiliary heat, 107, 109
Awnings, 21, 107
Azimuth angle, 132

Balconies, 19
Bamboo, 145
Barrels, 3, 114
Barrier, 35, 113, 150, 161
Batch processing, 7-8
Bazaars, 145
Beadboard, 100
Black, 26, 139-140, 147, 167
Blades, 142
Blinds, 29, 142
Blowing agent, 74
Blue, 42-43, 45, 97, 134, 148, 168
Board insulation, 101
Boat, 162
Boom, 37

Borosilicate, 163
Breeze, 87, 91
British, 127
Broiler, 29, 88, 119
Bronze, 42-43, 48, 97, 168
Brown, 139
BRS, 127-128
Building components, 63, 65, 162
Bulk insulation value, 12
Butt joint, 32, 34, 155
Butyl, 32, 160
By-product, 11, 108

Cadmium tin oxide, 30, 37, 59
Calendar date, 76
Calm, 113
Canada, 72
Canopy, 43, 106-107
Carbon dioxide, 39
Catalog, 91
Cathedral ceiling, 107
Cathode, 37
Catwalks, 144
Ceilings, 21, 107, 131, 134, 143-144
Cell, 163
Cellular foam, 145
Cementitious, 105
Certifications, 154
Chalk, 148
Charts, 2, 69, 81, 89, 101, 134, 139, 145
Chemical vapor deposition, 12, 37
Chimney, 40
Chlorophyll, 42-43
Chroma, 146
Cigarette, 148
Clerestory, 143
Cleveland, 100
Climate, 45, 48, 62, 69, 99-100, 167
Cloudy day, 21-22, 85-86, 90, 98, 100, 125-127, 129, 132, 134, 139-141, 147, 166
Cockpit, 5
Code, 4, 10, 20-21, 62-65, 70, 92, 97, 112, 139
Collapse, 164
Color fringing, 164
Colors, 45, 91, 105-106, 148-149
Columns, 167
Companies, 4-5, 8-10, 28, 69, 155, 160, 162, 164
Compass, 77, 82, 132
Composites, 36, 162
Computer program, 72
Concrete, 19, 90, 110, 120
Condensation, 4, 13, 35-37, 46, 49, 62, 69-70, 99, 104-105, 144, 161
Conductance, 92, 116, 119, 121
Conduction, 11, 13, 28, 38, 48, 50, 92, 104, 111, 149
Conductivity, 38-39, 50, 114
Conductor, 5, 10
Connecticut, 21
Containers, 115

Contrast, 127, 141, 144
Convect, 11, 26, 110
Convective heat, 107-108, 116, 163
Cooking, 69
Cool daylight, 2, 15, 19, 42, 86, 88, 95-96
Core, 162
Corrode, 6, 8-9, 12, 37
Corrosion, 7, 9, 32, 36-37, 56, 149
Corrosion-proof, 36, 38, 58-59, 105
Corrosive, 32
Creep, 34-35
Criteria, 46, 70, 96, 104, 156
Critical point, 164
Crystals, 165
Curators, 146

Damp, 8
Danger sign, 95
Daylight factor, 127, 129-132, 134, 139-140, 145, 147
Daylight transmission, 4, 12-13, 21-23, 29-30, 35, 39,
    42, 45-47, 50-52, 55-56, 58, 62-63, 74, 86, 96, 99,
    131, 139-140, 147-148, 158, 160, 162
Daylit, 68, 134, 146
Debris, 36
Deciduous, 107
Defogging, 10
Degree day, 65
Dehydrated space, 154
Deicing, 5, 11
Density, 62, 65, 67-68, 75, 93, 161
Department of Energy, 72
Desiccant, 32,157
Desiccated, 160
Design-a-Color Paint Chip Colors, 91
Detackifying overcoat, 36
Diffuse
    illuminance, 132
    light, 17, 100, 107, 126, 142, 167
    solar energy, 16
Diffuser, 142
Dimmers, 67
Dirt, 14
Disability glare, 140-141
Discomfort glare, 141
Diurnal heat capacity, 114
Doors, 16-17, 64, 143
Doped, 6, 30, 37
Double glazing, 2-4, 8-9, 11, 13, 16, 21-22, 29, 31-32,
    37-39, 42, 46, 48-49, 51-54, 56, 58, 63, 65, 68, 70-71,
    74, 81, 96, 100-102, 104, 120, 130, 149, 154-156,
    161-162, 166-167
Double-sided adhesive tape, 34
Drafts, 62, 104, 108
Drapes, 2, 15
Drywall, 107, 123
DSHGF, 119
Dual-seal units, 32
Duct enclosures, 144
Ducts, 19
Dwellings, 65
Dx definition, 47
Dyes, 165

Earth, 76, 139
Edge deletion, 37
Edge stripping, 58
Efficacy, 88-89, 96
Electric field, 5, 165
Electricity, 5, 30, 88

Electrochromics, 165, 168
Electronic thermometers, 74
Electro-optical, 166
Emissions, 88, 108
Emitter, 87
Emulsions, 165
England, 5, 9, 12, 16, 21, 63-64
EPS, 75
Equinox, 18, 83, 100, 103
Etched microgrids, 30
European, 4, 7-9, 11, 16, 39, 45, 51, 62, 72, 96, 99, 100,
    124, 132, 161
Evacuated glazings, 39, 163-164
Exotic gases, 49, 160
External reflected component, 126-127, 130
Extruded polystyrene, 75
Eye, 73-74, 141-142, 146, 168
Eyebrow, 107, 13

Fabrics, 52, 54, 56, 107, 132, 146
Facade, 81, 103, 142-144
Fade, 13
Fans, 21, 112
February, 22
Fiberglass, 142, 161-162
Fills, 12, 18, 32, 38, 49, 51-52, 54, 63, 160
Filters, 16, 42, 145
Finish, 142, 157, 161-162
Finland, 11
Fire, 21
Float process, 6
Floors, 64, 105, 110
Flowering plants, 44
Fluid, 115, 141
Fluorescents, 42, 88-89, 96
Fluorine, 37
Foam board, 74
Foamcore, 147
Foams, 163
Fog, 161
Fogging, 69
Foil, 35
Footcandle, 89, 127, 132, 134, 148, 158
Forest Products Laboratory, 161
Frames, 14, 73, 90, 141, 160-162
Freestanding water storage, 114-115
Fuel, 64, 102, 107

Gable end, 18
Galleries, 146
Galvanized steel, 157
Gaps, 32, 38, 40-41, 62, 96
Gas-filled, 15, 100, 102
Geilinger A.G., 8, 13
Gelcoat, 162
German, 9, 11, 16, 18, 32
Germination, 43
Glare, 16, 21-22, 24, 29, 125-126, 131-132, 134, 140-
    142, 144-146
Glass-reinforced polyester, 162
Glazing bar, 87
Gloom, 85, 86, 107, 141
Glossy surfaces, 140
Glue, 32, 35, 75, 145
Gold, 7
Granular microcells, 49
Graphic method, 108
Graphical solar positions, 77
Grass, 144

Gray, 27, 43, 50
Grease, 38
Greenhouses and the greenhouse effect, 25-26
Growing Plants, 22, 42-43, 134
Guide specification, 3, 151
Gypsum, 123

Hard coats, 37, 58, 148, 159
Hartford, Connecticut, 21
Haze, 37, 58, 141, 149
Header, 86, 129, 131
Health, 43
Heat
    flow, 38, 40, 49-50, 71, 75, 87, 161
    shrink, 34
    strengthened, 87
    transfer, 11, 28, 71, 99, 115-116, 119, 163
Heaters, 62, 107-108
Heat-reflecting silver layer, 12
Heat-rejecting, 86, 99, 134, 140, 165
Hermetically sealed glass, 154
High-iron glass, 42
Horizon, 77, 81, 129, 134, 144, 162
Hue, 146
Humid, 92, 165

Illuminance, 132
Incandescent lamp, 149
Incident solar energy, 91-92
Indices, temperature, 113
Indium, 30-31, 37, 59
Inert gas, 11
Infiltration, 112
Infrared, 1-2, 9, 25-32, 38, 43, 46, 62, 73, 86-88, 104-
    105, 107-108, 111, 149, 152, 162-163, 165
Inhibitors, 35
Inorganic electrochromic materials, 165-166, 168
Insulator, 40, 109, 162
Intensity, 44, 125, 141, 149
Interference effects, 6, 163
Internal
    gains, 85, 90
    heat gains, 109
    load density, 67-68
    mass, 103, 109
    reflected component, 126-127, 130
International style, 7
Ion beams, 8, 34
Iridescence, 6, 12, 37, 45, 57, 149
Isothermal mass, 109

Jamb, 84, 129
January, 17, 101, 111
Japan, 4, 10
June, 91, 106

Kilowatts, 167
Krypton, 11-13, 32, 35, 39, 41, 49-51, 54, 96

Labeling Legislation, 72
Lake Charles, 48
Laminated glass, 43,
Lasituku, Finland, 11
Latent heat, 92
Latitudes, 17, 76-77, 81, 91, 93-94, 100, 134
Latticework overhang, 107
Lawrence Berkeley Laboratory, 48
Leybold-heraeus A.G., 9
Libby Owens Ford, 12

Light scattering, 141
Lighting model, 134
Lightshelves, 86, 105, 132, 142-144
Light-tight joints, 147
Lightwaves, 164
Lightwell, 135-138, 140
Liquid crystals, 165
Local time, 76-77
Loft, 120
Longitude, 76-77
Longwave radiation, 25, 28, 36
Louver, 143, 145
Low iron glass, 46
Lumens, 88
Luminaires, 42, 152
Luminous ceiling, 131, 144
Lux, 44, 89-90, 96, 127, 132, 134, 147, 158

Madison, Wisconsin, 48
Magnesium fluoride, 165
Magnetic fields, 165
Magnetron, 9, 31, 37
March, 19, 103, 106, 110-111, 114, 120
Masonry, 110, 113-114
Massachusetts Institute of Technology, 43, 139, 166
Masterspec, 151-152
Matte, 22, 126, 139, 142-143
Metal foil tape, 35
Metalized glass, 7
Metallic oxide, 152-153
Microcells, 49
Microgrid, 30, 38
Microporous, 163
Microwave, 69
Migration, 160
Mirrors, 1, 7, 25, 27, 32, 148-149, 164
Molecular sieve, 157
Monitor skylights, 120, 140
Monolithic metallic coatings, 6
Monthly, 65, 91, 110-111
Months, 15, 17, 53, 62, 65, 77, 91, 101, 106-107, 110, 111
Moveable insulation, 101
MSDOS, 65
Mullions, 141, 145
Munich, 89, 95
Museum, 19-20, 146

Nature, 109, 131
Neon, 5
NESA glass, 5-6
Net
    annual heating, 100
    heat transfer line, 99
    radiation, 27
    seasonal heat gain, 13, 99
    solar intake, 101
Noise, 54
Nomograph, 130
Noon, 77, 81, 145, 147
North, 2, 13, 45, 51-52, 89, 95-96, 100, 124, 140, 145,
    151, 167
North America, 4, 9, 11, 161

Oak, 106
October, 91, 106-107, 111
Odor, 113
Offline, 159
Offshore oil wells, 3
Off-white walls, 86, 106

Ohmmeter, 149-150
Oil, 9, 149
On-line, 38, 159-160
Open-cell foam insulation, 163-164
Open-plan, 108-109
Operable louvers, 144
Outdoor illumination, 127, 132
Overcast, 124, 134
Overcoat, 7, 9, 36
Over-glazed, 103
Overhangs, 17, 81, 131-132, 143, 168
Overheat, 16, 63, 99, 103, 110, 123, 134
Owens-Corning-Fiberglass, 162
Oxidation, 6
Oxides, 37

Paint, 91, 106
Panel, 5, 139
Paper packaging, 34
Parabolic fluorescent fixtures, 89
Partitions, 90, 146
Pastel, 45, 148
Patterned glass, 142
Pavements, 28
Pedestrian circulation levels, 90
Perforated metal edge spacer, 32
Performance code, 63-65, 70
Permeability, 11, 32-35, 74, 160, 161
Phenolics, 161
Photosensors, 139
Photosynthesis, 42-43
Pilkington Glass Limited, 5, 9, 12, 149
Pine, 114
Pipes, 107
Pittsburgh Plate Glass Company, 5
Planter, 141
Plastics, 8, 34, 36, 56
Polyester film, 8-9, 13, 19, 23, 34-36, 54-56, 69, 152, 154-156, 162, 165
Polyethylene, 43
Polyisobutylene, 32
Polymer, 2-3, 9, 35, 37-39, 54, 160-161
Polymer-ceramics, 161
Polypropylene, 9, 36, 56
Polystyrene, 75
Polysulfide, 32
Polyurethane, 32, 34-35
Polyvinylchloride, 35
Pond, 17
Posttemper, 58, 155, 159
Power density, 65, 67-68
PPG, 5, 12, 91
Prescriptive code, 63, 65
Pressure, 9, 35, 39, 48, 51, 163, 165
Pressure-sensitive, 36, 145
Pretempered, 54
Princeton University Firestone Library, 21
Profile angle, 81-84, 107, 145
Projection factor, 67
Protractor, 127-130
Psychrometer, 69
Purple, 45
Pyrolytics, 5, 6, 37, 52, 59, 159-160

Quadrant, 130
Quadruple-glazed, 8

Radar, 5
Radiators, 28

Rainy days, 100
Reaction injected molding, 161
Red, 42-43
Reflect, 2, 16-17, 29-30, 36, 62, 123, 140, 142-143, 149
Reflectivity, 27, 60, 131
Reflector, 9, 27, 30, 87, 106, 126
Refract, 164
Refrigeration, 66
Refrigerator, 72, 164
Reinforced plastic, 142
Residence, 2, 16, 18, 28, 47, 63, 69, 85-86, 109, 127, 131, 160
Retrofit films, 9, 36, 38, 56-57, 87-88, 105, 151-152, 154-155
Reveals, 101, 141, 145-146
Robots, 39
Roll coating, 8, 13, 54, 56, 155, 159
Roof, 17, 19-21, 64, 90, 144, 139, 145
Rooms, 86, 89, 107, 109, 123, 127, 130, 140, 144
Rubber, 32, 34
Rugless, 107
Rugs, 110
Rule of thumb, 127, 140
Rupture by gas expansion, 41
R-value variation, 38
R-values, 13, 33-34, 41, 51, 61-62

Savings, 3, 34, 36, 48, 77, 99, 108, 167
Sawtooth, 140
Sealants, 11, 32, 34, 35, 53, 71, 149, 151, 154, 155, 157
Seasonal, 13, 16, 62, 86, 99, 106
Selective absorber, 42
Self-shading windows, 81
Semiconductor, 30, 37, 59
Sensible heat, 91-92
September, 106, 111
Shading coefficient, 13, 21-23, 29, 32, 45-47, 51, 54, 56, 58, 60, 63, 67-68, 73-74, 85, 87, 89, 92, 95, 99-100, 103-105, 111, 119-120, 153, 160, 162, 167
Shadow mask, 81, 84
Shelf life, 34, 53
SHGF, peak, 92, 96
Shortwave radiation, 25, 28
Shutters, 2, 15
Side-lit rooms, 130, 140
Silica gel, 157
Silicone, 32
Sill, 128-129, 146
Silver-based coatings, 2, 10, 12, 21-22, 42
Single glazing, 9, 12, 31, 37-38, 49, 56, 58-59, 63, 65, 73-74, 87-88, 105, 149, 160, 165
Sky component, 126-132, 147
Skylight, 40, 43, 86, 120, 134, 140, 164
Slab, 109, 120
Smoke exhaust fans, 21
Snow, 144
Softcoat, 101, 149, 159-160
Sol-air temperature, 90-92, 95
Solar
    altitude, 76-77, 81, 132, 134
    azimuth, 76, 83, 132
    collectors, 52, 58, 120, 164
    exposure, 109, 125
    gain, 4, 15-16, 19, 21, 27, 29, 42-43, 47, 51, 65, 81, 85, 90, 92, 95-96, 99-100, 103, 105, 120, 123, 125, 134, 142, 162-163, 165, 167
    geometry, 61, 76
    heat, 2, 4, 6, 12-13, 16-19, 25, 29-30, 42, 46, 73, 85-